ALSO BY HARVEY COX

God's Revolution and Man's Responsibility

The Secular City

On Not Leaving It to the Snake

The Church Amid Revolution (editor)

The Situation Ethics Debate (editor)

The Feast of Fools: A Theological Essay on Festivity and Fantasy

THE
SEDUCTION
OF THE
SPIRIT

*The Use and Misuse
of People's Religion*

HARVEY COX

Simon and Schuster / New York

Embryonic expressions of some of the ideas presented in this book have appeared at various times in such places as *The Christian Century, Commonweal, Soundings* and *The National Catholic Reporter*. Parts of the chapter on *The Virgin and the Dynamo* came out in *Humanities, Religion and the Arts Tomorrow*, edited by Howard Hunter (Holt, Rinehart and Winston, Inc., New York, 1972). I am grateful to all concerned, both for the opportunity to air new ideas on their pages and for the permission either to carry them forward or to adapt and reprint them here.

SBN 671–21525–6
Library of Congress Catalog Card Number: 73–2314
Designed by Irving Perkins
Manufactured in the United States of America
Printed by Mahony & Roese, Inc.
Bound by American Book–Stratford Press, Inc.

1   2   3   4   5   6   7   8   9   10

For Doll

Contents

Preface: Religion as Story and Signal   9

PART ONE: TESTIMONY

ONE   *The Tribal Village*   23
TWO   *The City of Light*   53
THREE   *The House of Intellect*   91

PART TWO: PEOPLE'S RELIGION

FOUR   *Viva Jesús, Quetzalcoatl and Zapata!*   115
FIVE   *Beyond Bonhoeffer*   123
SIX   *Learning from People's Religion*   144
SEVEN   *People's Religion and Radical Theology*   169
EIGHT   *Naked Revival: Theology and the Human Potential Movement*   197
NINE   *The Search for a New Church*   226

PART THREE: THE ELECTRONIC ICON

TEN   *The Image and the Icon*   261
ELEVEN   *The Virgin and the Dynamo Revisited: The Symbolism of Technology*   280
TWELVE   *The Flintstones in Recife*   302
THIRTEEN   *The Future of Theology: A Poetic Postscript*   317

Notes on Sources   331

Index   335

Religion as Story and Signal

ALL HUMAN beings have an innate need to tell and hear stories and to have a story to live by. Religion, whatever else it has done, has provided one of the main ways of meeting this abiding need. Most religions begin as clusters of stories, embedded in song and saga, rite and rehearsal. Go back as far as the bloody Babylonian epic of Gilgamesh or to Homer's accounts of the gods and heroes of Hellas. Or read the tales told by Bantu priests, Cheyenne holy men or Eskimo shamans. They are all, in their own way, stories. The Hebrew Scriptures are largely stories; so is the New Testament. Rabbis, saints, Zen masters and gurus of every persuasion convey their holy teachings by jokes, *kōans*, parables, allegories, anecdotes and fables. There has never been a better raconteur than Jesus of Nazareth himself.

There are two kinds of stories that are especially important as vehicles for religious expression. The first is *autobiography*, or "testimony," the first-person account of the teller's struggle with the gods and the demons. It begins inside the speaker and says, "This is what happened to me." Recently neglected, testimony deserves reinstatement as a primary mode of religious discourse. It is a genre which celebrates the unique, the eccentric and the concrete. I suspect its decline in recent years is related to our industrial society's emphasis on interchangeable units, both human and mechanical, and its consequent suspicion of the particular and the irregular. But that is just what is valuable about autobiography. It reclaims personal uniqueness in an era of interchangeability. In an age of externality it uncovers what the classical mystics once described as "interiority." Autobiography is *my* story.

The second religiously significant mode of storytelling is what

I call "people's religion." It is the collective story of a whole
people. Like popular music and folk medicine, people's religion is
usually mixed with superstition, custom and kitsch. Specialists
and professionals view it with suspicion. But along with autobiography, it is an essential form of storytelling, a kind of
corporate testimony. People's religion includes both the folk
religion of ordinary people in its unsophisticated form and the
popular religion that occurs outside formal ecclesiastical institutions and ad hoc rituals and do-it-yourself liturgies. I call both
folk and pop varieties "people's religion" because they are both
variant expressions of genuine collective interiority. People's
religion is *our* story.

There is a third type of religion which is neither testimony nor
folk expression but which also serves an important purpose. It is
the religion that is coded, systematized, controlled and distributed
by specialists. Religion in this form, though it still bears certain
marks of a story, has actually become a system of what I call
"signals." Most of the great religions of the world are a mixture of
story and signal.

The distinction between story and signal is important, not only
for understanding the various forms of religion but for grasping
the very nature of contemporary societies. Stories reflect those
forms of human association which blend emotion, value and history into a binding fabric. Signals, on the other hand, make possible large-scale and complex types of human association where
such binding would not be possible. Stories amplify. They elicit
emendations and embellishments from their hearers and often tell
us more about the narrator than about the plot. Signals specify.
They cue a single patterned act and tell us nothing about the
signaler. Stories enrich the fund of common recollection and
stimulate shared imagination. Signals permit people to move
around in systems that would grind to a halt if all communication
had to be deep and personal. Stories depend for their zest on
eccentricity, hyperbole and local color. Signals must be clear,
and their clarity requires the paring away of all extrinsic data.
Jokes are stories. They convey multiple layers of information all

at once and can be told and interpreted in several different ways. Traffic lights are signals. They transmit one unequivocal message and discourage all but one response. Both jokes and flashing yellow lights have a place. Jokes do much more than merely make us laugh, and signals not only prevent cars from crashing into each other, they also serve a thousand other indispensable functions.

All societies need both stories and signals. Large societies like ours especially need both the autonomous activities people engage in without anyone else's planning these activities and also the impersonal procedures that make possible the constant flow of ideas, goods and persons. Religions also serve their purpose best when they include both the spontaneous personal aspect and the inclusive consensus on value and vision that makes whole civilizations possible. The problem, however, is one of proportion, and what has happened in most modern societies in recent decades represents an ugly distortion of the symmetry that should obtain between story and signal, between people's faith and clerical religion. We have contracted the cultural and religious equivalent of leukemia. In leukemia, the balance between white and red blood cells is lost. The white cells first outnumber, then begin to cannibalize the red ones. In time the victim invariably dies. Similarly in our social body, institutionally programmed forms of activity which should be balanced with random, capricious and inwardly initiated forms of human action now threaten instead to devour them. This is happening in everything from travel to education and from religion to making love. Organized sports replace play. Prefabrication makes building something obsolete. Tourism takes the place of travel. Religious faith is channeled into the institutional expansion of churches. No human impulse seems safe from the omnivorous onslaught of programming.

The swamping of stories by signals concerns me because I think something fundamental is at stake. Although signals multiply in dense, bureaucratically organized cultures, they are actually a less human form of communication. Animal language consists almost entirely of signals—the screech, the bark, the howl—but human beings are storytellers, and without stories we would not be human. Through our stories we assemble our pasts, place ourselves in a present and cast a hope for the future. Without stories we would be bereft of memory or anticipation. We know we are something more than mere hairless bipeds, because of our parables, jokes, sagas, fairy tales, myths, fables, epics and yarns. Not only have we created innumerable stories, we have also found endless ways to recount them. We dance them, draw them, mime them with masks and carve them on rocks. We sing them around tables stacked with the cold remains of a dinner. We whisper them in the ears of sleepy children in darkened bedrooms. We stammer them out to confessors and therapists. We inscribe them in letters and diaries. We act them out in the clothes we wear, the places we go, the friends we cherish. As soon as our young can comprehend our words we begin to tell them stories, and the hope we harbor for our elders is that we will be able to hear their full story before they go.

Religion should be the seedbed and spawning ground of stories. But today religion is not fulfilling its storytelling role. Like the society it inhabits, it has become top-heavy with signals and systems. Meanwhile the stories, without which there would be nothing to systematize, grow fainter. This is true at both the individual and the corporate level. It is time for a rebirth not just of testimony but also of people's religion.

At first glance it would appear that the principal threat to story religion comes from the huge organized churches and denominations. Actually I do not believe this is the case. There is another form of "signal religion" abroad in the land today which is even more hazardous because it is not generally recognized as a religion at all. It is the "religion" propagated by the mass media.

I realize that the use of the word "religion" to describe the content of network TV and popular magazines may seem confusing. We think that the mass media inform or entertain us, and in the modern world we have gotten used to making sharp distinctions between "religion" on the one hand and news, entertainment or advertising on the other. But these distinctions have already outlived their usefulness. True, the "church religion" of our modern Western society is usually distinguishable from our commercial, artistic and political institutions. But ours is a highly unusual pattern. Preliterate peoples and traditional societies rarely have a separable set of "religious" activities. For the ancient Hebrew or the contemporary Eskimo, such distinctions are meaningless. In most cultures, religion is not separable. It is an integral part of healing, planting, learning, hunting, dying and giving birth. Only in the modern industrial West have we delimited the term "religion" to describing what goes on in and around churches, synagogues and mosques. But even that habit is now changing. Scholars are beginning to recognize that "religion" can no more be equated with what goes on in churches than "education" can be reduced to what happens in schools or "health care" restricted to what doctors do to patients in clinics. The vast majority of healing and learning goes on among parents and children and families and friends, far from the portals of any school or hospital. The same is true for religion. It is going on around us all the time.

Religion is larger and more pervasive than churches. Nowhere is this fact more evident than in those areas where this book's themes have led me: in personal life history, in collective memory, and in the content of the mass media. When, for example, we examine our own or another's personal history, including the night dreams and the day fantasies, it soon becomes obvious that we are wandering in a religious realm. However unreligious or "secularized" someone may claim to be, he instantly relapses into being a mythic and symbolic creature as soon as he falls asleep and begins to dream. Our interior stories are sagas teeming with monsters and ghosts, magical flights, bloody ordeals, violence and primitive passion. The same epic religious quality with its heroes, demons and elemental urges also surges through in the group consciousness of human communities and pours out of the mass media. Whether as story or signal or a mixture of the two, religion is everywhere around us. But if we are to avoid the narrow Western reduction of the meaning of "religion," what does the term mean?

"Religion" is that cluster of memories and myths, hopes and images, rites and customs that pulls together the life of a person or group into a meaningful whole. The cluster need not be very systematic, although theologians spend a lot of time trying to make it so. A religion can be creative or demonic, theistic or nontheistic, consciously held or only dimly recognized, static or mercurial, spontaneous or imposed, story or signal. Whichever it is, it lends coherence to life, furnishes a fund of meanings, gives unity to human events and guides people in making decisions. Religion, as its Latin root suggests, is what "binds" things together.

Any religion, whether story or signal, has three identifiable components. First, it tells us *where* we came from and in connection with that often tells us what is wrong with us and how we got that way. Theologians call this part of religion its "myths of origin, creation and fall." Second, religions hold up some *ideal* possibility for humankind. They project the blessed condition of salvation or satori or nirvana. They portray what it would mean to be fully saved or liberated, and sometimes this ideal is personified in saints and holy people. Third, a religion tells us *how* to get from our present fallen state (sick, alienated, lost, in captivity) to what we can be or ought to be or already are if we only knew it. This is the "means of grace."

With this definition in mind, it now becomes easier to see why I think the signal clusters of the mass media can also be understood as religion. TV shows and magazine ads seethe with myths and heroes. They guide decisions, inform perception, provide examples of conduct. Does that make our mass-media culture "religious"? I do not think we can explain its grip on people in any other way. Its preachers tell us what our transgression is: our armpits are damp, our breath is foul, our wash is gray, our car is inadequate. They hold up models of saintly excellence before our eyes: happy, robust, sexually appreciated people who are free, adventurous, competent, attractive. These blessed ones have obviously been saved or are well on the way. And the sacramental means of grace that have lifted them from perdition are available to you and me—soaps, deodorants, clothes, pills, cars. If, despite our devoted attendance at the sacraments, we never seem to attain the promised bliss, well, salvation can be the quest of a lifetime. Mass-media culture is a religion, and we rarely get out of its temple.

Some critics complain that this broader use of the term "religion" only confuses people by violating the usage of ordinary language. They point out that we normally use the word "religion" to designate what people do in churches, or to describe belief in a supernatural being. To broaden the usage, they argue, merely sows confusion.

But surely this narrow usage of "religion" confuses people even more. It blinds us to the fact that we live today in the midst of *competing* religions and value systems and that we are being pressed by this warfare of the gods into making choices we would rather avoid. If we exempt mass-media images from religious definition and evaluation, we allow them to influence us unconsciously, while we continue to dismiss them as trivial. We fail to notice that the behavior models they promulgate often directly contradict the life goals Christianity celebrates. By assigning "religion" and "mass media" to separate spheres we think we are avoiding painful choices, but the fact is that the two are competing for the same loyalties. We should see the mass media instead, I believe, as disguised forms of religion. When we do, we become aware that life is a never-ending series of choices among conflicting values and disparate beliefs, and that when we do not make those choices ourselves, someone is always ready to make them for us.

So far I have touched on the three forms of religion this book is about—testimony, people's religion and the value patterns promulgated by the mass media. I have argued that religions serve the human spirit best when they nurture a lively mixture of stories and signals, but that our society is suffering from a lethal overload of signals. There is still another distortion in the relationship between story and signal, however, one that damages the fabric of the human community even worse than disbalance does. It appears when signals begin to *pose* as stories, when control cues *pretend* to be something other than what they are. This is what I call the "seduction of the spirit."

The term "seduction" as I use it here is not intended to conjure boudoir scenes. To seduce means to mislead or to deceive, and although the word has been used most often to refer to affairs of the heart, most of the so-called seductions that occur between men and women are probably not seductions at all. With rare exceptions, both people are usually fully aware of what is going on. What interests me about the idea of seduction as applied to the spirit, however, is that the great seducers of history all had one thing in common: they could use the natural needs and instincts of another person for their own selfish ends. Seducers employ the language and gesture of dialogue, trust, intimacy and personal rapport with consummate skill. They do it, however, not to develop personal intimacy but to subvert it, not to nourish human community but to undermine it. Seduction is the most callous form of exploitation because it tricks the victim into becoming an unwitting accomplice in his own deception.

The seducer is a signaler wearing the garb of a storyteller. What he tells sounds like a story and has all the marks of a story, but it is really a "line" or a spiel or what is now called a "cover." In this book I use the word "seduction" to refer not to the misuse of romance but to the misuse of religion, not to sex but to the spirit. The seduction of the spirit, in short, is the calculated twisting of people's natural and healthy religious instincts for purposes of control and domination. It is the cruelest abuse of religion because it slyly enlists people in their own manipulation.

When we look at the religious situation of the late twentieth century in the light of a broadened view of what religion is and how it is used and misused, it turns out to be a complex picture indeed. After centuries of enlightenment and skepticism modern man is now evangelized, catechized and proselytized more than ever; but he does not perceive the process as a religious one, so he fails to see what is happening. There are some people who are zealously critical of "religion" in the narrow sense, but they remain vulnerable to religions they do not recognize as such. Meanwhile another irony has appeared. To many skeptics' surprise, "religious" practices and ideas they had thought were long since discarded or outgrown have begun to reappear, often quite noisily, on the streets of our secular cities. From astrology to Zen, from mysticism to Pentecostal healing, from ecstatic dance to chanting—a massive rebirth of spiritual energy is occurring, albeit mostly outside the walls of the institutional churches. Organized religious groups seem bewildered by this unforeseen turn of events. In their justifiable attempts to infuse some moral content into the massive signaling structures of our civilization they have themselves become signal-heavy bureaucracies, cut off from the freshening sources without which both religion and culture die. Understandably they seem startled and frightened by the spiritual outbursts of recent years. When churches are stunned by a revival of piety, and TV commercials take over the indoctrinating once handled by priests, no wonder the picture is confusing.

The situation will become less perplexing, however, if we stop trying to understand it as a battle *between* faith and reason, emotion and intelligence, religion and science. We will make sense of our scene only if we begin to view it as a rebellion by story and symbol against a culture which had gone much too far in the direction of cues and signals. What we are witnessing is a reassertion of the small-scale, the spontaneous, the particular in response to a surfeit of the large-scale, the programmed and the prepackaged. When these terms become clear, religion can no longer be cast as hero or as culprit. It can be both, neither, or a little of each. Healthy religion, like healthy culture, requires a balance of energy and form, of spirit and structure, of story and signal. In an era like ours, where the balance is dangerously wrong, religion can either worsen the disease or help contribute to a recovery. This is the only sound basis on which religious movements, new or old, established or exotic, overt or covert, can be judged.

What role would religion play in a healthy culture? It would spawn both visionaries and codifiers, both prophets and priests. It would be a source of energy and a basis for moral consensus. It would celebrate both heart and head. When the personal, small group and civilizational levels are feeding one another properly, a robust interdependence appears. Stories and symbols enrich memory and conjure new fantasies; prayers and rituals nourish alternative forms of consciousness; signals and structures solidify past gains and provide the necessary stability. Religion as personal testimony, group ritual and civilizational self-image nourishes the spirit at every level.

The problem is that despite the current renaissance, our culture still remains grotesquely out of balance; so consequently religion must play a different role. It must become corrective and critic. If the freeing of persons and groups from the intrusive control of their lives by outside forces is what our benumbed era needs more than anything else, then in our time we must reclaim testimony and people's religion, if necessary at the expense of organized and coded religious systems. Let the apostate, the miscreant and the dissenter thrive! Just as important, we should expose those forms of religion which, posing as entertainment, education or something else, nonetheless stupefy our psyches with vacuum tube demigods, consumer panaceas and mock-up visions of supernal bliss. The actual stories of men and women and the shared memories of living groups could be silenced forever by seductive signals; so we must become partisans instead of onlookers. People's religion is in danger and testimony is discouraged. But without these forms of storytelling we would cease to be human. Therefore religion in our time can best restore balance by being partisan, by supporting the storytellers against the signalers.

I realize that one more book on what religion should do or be will not make much difference in how things eventually turn out, especially if it just describes, exhorts and recommends. It can only help if it becomes itself a part of the counterattack against the discrepant power of signals. In order to make a difference, it must be itself a kind of refusal—a refusal to be quieted, entertained, controlled, directed, informed or cajoled by massive organizations, prepared programs and external signals. It must itself be both a testimony and an endorsement of people's religion. So I will not register here the conventional apology for all the "personal references" in the pages to follow. My telling my own story is in part at least just what the whole book is about.

PART ONE

TESTIMONY

CHAPTER ONE

The Tribal Village

Just as I am, without one plea
But that thy blood was shed for me
And that bid'st me come to thee
O Lamb of God, I come, I come.
—Hymn by Charlotte Elliot
(1789–1871)

IN 1935, when I was six years old, the town of Malvern, Pennsylvania (Chester County), listed a population of 1,555. Apart from this fairly modest demographic aggregate, it had little else to boast of, at least as measured by this fallen world's avaricious calculus. Even in 1935 the world seemed to have left Malvern behind. Like a line drawn by a steel scalpel, the four-track "mainline" of the Pennsylvania Railroad bisected the town into "this side" and "across the bridge." But the trains didn't stop. Like arrogant, preoccupied strangers, they screamed through on their way east to Paoli or west to Harrisburg, bypassing Malvern. There was a persistently whispered rumor that the PRR had once offered to build its passenger depot at Malvern but that the conservative Quaker town fathers on the borough council had turned it down, so the depot was built two miles east in Paoli. Whether this oral tradition is true or not, today Paoli is blessed not only with the passenger depot but with a four-lane highway for its main street, plus more supermarkets, shopping plazas, parking lots and specialty shops than Malvern could ever dream of. Richard Nixon spoke in Paoli during his unsuccessful Presidential campaign against John F. Kennedy in 1960. He bypassed Malvern on his way to his next stop, which was, I think, Downingtown. No Presidential candidate has ever visited Malvern, the constantly cold-shouldered little borough of my birth. I feel sure none ever will.

Even the highway bypassed Malvern. Up until the New Deal, a curving macadam road, then called the Lincoln Highway, ran through Malvern a quarter of a mile on the "other side" of the tracks in the section where most of the few blacks and all of the very few Italians in Malvern then lived, separated from each other by the highway. But during the 1930s a new concrete four-lane highway was constructed to link Philadelphia to Harrisburg via Paoli, Downingtown and Coatesville. Malvern was bypassed. The old Lincoln Highway deteriorated and became neglected, in places even unused. Children played ball on it, and alfalfa shoots poked through the cracked tar. The tunnel it had run through, under the Pennsylvania Railroad tracks, was filled in with shale and dirt, creating a puzzling dead end for later generations of drivers unfamiliar with local history, and a relatively unpoliced nighttime parking area for couples intent on lust.

Industry had also bypassed Malvern. There was a small steel-tubing factory where a lot of people in town worked. But part of the sorry psychological history of the town was its rebuff and abandonment by the Hires root beer people. It seems to have been a case of downright desertion, and during most of the years of my childhood an ugly daily reminder of the humiliation stood on the corner of King and Bridge streets, at the very center of town. It was the large red-brick building once used by the Hires company but now empty and falling apart. Its windows broken, doors bashed in, walls collapsing, the building was finally decreed a safety hazard and razed. But for reasons I've never learned, even the razing was never finished. Maybe the money ran out, maybe the company lost interest. For whatever reasons, it was to remain for decades a half-destroyed, hence even more perilous, ruin. I can still remember a large glob of brick and cement, as tall as a man and three times as thick, hanging by a strand of cable from a half-exposed third-floor girder, like a grotesque sword of Damocles. I had been solemnly warned time and again by my parents never to play around the wrecked building. I'm sure they were right. It was not only unsafe, it was an open shame, and the bypassed people of Malvern would just as soon have forgotten it.

Still, the presence of the old Hires ruin provided the one occasion in my childhood memory when Malvern was not bypassed. During World War II, when the Civil Defense authorities of the neighboring towns wanted to stage a realistic air-raid drill, they selected Malvern as the site. Although it seemed at the time like an honor, in retrospect I wonder: Malvern was picked for the affair because, more than any other town anyone knew of, it looked like one of those bombed-out cities we saw pictures of in *Life*. Obviously Malvern was good for *something*.

Well, the Civil Defense drill was a great success, staged with theatrical realism and gusto. People came from miles away to watch, and the old Hires wreck served as a perfect smashed and twisted backdrop. Smoke bombs transformed it into a nearly believable Coventry. Sirens wailed. Once the crowd gasped as a dummy was thrown off the top of the ruin near the Damocles sword and into a fireman's net. Civil Defense wardens, aides and anybody who could somehow obtain an armband rushed to and fro shouting orders and caring for the wounded, whose injuries, typed out on sheets of paper, were safety-pinned to their chests. I was selected as one of the victims. I still remember a youngish Dr. Jacob Sherson, who years later attended my father while he was dying of cancer, pretending to take care of the fictional injuries described on my paper. He was young, new in town, the only Jew anybody in Malvern knew; and he was obviously trying to do his bit. I remember well because I was embarrassed that my injuries ("bruises and contusions") were not nearly as serious as those of the girl next to me. She had a broken neck and internal bleeding. Some people have all the luck. Anyway, it was a great day for Malvern, even if the reasons our town was selected were a little ambiguous. At least once we had not been bypassed.

I know that nowadays towns *like* to be bypassed. Perhaps the somewhat isolationist decision of our curmudgeonly town fathers to let Paoli have the honor, noise and congestion of the train depot might be viewed today as progressive, even ecologically sound. I know too that city officials today *try* to get highways out of the center of town and to move factories off Main Street, though I doubt that today Hires or anyone else could get away with leaving a teetering eyesore and firetrap in its wake. But in those days, especially for the kids, it seemed that Malvern was a place the whole world had left behind. Unlike our great-grand-parents, many of whom had lived in or near Malvern, we were constantly reminded of the big world outside by radio shows and magazines. But that world was somewhere else, or so we thought. We had to leave town to see a movie, board a train, visit someone in the hospital or even (after ninth grade) to go to school. Since the world had bypassed Malvern, it seemed to many of us, or at least to me, that a kid would have to leave Malvern to find the world.

I'm not so sure about that today. When I wrote *The Secular City* nearly ten years ago, I was still living in the heady ecstasy of escape from Malvern, the gossip-ridden small-town "fish bowl," where everybody knew everybody else. I even constructed an improbable typology of tribe-town-technopolis, ostensibly to make sense of the course of recent world history, but more probably to make sense of my own autobiography. Recently it has seemed to me that tribe, town and technopolis are *not* stages in the maturation of the species at all, even though they did appear historically in that order. Rather, they are different ways of being in the world, each with its own richness and value, each with its faults and limitations. At this stage, there is a little of each in me.

Malvern, for me, represents tribe more than town. It is my ancestral taproot, my *axis mundi*, the cosmic navel, the sacred grove where I first discovered sex and work and death and love. It is where I first felt the unbearable cold that attacks your toes when you trudge home and pull off icy wet stockings after a day of sledding. It is where I first tasted the blood from my own lip, bashed into my irregular teeth by a big kid everyone called Ikey. That must have been in 1936, because he had caught me a block from home wearing my Landon sunflower, a gift from my grandmother, our family's most successful politician. (Politics in the 1930s had also bypassed Malvern, which had remained serenely Republican, at least on "this side" of the tracks, without interruption since the founding of the GOP in 1856.) It is where I first discovered myself alone in the woods on my stomach during an autumn game of hide-and-seek and heard the beat of my own heart against the earth and found that the soil has a dense, dark smell and that under every rotting branch there lives a whole subuniverse of scurrying midges who show little regard for passenger depots and four-lane highways. And Malvern is where I first learned about God. For if the world had bypassed Malvern, He certainly had not.

Even in the 1930s you didn't have to leave Malvern to find God. For a town with fewer than 2,000 souls we were more than amply blessed with churches. We had more churches than filling stations, more churches than saloons, more churches than restaurants. In fact, if I count correctly, there were more churches than all of those things put together. Which is cheating a little, because in those days we didn't have *any* restaurants. We did have two saloons and three gasoline stations. We had, however, eight churches. God had not only not bypassed Malvern, He had also generously provided a rich, if somewhat bewildering, variety of ways to approach Him. The tribe had several clans, and although there was sometimes suspicion and sniping among them, there was never intratribal war. Maybe that is why I've always been a pluralist. When you grow up in a town where on a warm Sunday with all the church windows open you can hear gospel hymns being sung and the Mass being chanted at the same moment, pluralism comes easily.

The churches of Malvern during the 1930s reflected, of course, what my scholarly mentors have since taught me to recognize as "class and ethnic lines." To start at the top of the pecking order, there was a lovely limestone meeting house, with nearby antique stables. It was used by the diminishing but stubborn band of Quakers. Inside were hard wooden benches, appropriate, I always thought, to the parsimony and severity of the Quakers I knew. I only saw those benches through the windows, however. Although the meeting house stood only a block from where I lived, and I often cut across its lawn on my way to my grandparents' house, I never once entered it. That seems strange to me now, especially as I remember being in all but one of the other churches at least once. Maybe it's because the congregation was so small and the meetings took place, I think, only once a month. Maybe it's because they never held youth meetings, community Christmas services or even weddings—which provided the occasions for my visiting other churches. More likely I absorbed from my parents a feeling that the Quakers, who had founded Malvern after all and represented the closest thing we had to a nobility, were a cold and inhospitable lot. They had some personal reasons too. My paternal grandfather, John Foreman Cox, had been "separated from meeting"—that is, excommunicated—in 1898 for "marrying out of meeting"—that is, taking a non-Quaker girl to wife. Grandfather immediately became a not particularly devout Baptist and hated the Quakers ever after. Grudges among the clans do last a long time in bypassed villages, even unto the children's children.

Well, to slide down one notch on the scale, we also had a small Presbyterian church in Malvern. During the whole period of my boyhood its congregation persevered patiently under the preaching of a pleasantly intense and lively man cursed with the most rasping, abrasive voice I have ever heard and given to forty-five-minute sermons. Why, I often wondered, did they stay? I think I know now: They had no place to go. The Presbyterian church provided the niche for that minuscule stratum of the upper-middle who were not "birthright Quakers" (and surely no one *else* would attend meeting) but who would have felt miserably uncomfortable with the altar calls and teary revivals at the Methodist and Baptist churches. Far better the predictable drone of dependable moralisms that you could cope with, at least, in your pew than to be asked to "come forward" or to testify. John Calvin would have been mildly pleased to see that his God cared for the elect even in Malvern. You had to leave town during the 1930s to be an Episcopalian. The closest Episcopal church was in Paoli, two miles away. The only family I knew in Malvern who went there was that of the president of the town's only bank. No, there was also my Uncle Harry, the town's only undertaker. A marvelously genial man, he was, however, seen by some people, including my parents, as something of a social climber. He was the one person we knew who belonged to a golf club and drove a Cadillac. When he retired from his mortuary business a few years ago, he also became a bank president.

We all admired and liked Uncle Harry despite his upward mobility. Maybe it was the *way* he did it. Although the Episcopal church smacked to me in those days of the society pages, coming-out parties and people who wore red coats and rode horses after foxes and dogs—a very distant world indeed—Uncle Harry had been a poor up-country Episcopalian from a very pious family *before* he got rich, so he never got snooty about it. Maybe because he saw so many dead bodies he seemed to have a kind of jocular contempt for worldly rank and privilege. He made it big, but he never forgot old friends or kissed anybody's ass. And he was a vestryman at the Church of the Good Shepherd, Episcopal.

There were two churches for blacks, or "colored people," as every well-mannered kid was taught to say in those days before Malcolm X and Stokely Carmichael. On "this side" there was an African Methodist Episcopal (A.M.E.) congregation housed in a tiny brick building on an unpaved street in a section of town where, to this day and in seeming disregard for the changing tides of racial integration, separation and the rest, black and white families live cheek by jowl. My Grandmother Cox often took me to church suppers at the A.M.E. church. It never occurred to me then that the black townspeople at the suppers, enjoying that savory ham, corn on the cob and fried chicken, were also voters, and that her being there might have helped her to get re-elected year after year to almost any office she wanted, or that she went there for that reason. I don't honestly think it occurred to her either. For Maud Cox it was one way to get away from cooking dinner and to chat for two hours with willing listeners.

The other black church remains a mystery to me even today. It stood across the bridge, not much more than a shack clinging to a corner of land near the abandoned section of the old Lincoln Highway. It housed a Baptist congregation made up mostly of the poor, mainly darker-skinned, black people who lived nearby. It represented then, I suppose, the end of the class-ethnic spectrum opposite the Quaker meeting. Maybe that's why it is the only other church in Malvern I have never been inside. But I still feel sad and cheated about that. I went to school and played and fought with kids who went to that church, but not until I was in my teens did I see anything odd about their having completely separate ways to God. I sometimes wonder now if that strangeness ever struck them.

St. Patrick's Roman Catholic Church, a large stone Romanesque structure, stood next door to the rambling brick-and-frame double house I lived in. On the other side of the house stood the large brown Baptist church where I belonged. When people find out today that I spent the first seventeen years of my life living in the only house standing *between* the Baptist and the Catholic churches of Malvern, they often make some quip to the effect that I was fated or predestined to become an ecumenical theologian. I'm not so sure about that. I am sure, however, that the location has a lot to do with the way I *felt* about the Catholic Church. The way I felt, and still feel, expressed in a few words, is "close, but outside."

During the 1930s Vatican II, the ecumenical movement and all that could hardly have been anticipated in anyone's wildest fantasies. Catholics were busy building up the separate school system so many of them would now like to unload. In Malvern the parochial school was a tiny affair, housed in an old residence across the street from the church. The pupils, always clothed in black and white uniforms, played during recess on a gravel lot next to our side yard. They were pretty noisy during their games but got very quiet amazingly fast, I thought, when the nun rang a large silver bell. I grew up thinking there was *something*—I was never really sure what it was—*different*, either about me or about them. In the 1930s there were probably more reasons for the Catholics to feel different from me than vice versa. The bitter memory of Al Smith's defeat in 1928 still rankled. Catholics and Protestants lived in overlapping but still somewhat separated worlds and heard piles of rumors and nonsense about each other, some of which is still there in our heads. Most of it we just forgot as soon as we heard it, but the impression of a real difference persisted.

Many years later, in 1959, when I was a graduate student at Harvard, I helped organize a group in which Catholics and Protestants could meet to discuss theology and politics. How daring the idea seemed in 1959! Since then I have taught Catholic (as well as Jewish, Buddhist, Mormon, Muslim and atheist) students; lectured at the Pontifical Catholic University of Peru in Lima (the first non-Catholic theologian to do so); been personally received (and mildly condemned) by Pope Paul VI; preached in Catholic churches; celebrated communion jointly with priests; been arrested in peace demonstrations with priests and nuns. Together with one Catholic priest, Nicolas Spagnola, I officiated at one of the first ecumenical wedding services ever held in Boston, the marriage of my youngest brother, Phil Cox, to Mary Ellen, née de Stefano. It took place at the Sacred Heart Church in Newton. I suspect that at least as many Catholics as all other people put together read my books.

But despite all this welcome ecumenical thaw, and despite our natural desire to emphasize similarities, we are now at the stage, I think, where we can not only admit to but celebrate our differences. They make the stew more succulent. A lot of those differences, I am discovering, have to do not with doctrine but with feeling. And a lot of them root in our childhood.

My own childhood impression about Catholics was that they were just that: different. Not that they had guns in their church basements or were going to take over the country, but that their religion seemed like an unnecessarily elaborate caricature of what I had been taught was quite simple and that the rules they followed, like not eating meat on Friday, were not only very strict but pointless. It really wasn't the Friday abstinence I minded, it was the impression they conveyed, usually subtly, but often explicitly, that somehow they were closer to God because they devoutly ate tuna fish while I ate salami. What bothered me, I guess, was not the difference itself but that they seemed very sure they were right and, at times, even arrogant about it. By high school it was a commonplace among the rest of us that it was just plain useless to argue with Catholics about religion, because no matter what you said, they *knew* they were right, or at least they seemed to know.

I don't think all that would have irked me so much except that I harbored a secret suspicion from a very early age that they just might *be* right. Sometime very early on, just after I had learned to read, I noticed one day that their church had engraved on its cornerstone an inscription stating that it had been founded by Jesus Christ Himself. Himself! The comparable stone in our church said "Founded in 1846," which even as a small kid I knew was considerably *later* than Jesus Christ's time. Besides, when men walked by the Catholic church some of them took off their hats. They didn't do that in front of ours. And whenever I peeked in the half-open doors of St. Patrick's while on my way to Stackhouse's grocery store or the post office, I'd catch a glimpse of a mysterious darkness broken only by an even more mysterious flickering red lamp. Catholic playmates assured me in hushed tones that Jesus Christ Himself was up there on the altar. We didn't even *have* an altar, let alone one with Christ Himself on it. Many times I would like to have ventured into the dim recesses of St. Patrick's, but I was scared. It seemed so foreboding, so dark and awesome. I wondered to myself sometimes how it would feel to be inside that fearsome place, not to be viewed as an outsider, how it would feel to be at home there, protected by those uncannily powerful mysteries instead of threatened by them.

I never got into the main section of that Catholic church until my cousin Phyllis married a Catholic man when I was in my late teens. The closest I got were those occasional peeks plus attending musicals in the church basement. Again it makes me a little sad to think about that. I had cousins and playmates right on my street who were Catholics. They wore medals, crossed themselves now and then, went to confession on Saturday afternoons and, of course, didn't eat hamburger on Friday. But we never once visited each other's churches. They had been taught, at least they told me then, that it would be a sin for them so much as to *enter* our church. There was even some question, I remember, about whether they would be endangering their souls to come into the social hall of our church for a covered dish supper on Wednesday night. Naturally I could not help wondering what it was about our church that posed such a terrible threat.

All the same, I was secretly a little relieved that they were not allowed to come in, because I was afraid they'd see right away that there wasn't much to it. We had no little red lamp, no rose windows, no exotic darkness. Our windows were plain glass. I wasn't exactly ashamed. I just didn't think they'd understand what was important to me about my church, and I knew I couldn't tell them. So they might get even more smug. Better they shouldn't know.

No one ever told me I'd go to hell if I went inside the Catholic church. I did get the clear impression, however, from both sides, that my presence was not sought and that I would not be very welcome. I still remember a dream I once had as a child in which I found myself sitting and trying to appear unobvious in the last row of the Catholic church—very dark and terrifying in the dream—during a Mass. Suddenly I was being singled out by the priest and commanded in a sepulchral echo-chamber voice to kneel. When, years later, I read Kafka's *The Trial*, I was astonished to find a very similar theme there, K.'s strange experience in the cathedral of Prague. Maybe it's an archetype.

In any case, archetype or no, I grew up with the feeling that Catholics either knew something I didn't know or thought they did. And I really wanted to know which it was. I think I still do. Though I hated to admit it, it often seemed to me that our Baptist church, which with an average Sunday attendance of fewer than a hundred people was still the most "successful" non-Catholic church in town, nevertheless looked somehow amateurish, precarious and insecure when compared to the Catholic one. That would have been all right too, I guess, but what really hurt was that my Catholic playmates always seemed so sure. They seemed to have no doubts whatever, and I had had doubts ever since I could remember. Was there *really* a God, or were people just wishing? Did we really go somewhere better after Uncle Harry had drained our blood and we'd been put in a satin-lined casket, lowered into a grave and covered with dirt, or did we lie there forever and ever, the worms devouring our flesh? I lay awake many sleepless nights over those questions, even at nine and ten—and I still sometimes lose sleep over similar questions today. Maybe my Catholic friends and cousins had doubts too after all. Or maybe they didn't. In any case, they *talked* and *acted* as though they didn't, and that's what bothered me most about them.

Today, decades later, when I talk honestly to Catholics, I get the feeling that, although they belong to the Catholic Church, they know now how I felt then. For now, even on the inside of their church, that serene assurance is gone. So is that secure conviction that it all goes back directly to God Himself. Catholics too now know that awful sense of precariousness. The flickering red light is still there, at least in some parishes, but doubts and uncertainties inhabit the darkness around it. The Catholic Church I knew from the outside, and they from the inside during those now long-gone days, just doesn't exist any more. In that sense we are all "outside" now, and our task is to learn how to live with it.

There was also a Methodist church in Malvern, quite small, where the people sang a little louder and took revival a little more seriously than we Baptists did. They sang hymns that might have seemed a little too emotionally explicit to the more dignified pillars of our church. On a warm Sunday evening, from two blocks away, you could hear the Methodists singing:

> What a wonderful change in my life has been wrought,
> Since Jesus came into my heart!
> Floods of joy o'er my soul like the sea billows roll,
> Since Jesus came into my heart.

It was one of their favorites. They would sing the verse and then hold the word "since" a long, long time, coming down and then bouncing ahead on the word "Jesus." Their singing was often accompanied by a trumpet or even a trombone. In our church, musical instruments—other than the organ—were generally used only for solos. I have since learned that the 1930s and 1940s were a period of great emphasis on social action in American Methodism. Somehow that emphasis never seemed to reach Malvern. But I don't really mind that very much. It was a happy, warm church where nobody looked at you funny if you really poured the volume into a gut-busting hymn: "*Since* . . . . . Jesus came into my heart. . . ."

My own family belonged, more or less, to the Baptist church next door. My parents, during my boyhood, rarely attended, although later on, after I went to divinity school, they went more often. But they were never very regular churchgoers. Still, all through the 1930s they did send us to Sunday school, where my excommunicated ex-Quaker grandfather took the class roll and counted the nickels and pennies in the collection. But that was about all the religion he could take. He left the church building after his Sunday school treasurer's duties were done and sat on his front porch reading the Sunday edition of the Philadelphia *Inquirer* and smoking a cigar. He never once attended church services, so far as I remember, during his entire life. My grandmother never missed. A large handsome woman reputed to have been a famous beauty in her youth, she was kind, jolly, easygoing and totally untheological. For her the Baptist Church, the Fire Company Women's Auxiliary and the Women's Republican Club were all overlapping tents in the same big county fair, and she loved to be in the center of it all. Although she was at times a member of various county and even state Republican committees, her politics was as nonideological as her religion was nontheological. She hated cooking, rarely cleaned house, dressed haphazardly and spent most of the day wandering the streets of Malvern conversing cheerfully with everyone she met. She never lost any election she ran in and she died of a heart attack in her seventies one blistering July afternoon while buying the rolls and hot dogs for the annual volunteer fire company fair.

My own recollections of the First Baptist Church of Malvern are a mixture of warmth, boredom, awe, guilt and fascination. We sang hymns about crosses and blood and pilgrims and diadems. We heard time and again stories about David and Goliath, Saul and David, Adam and Eve, Cain and Abel, Jesus and Judas. At unforgettable moments other people, and eventually myself, would be immersed in the sloshing waters of the baptismal pool, with the congregation singing "Just As I Am." I remember especially the second verse of that hymn:

> Just as I am, though tossed about
> With many a conflict, many a doubt,
> Fightings and fears within, without,
> O Lamb of God, I come, I come.

That was just how I felt, and it seemed good to be able to sing it. I was at home in church since before I can remember.

I know, probably better than most people, how narrow and mossy Baptist churches, maybe all churches, can be—how intolerant, ignorant and all the rest. When I went to college I was sometimes embarrassed when people would ask about what they usually referred to as my "religious background." It seemed to be assumed that having something like that in your childhood, though unfortunate, could be outgrown. But since I've gotten beyond that sophomore intellectual stage, I have never wanted to disavow that so-called "background," because when all is said and done, it remains the way I met the holy, and I've never been able to shake that off. I doubt that I'll ever want to.

I got baptized myself when I was ten, going on eleven. That seems a little young, and in retrospect I can scarcely claim to have reached the age of consent. I can't say that I'd had a deeply emotional salvation experience beforehand or anything like that. I had not. I hardly knew what was happening.

One Sunday our minister, Mr. Kriebel, visited our boys' Sunday school class and asked how many were now ready to follow Jesus into the waters of baptism. We all liked Mr. Kriebel immensely. A youngish man at the time, he was a somewhat uninspiring preacher but an incomparable small-town pastor. He was always on the spot when people were down with flu or stomach trouble or when someone died. Besides, he took us swimming in his rattling 1935 Ford and both coached and pitched for the church's softball team. He had a way of standing stiffly in his tight Sunday clerical clothes which made you think he would be more comfortable in a cotton pullover and sneakers. He read a lot though, especially biography, and peppered his sermons with stories from the lives of great painters, explorers and composers. Mr. Kriebel in 1939 made $1,600 per year plus use of parsonage and car expenses. We boys all admired him, and it seemed important to him that Sunday that we be ready to follow Jesus. So we all said we were. It sounded like a small thing to do.

There were only six of us in the class, so Mr. Kriebel had us all come over to his parsonage for three or four weeks for a baptismal class where, mainly, we learned what we were to say when the deacons examined us and how to respond to the questions the minister himself would put to us in the baptismal pool. Our preparation, however, was not very adequate, since it did not include instructions on how to handle the situation that would arise if one of us got the giggles during the prayer part of the deacons' meeting, which is exactly what happened. Our examination by the deacons was a disaster, but they were not of a mind to turn down candidates for baptism, I guess. So they accepted us.

I was baptized not in a white robe as the pictures of old-time baptisms show but in a pair of worn white slacks and a loose white shirt. The minister wore a black robe, weighted at the bottom seam to keep it from floating up, and hip boots. At baptisms that I'd seen before I knew about those boots I was always astonished at how quickly he could reappear in the pulpit, perfectly dry, after conducting a baptism, to dismiss the congregation. The baptismal pool itself, as in most Baptist churches, was located behind the pulpit and built in such a way that you could both enter and leave it from its sides without having to walk through the congregation. I've been told that in old Baptist churches this architectural concession to the modesty of candidates for baptism was not the custom, that the pools were often built near the center and that when you came up dripping and sputtering from the waters you could not disappear discreetly into a wing but had to make your way, with lots of help of course, right through the waiting congregation to wherever you got dried and reclothed. Of course in the really old days baptisms occurred in rivers. By 1940, however, in the First Baptist Church of Malvern, they had become considerably more decorous.

I entered the pool that Sunday with very little sense of what I was doing or why. The choir and congregation sang very softly, "Just as I am, without one plea." The water came up to just above Mr. Kriebel's waist. It came up to my armpits. He stood facing the congregation over the edge of the pool and read something from the Bible. I think it was about the baptism of Jesus by John the Baptist in the River Jordan. I stood with my side to the congregations on his right. When he finished the reading, he closed the Bible and asked me in quiet serious tones whether I accepted Jesus as my personal saviour. I said I did. He then said, in a somewhat more public voice, that he was baptizing me in the name of the Father, Son and Holy Spirit, placed one hand behind my back and lowered me backwards into the water while I held a white handkerchief over my nose and mouth, as we'd been taught, to keep the water out. He held me under only for a second, then pulled me back up, turned me around and handed me to the deacons who were waiting in the wings to help me dry off and return to the main section of the church to be welcomed into the congregation as a full participant.

I tried to be as nonchalant as possible about my baptism, even to joke about it as soon as I could. I even remember quipping lamely to the elderly deacon who helped dry me that I wouldn't need a bath that night. But I just couldn't pass it off as glibly as I wanted to. It made a telling impression on me. I'd be very sorry if in some future ecumenical version of Christianity that terribly primitive rite, so archaic and so incontrovertibly "out of date," were to disappear. I say that even though I was baptized long before I should have been. My real religious crisis, when I agonized over whether I was saved, going to hell, and all the rest, came during my late adolescence. I even resented at that time that the minister and deacons had allowed us to get baptized, maybe even pushed us into it before we were ready. I don't resent it now. They were doing the best they could. They probably wanted to get us all into the church before we dropped out of Sunday school, which a lot of boys did in their teens. And with me, it worked. I did drop out of Sunday school soon after I was baptized, but I hardly ever missed church. I went, not because I had to, but because I wanted to. I don't know why for sure. Somehow it just seemed important.

My resentment at being baptized at ten before I was ready and then having no ritual available to mark my adolescent religious crisis may help explain some of my current interest in ritual. I believe that as a culture we are ritually out of phase. We are dragooned into rituals that mean little or nothing to us—saluting flags, national anthems, commencements, even bar mitzvahs and confirmations—yet when we need the symbolic deepening of an important experience, we somehow lack the necessary gestures and images.

Nothing is easier to make fun of than the sloppy, improbable form of baptism I experienced at ten, the awkward effort, complete with hip boots and warmed waters, to keep something of the primitive in a modern hygienic setting.

But maybe we laugh too soon. Remember *your* emotional state at thirteen or thereabouts? Remember your need to deal all at once with anxiety and awkwardness, identity and faith, finding your way out of childhood, facing your own death, finding something to live for? Is it any wonder that nearly every culture in the world has devised rites of passage—initiation and puberty rituals—to deepen and resolve this perennial crisis? The Cheyenne lad goes out to the forested hills alone, sleeps on the ground, lives without food, suffers cold and loneliness, sees a vision and then returns to the tribal circle to become a brave and to receive a new name. He has endured his ordeal and is now an adult.

Today in America we have few if any puberty rites. Children pass awkwardly and without ritual through sprouting pubic hair, menstruating, changing voice, having wet dreams, getting hold of the family car keys. No wonder we undergo "identity crises" until we die. Rituals should mark and celebrate the transition from one phase of life to the next. But our lives are phaseless, like an automatically geared car shifting noiselessly from one speed to another. And the result is that we never know for sure what gear we're in now. Children try to act like adults and adults like children.

For me, despite its being too early and only fully appreciated much later, my baptism was what some young people today might call a "real trip." There were all the symbols of blood and suffering (sharing the death of Jesus), the physical act of going under the water, the facing of embarrassment, fear, the triumphant emergence, the feeling that I'd been through something and was starting a new phase.

The word "trip" here is not accidental. I wonder sometimes how much drug trips have begun to take the place of our culture's forgotten or abandoned puberty rites. The experience is similar in many ways. You expose yourself to danger and death. You make a break from the world of childhood. You see visions. You may suffer pain. You come back, usually, and are received into a new phase of life by those who have undergone the ordeal before you. You may even feel you've seen God or have found a way of life.

I don't believe for a minute that all those terrifying "drug education" spots on TV will scare kids out of trying drugs. In fact, they may have the opposite effect. Everyone longs, sometimes secretly, to experience altered states of consciousness. Adolescents are intrigued by death and danger, *not* repulsed. How can people lure them *into* movies with the same symbols they somehow think will *repel* them from drugs? Our drug epidemic may or may not be a serious one. But I believe it is the symptom of a deeper cultural disease—the disappearance of legitimate occasions for ecstasy, trance, emotion and feeling, and the erosion of traditional rituals. When I was a kid, people got "high" at revivals and during other religious events. Everyone needs to experience that special kind of mental elation now and then. If we don't do it one way we will do it another. We won't outgrow drug abuse until those needs too, not just our needs for bread and housing, are cared for. Man does not live by bread alone.

In recent years I've become much more interested in this issue of "ritual" (a word I usually define as "symbolic action," in contrast to myth, which is symbolic thought. The two go closely together and are seldom discovered in isolation from each other). I forget just when the word "ritual" ceased having a negative, sticky-sanctimonious connotation for me and began serving as a pivot around which I could organize a lot of the loose ends not only in my thinking but in my life. Maybe it happened in the middle 1960s when I first fell in with the "radical Catholics" like Corita Kent, Dan Berrigan, Ivan Illich and the people from Emmaus House. Maybe it happened during that period of the anti-war movement when the immolation of draft cards in altar-candle flames was going on. In any case, the power of symbolic acts, "the politics of gestures," certainly became a central concern for me by the time the peace movement began using rituals like coffins, mock burials, fasts, sanctuary vigils and the rest. After participating myself in many of these rites, and seeing the impact they had

on all kinds of people, I couldn't really go on claiming that man is
leaving behind his "religious stage," including ritual and myth. I
just could not believe that idea any more after, for example,
watching dozens of young men come forward and solemnly burn
draft cards at the altar of the Arlington Street Church. It was all
there again—puberty rite, sacred flame, ordeal, risk, the symbolic
act of cutting oneself off from one community and becoming
part of another, the choosing of a new way of life. The boy becomes a man with a new name. As those draft cards crackled in
the candle flames, I could see in the smoke the shadows of rites
that reached back to the infancy of the species. I became convinced at that moment that although modern urban man was certainly not religious in most conventional senses of the word,
neither was he secular in the way I had once thought. I could see
that ritual and religion were *not* going to wither away, and that
the real issue now was whether they would be used for man's
liberation or to keep him in bondage.

The Berrigans and many others had seen all that and felt it long
before I did. They knew the potency of gestures. They acted on
it in the blood pouring and the burning of draft records. In their
melding together of ritual and revolution, the politics of symbolic gesture again began to play a decisive role in the American
consciousness. I'm convinced now that man never "outgrows"
rituals, although he certainly uses them for vastly different
purposes and relates to them in ever-changing ways.

Until quite recently I was deeply confused about the sources
of my interest in ritual. Hadn't I come from a notoriously "anti-
liturgical" and "non-ritualistic" church? Was I regressing into a
primitive stage of my own, and maybe even mankind's, religious
development? Was it a loss of nerve?

I think the answer to all those questions is no. I grew up in
a church which I was told time and again by those inside it and
outside it was "anti-ritualistic." But it is no such thing. It holds at
the core of its life one of the most powerful rituals anyone has
ever undergone—identification with the burial and resurrection
of the God through a deathlike total immersion in water. It fairly

crawls with archetypes, and however much Baptist preachers may inveigh against "ritualism," and I've heard it inveighed against hundreds of times, people who, like me, have gone through the waters at an impressionable age can never honestly deny the uncanny power of that experience, even if they have junked all the doctrinal interpretation long since. Archetypes touch you at a level far deeper than doctrines.

What I am saying is that I no longer view my recent increased interest in ritual and myth as a deviation from my "background" but as a rediscovery of its essential quality. Mircea Eliade says somewhere that initiation is the most pervasive and perennial of all forms of ritual. I think he is right. Even more importantly, an initiation rite like the one I experienced, even when shorn of its particular denominational interpretation, still creates a life paradigm of enormous potency. Plunging under the water says that life is made up of one risk after another, that maturation requires the continuous surrender of familiar securities, that I can't breathe free unless I have taken the leap.

But church was not just terror and purgation for me. It was also a groove: taking up the collection in wooden plates with green felt bottoms and discreetly trying not to notice who put how much in; thumping out the bass line in choir anthems like "Jerusalem" and "The Stranger of Galilee" after my voice changed; consuming enormous amounts of baked ham, candied sweet potatoes and lemon meringue pie at potluck suppers. But, more than anything else, what got to me about church was the ministers.

The ministers who came to our little congregation for what was usually a short pastorate, probably because they were paid so poorly, were a varied, eccentric and completely unstereotyped lot. They could hardly have been cum laude seminary graduates to find themselves in what must have been an unprestigious outpost even in its own denomination. Still they were always larger-than-life figures to me. Their black suits and booming voices set them apart from other mere mortals. Their sheer knowledge seemed amazing to me and their confidence and poise unbounded.

But at the same time they were invariably friendly and accessible. They even *wanted* to know me. They were a little like God. Although ministers obviously commanded respect and even deference, they also weeded their tomatoes, had sickly wives and squawking children, and sometimes seemed discouraged or angry. Besides, they had huge collections of books, were actually *paid* to read them and to prepare sermons. They knew, it seemed to me, almost everything, and they didn't seem to be afraid to die. How else were they able to talk about it when nobody else did? I can't remember when I didn't want to be a minister when I grew up.

When I think back, there were obviously other things about the ministers that attracted me. For one thing, they were never completely at home in Malvern. Most people in our town were born there or close by and lived there until they died, although even in the 1930s they were beginning to leave town to die in the hospital in the county seat seven miles away. But the minister always came from somewhere else, stayed a few years, then left. He was always something of an outsider, without cousins and uncles in town. He was *in*, but not *of*, our world, to paraphrase St. Paul. His coming and his going reminded me of that vast larger cosmos in which little Malvern was located. The preacher, even if he stayed five years, was always to some extent a stranger in a strange land. Maybe that gave him a little of the aura of transcendence or at least of the "otherness" the representative of God must always signify, whether he likes it or not.

The fact that ministers came and went or, as it was always put, were "called" and "went on to larger fields of service" also made its impact on the congregation. We knew the church was not his but *ours* in a special, rather disquieting way. We knew we couldn't ultimately depend on someone else to solve our problems. Because Baptists have a congregational form of church government, we came to sense very sharply, especially during the times of preacher transition, that our choices were real and important. This was true even among the kids, since anyone who had been baptized could vote in a church election. It was one of the few things we did not giggle about. No one *sent* a pastor, as happens in Catholic and Methodist churches. We had to "call" him, and this meant appointing a pulpit committee that would go around interviewing prospective candidates, listen to them preach, and then recommend one, or sometimes two, for a vote by the full congregation. I know all this well because my first real experience in participatory democracy came when I was thirteen. That year, because I was a little precocious and president of the youth group, I became a full voting member of one of these periodically necessary pulpit committees.

When the preacher left we were on our own, abandoned in a sense like Christ on the cross by what classical theologians call the *deus absconditus*. We had to take things into our own hands and start over. It was sobering to sit with all those adults, some of them sixty years older than I, and to know that my thirteen-year-old vote would help determine who would lead our church for the next few years. But I also felt a heady tingle of power. No mere student council or Boy Scout election this. We were charged with the awesome task of choosing the man to represent God in our midst. And we did it. Ever since then I've been less apprehensive about sharing power with nonspecialists, letting the people themselves make decisions. I've been more skeptical of a god who does everything for us or to us and more willing to imagine a divine-human partnership than many theologies allow. Maybe that's why I'm more intrigued by people's religion and popular culture. I can honestly say that as a kid I absorbed more about God and man from participating in congregational life than I did from the worship and preaching.

There was even a kind of paradox between the preaching and the practice that set up a tension I have felt ever since. The preaching tended to be vaguely Calvinistic, spiced with generous doses of pietistic flavoring. Basically, however, we were told that God saved man by grace, that grace was unmerited and that there was nothing at all we needed to do to earn it, just accept it. The analogy of a gift versus a purchase was used all the time by the preachers, and people giving testimonies would frequently repeat the idea that they had tried to do this or that with no satisfaction and had finally been saved only when they realized that God's love was absolutely free, that Christ had already died for our sins and that all we had to do was to "open our hearts and receive Him." But in contrast to this God-does-it-all preaching there was the evident fact that *we* had to keep the church going, organize its programs, select its leaders, pay its bills and paint and repair the building. God did not do that, we did; though when we were finished we always thanked God for what He had done. The ancient riddle of faith and works, activity and acquiescence was built into my consciousness from the start.

It is an eternal riddle. In various guises it has charmed and pursued me throughout my life. I am intrigued by the multiple ways people form and are formed by their cultures. It is not only true, as Churchill once said, that we first shape our buildings and then are shaped by them. It is also true, I believe, of our symbols, our institutions, our culture and our religion. My fascination with this unending interactive process goes back, I am sure, to that portentous experience of power and weakness, of selecting preachers and then being taught by them, of molding and being molded by a religious community—all of which took place with such a vivid quality in the life of a small religious congregation like the First Baptist Church of Malvern.

The reason why I focus so sharply on the issue of activity versus acquiescence or, put in a stronger way, rebellion versus resignation is that in the past few years it has become a central issue in theology. Several recent religious writers, motivated in part by the ecological crisis and inspired often by Oriental religious traditions, have argued that Western man sacks and pillages the planet largely because of his drive to master, subdue and dominate and his seeming incapacity to merely let things be. This frenzied Western man, so the allegation runs, pushed by an overdose of activistic earth-denying Judeo-Christian religiosity, must tear up, shovel around, intervene and alter. He cannot simply fit into the way things are. It is not a theologian but a landscape architect, Ian McHarg, who puts the indictment most tellingly:

> On the subject of man-nature, however, the Biblical creation story of the first chapter of Genesis, the source of the most generally accepted description of man's role and powers, not only fails to correspond to reality as we observe it, but in its insistence upon dominion and subjugation of nature, encourages the most exploitative and destructive instincts in man rather than those that are deferential and creative. Indeed, if one seeks license for those who would increase radioactivity, create canals and harbors with atomic bombs, employ poisons without constraint, or give consent to the bulldozer mentality, there could be no better injunction than this text. . . . When this is understood, the conquest, the depredations and the despoliation are comprehensible, as is the imperfect value system.

Since the source of the infection is religious, some writers urge that the antidote this haplessly driven Western plunderer needs is also religious. Ivan Illich in *Deschooling Society* prescribes a rebirth of what he calls "Epimethean Man," the mirror-opposite of that type of person whose ideal is Prometheus (who was the brother of Epimetheus). Instead of storming heaven, stealing fire, conquering and subduing in a Promethean mode, humankind should now renounce its obsessive need always to smelt old ways and forge new policies. We should make our home on earth. Illich locates the wrong turn our civilization took not with the Hebrew creation myth but with the rational and authoritarian Greeks of the classical period, whose priests of Apollo, identified by Illich with purpose and utility, stole the sacred site at Delphi from the Earth Goddess and installed their oracular policy consultants. This fatal fall from the Epimethean Eden reached its Greek extreme, for Illich, in the rigid human-engineered state described in Plato's *Republic*, a place from which poets and flute players were banned. Other writers place the ecological fall not with Genesis or the Greeks but with Western Christianity, Protestantism or modern liberal religion.

I take a special interest in the current and somewhat fashionable attack on Western culture and its Greek and Judeo-Christian sources because I am occasionally singled out as one of the main contemporary perpetuators of this tragic error. One theologian has devoted a sizable part of his book to a criticism of Teilhard de Chardin and myself as "extrinsic" theologians, who allegedly place man so far outside of, above, or in opposition to nature that he must see nature as a foe to be vanquished. Some critics, including Illich, attack the idea of *homo faber*, man the maker, as the most vivid symbol of what is wrong in Western man's view of himself. "Something," says Illich, "is structurally wrong with the vision of *homo faber*."

My suspicion, however, is that the critics of *homo faber* and of man's creativity have themselves become unwitting victims of the same technological imperialism they correctly deplore. They have done so by allowing the very terms of the debate to be dictated by the other side, always a fatal error. They have done it in this case by accepting a reduced, technologized definition of *homo faber* and then turning against it. But this is a historically shortsighted error. The truth is that human creativity is not mainly a technological or even material faculty at all and that the technicians and institutional operators have stolen the joyful task of creating from the artists, visionaries and poets, shouldering them to the edges of society where they can make no real contribution to the spiritual renewal of the culture. There is nothing essentially wrong with the concept of *homo faber* itself. Human beings are in fact creators and shapers as well as enjoyers and receivers. What is wrong is that those with a narrow and external view of man's capacity to make have kidnaped the concept and now insist on using it to describe only their own arrogant attempts to impose their plans on everyone else. What they would like us to forget is that men and women not only make space capsules, they also make myths; they not only construct bridges, they also construct limericks and legends. They not only invent welfare schemes, they also invent plots. Notice how even the terms we use, like "construction" and "invention," which once had a wide cultural sense, are now used almost entirely to refer to a much narrower range of artifacts. But the defeat is not yet a rout. The imagination of one person is still a thousand times more capable of creating things than all the factories in the world. In our rightful need to move away from images of man the plunderer of nature and man the programmer of his neighbor we should be careful not to throw away our last weapon; we should refuse to allow the enemy to define for his own convenience what our capacity for creation is or is not.

The primal confrontation today is not one between the active shaper and the passive, unassertive recipient. It is not, I hope, between creating man and receiving man. It is between those people who quietly insist on telling their own story and creating their own styles, and those who try to seduce, impose and inculcate. In such a world, where life styles are so often prepackaged, let us avoid using arguments that weaken anyone's capacity to roll his own. That capacity is itself a part of being *homo faber*. What we must do now is not to swear off designing our environment but, as McHarg himself says, to "design *with* nature" instead of against her. Let us not slay the creative urge in man because a misguided elite has wrongly channeled it into devising endless programs and useless consumer products. It can do better.

Some of the critics of *homo faber* suggest that people today are dispirited mostly by the fact that they see themselves in a world made entirely by man. I disagree. Such a world would indeed be dispiriting, and its horror supplies a further reason for us to design with full cognizance of how nature can be preserved and enhanced. What dispirits most people today, however, is not that their homes and institutions are man-made but that they live in a world made by someone else. Their inner desires are anticipated and exploited, their daily schedules are printed out for them, their career trajectory is mapped by benevolent institutions. But they are losing, and they know it, because their inherent need to share in the shaping and creating process is being taken away from them

I will not recant my belief in the capacity of human beings to play an active part in shaping a world that will, of course, then shape them in return. I do not believe we will stem the plague of pollution by abdicating our role as the earth's stewards but only by doing it more compassionately and imaginatively. But a lot of the difference between myself and other theologians on this issue goes way back to those early childhood experiences. In the Catholic Church thirteen-year-old boys must absorb a lot about the mystery of the Mass, the power of gesture and sacrament, the objective *otherness* of the holy, by serving as altar boys and acolytes. The Catholic religious sensibility includes, from very early on, the feeling of being *part* of a vast, ancient and relatively fixed reality. Like the grace that was promised to me in those sermons, the church itself, for Catholics, was not something you had to do anything about. It just *was*, and all you had to do was accept it. I could sense that even in my Catholic cousins and playmates.

But my own experience was quite a different one. At thirteen I had to sit late into dark winter nights with the troubled elders and choose, amidst growing uncertainty and confused counsel, the man who would open the mysteries and interpret the Word. The contrast becomes even more dramatic when one realizes how central the minister is in a church where, within limits, he can alter the liturgy and modify the church's practices without the objective structure of the Mass to provide continuity. Baptists have no standard Mass, no recurrent liturgical year, fewer visible assurances of the universal scope and ancient credentials of their sacred cosmos. Much, much more depended on the preacher. And *we* had to choose *him*. We knew how ill equipped we were to make that decision, and how terribly precarious the whole thing was. And we knew how all of us would be changed in ways we could hardly imagine by the choice we would make. But we did it. Although I've sometimes longed for a community, even a world, I could simply accept without also having to constitute it, my experience has never allowed me to have it. As the old Presbyterian catechisms used to state, the chief end of man is to glorify God and enjoy Him forever. "Glorify" is an active word, but even for those activist Calvinists it was only half. "Enjoy" means savor, receive, delight in. To use a different metaphor, life for me is a two-step saraband of creating and letting be, of making and simply enjoying, of molding and then being molded, of work and play, prayer and politics, telling and listening. If you reduce it to a one-step, you might just as well stop the music, because it isn't really a dance any more.

I left in 1946 to get out to see the world that had bypassed Malvern. I did it by spending a few months on the horse and cattle ships being run after the war by UNRRA and the U.S. Merchant Marine. During those months I sailed to England, Germany, Poland and Belgium, first on a dilapidated Liberty ship called the *Robert Hart*, named for the captain of a previous vessel who, in defiance of a new regulation, had insisted on going down with his ship instead of abandoning it; and then on a newer ship called the *Pass Christian Victory*, named after a small Gulf port in Mississippi. Malvern seemed very far away, but everywhere we tied up I visited churches, many of them still in ruins. I never told my shipmates about my boyhood hope to someday become a minister. I felt they wouldn't have understood, and besides in those days I often wondered about it myself.

I came back to Malvern for a short while before I went away to college at the University of Pennsylvania in 1947. But after I'd crossed the ocean a few times Malvern didn't seem the same. No one in my family had ever crossed an ocean. Most had rarely ventured outside Chester County. Before I left I had wanted to get away from Malvern. Now I'd been away, but I didn't really want to come back. Besides, everything was changed. Ministers had come and gone in the Baptist church. The old brown coloration I remembered, somber and serious, was gone. It was now painted white and had a new "religious education" wing. Later on, after I'd graduated from divinity school, my father died and my mother sold our old brick and frame house to the Catholic church next door. It is now occupied by the Sisters of St. Joseph. The last time I was in town I noticed that the old Hires ruin had been removed, and a small clean plastics factory stands on that once shameful spot. An independent fundamentalist group has bought the limestone Quaker meetinghouse. The trains still bypass Malvern, but now that everybody drives cars the townspeople feel more mobile, if not as involved with one another. A couple of housing developments have added five hundred souls to the population, so it is now actually possible to see someone in the post office no one knows. Even Malvern has edged over the line and is now almost a *suburb*, no longer the tribe or, more accurately, the *village* where I grew up. The tribe is gone, at least physically, especially for the people who still live there. But for me, Malvern will never change. The tribal village is eternal. The old Malvern which is gone forever is more real for me than the new one that now exists. It molded impulses and instincts that still move me every day. It aroused obsessions that still haunt me. It kindled longings I will feel until I die. Malvern was the place where, as I might once have said, and can still say in another way, "Jesus came into my heart," where the awful sense of the fathomless mystery and utter transiency of life first dawned on me, and where I discovered that in the midst of all that terror and nothingness I was loved. What more could anyone's tribal village do for him?

CHAPTER TWO

The City of Light

Hail the glorious Golden City,
Pictured by the seers of old!
Everlasting light shines o'er it,
Wondrous tales of it are told.

And the work that we have builded,
Oft with bleeding hands and tears,
Oft in error, oft in anguish,
Will not perish with the years.

It will live and shine transfigured
In the final reign of Right;
It will pass into the splendors
Of the City of the Light.
    —Hymn by Felix Adler
    (1851–1933)

By building a golden temple one is freed from all sins.
He who built a temple of Vishnu reaps the great fruit
which one gains by celebrating sacrifices every day.
Vishnu is identical with the seven worlds.
He who builds a temple for him saves the endless worlds
and himself attains immortality.
    —*Agni Purana* XXXVIII : 48–50

THE TREAT of the year for my younger brother and myself in the
days when we attended the Malvern Public School happened
early every December: my father kept us out of class for a whole
day and took us on an annual Christmas outing to Philadelphia,

twenty-two miles from Malvern by train. We always said we were going "to see Santa Claus," and when I was very young we did, standing in those endless lines at Gimbels or Strawbridge's and then crawling up on the lap of a tired red-suited employee we knew was a phony to whisper what we wanted for Christmas. After I was seven, that part of the expedition dropped out and the three of us spent the day riding subways, taking in movies or listening to one of my father's favorite big bands like Count Basie at the old Earle Theatre on Market Street, eating at the automat and looking at the Christmas displays. But we still referred to the trip as "going to see Santa Claus." We all knew what it meant.

No wonder "the city" has always been a positive symbol for me, despite all the bad things that happen in and to cities. Nor do I see any contradiction between the theme of *The Secular City* (urbanization) and the themes of *The Feast of Fools* (festivity and fantasy). The first real city I knew was the place we went to celebrate the most colorful festival of the year. Pathetic sooty old Philadelphia was both my first technopolis *and* the setting for my first feast of fools.

After I left Malvern at seventeen, with the exception of a few years in Oberlin, Ohio, I have always lived in cities. When I finally moved from Malvern to Philadelphia in 1947 to attend Penn, I got addicted instantly to city life. I worked once a week with a boys' club in a leaky settlement house at Third and Reed, mainly with impoverished Italian kids who smoked cigarettes at ten, masturbated in the shower stalls and screamed homicidal threats at one another after every play on the basketball court, while I stood by ineptly. I handed out leaflets at Thirty-seventh and Spruce for Joe Clark, the 1950 Reform Democratic mayoralty candidate. I rowed with the freshman crew up and down the Schuylkill River past boathouses, factories, tenements and the huge Greek-pillared museum of art. I roamed the bars on Market Street, took dates to Fairmount and Wissahickon parks, and explored Philadelphia's many riches—its movies and the old Troc burlesque house at Tenth and Arch, its jazz emporia, bookstores and slot machine arcades. And its churches. But what impressed me most was just the city itself—its sheer scope and immensity, its variety, its infinite possibilities. Philadelphia in the late 1940s, the noplace so many nightclub comedians have joshed and belittled, was *not* Malvern. It was still *The City* for me. It was where I could light a cigarette on the street, wear any kind of affected clothes, stay out all night without being missed. It gave me my first taste of that liberating anonymity I was to salute years later in *The Secular City*. It was where I began to become, and *like* being, an "urban man."

If these postadolescent high jinks appear to have introduced me only to the fun-and-games side of the city—the jovial Elysium where conventioneers slip away to drop bags of water out of hotel windows—then the appearance is misleading. During my time in the Merchant Marine I walked for hours in the endless devastated streets of Gdansk, Poland (the "Danzig" of the period between the wars), followed by bands of children begging for food. During the three years supposedly spent at lectures at Yale I also worked in ward politics and got up at five-thirty on freezing Connecticut mornings to distribute leaflets as a part-time union organizer outside the gates of Winchester Repeating Arms. I lived and worked one summer in the early 1950s in Stepney, the poorest part of London's east-end dock section. In the early 1960s I lived with my wife and children in perhaps the most cosmopolitan and tragic city of the world, Berlin. After that we lived for nearly seven years in Roxbury, Boston's black ghetto. We were the only white family in sight. During that period I saw muggings in open daylight and police firing guns at people within one block of our front door. The house itself was burglarized eleven times during our last two years in it. I have visited not just the tourist brochure settings of Rio and Lima and New Delhi, but also their *favellas, barriadas* and alleys. I have not just nibbled at the frosting of urban life. My feeling for the city and my hope for its future have some basis in a more varied experience. But my hope is based on something more than experience. It grows out of a vision of the destiny of the human species in which the city plays a central role.

The religion of *homo urbanitas*, the dweller in the city, is a special kind of religion. Regardless of his or her religious past, once the city really makes its impact on the psyche, any city person's religion begins to have more in common with that of other city people than it does with the faith of people of his own tradition who still live, either physically or spiritually, in the countryside or in small towns. The phenomenon of urban religion has been known for some time, even though I myself first began to discover it only as a college student home from my wanderings at sea. But since then I have become more and more convinced of its reality. There is not only a distinctive urban mentality, there is also a characteristic form of urban faith and a peculiar way city people feel the basic religious question.

This should not come as any real surprise. No religion floats above its terrain without touching. The faiths people hold to invariably bear the telltale marks of the places where they originated and developed. For centuries before the rise of cities people met their gods in forests, grottoes and hills. My experience of the holy had come in a bypassed hamlet with eight churches, an abandoned root beer factory and a main street where you rarely met a stranger. But for the noisy kids I vainly tried to supervise in South Philadelphia, and for increasing millions of people everywhere, the forests and grottoes and villages are gone. The man-made metropolis itself is now their *axis mundi*. This has been true for *some* people for centuries. But they have always been a minority. In our own time the balance has tilted. More people, and a higher proportion of people, are "urbanized" today than ever before, and the process proceeds apace. The religious implications of that fact are enormous.

Of course the process goes both ways. Not only do cities markedly alter the faiths people bring to them, religious visions and values also influence the character of cities. The interaction is never ending. Imagine first how a religious change or awakening can influence a city. A new charismatic prophet arises—a Gotama or an Amos or a Mohammed. Or a new revelation comes. Encounter with another people and their gods through conquest, defeat or simple peaceful coexistence brings new stories and symbols. Religions change. But since the religious vision anchors a whole way of seeing the world, changes in religion alter the way people experience what is around them. Not only does religion provide the symbols people live by, it also reflects itself in the layout and mapping of their settlements, in their government, customs and art. Geneva under Calvin, Baghdad under Haroun-al-Raschid, and Rome under the Renaissance popes all changed dramatically from the cities they were before the new faiths took hold. Inspired by new religious vision, reformers have torn down and rebuilt entire spatial environments.

Sometimes they have started all over. The emperor Constantine simply forsook Rome and erected a new capital on the straits of Bosphorus, not just because the Franks were at the portals but because he wanted a capital whose streets and temples would not bear the taint of the pagan past. He believed the new faith required a new city. Many other cities have had comparable beginnings. My own Philadelphia began as a "holy experiment" in the mind of an eccentric English Quaker.

But the other side is also true. The relationship between earth and heaven is reciprocal. Just as new religious insight can change man's experience of space and time, so can a new experience of space or time alter his religious vision. Imagine an American Indian tribe living amidst steep cliffs and swift mountain streams, each with its spirits and daemons. Imagine this tribe now forcibly resettled on a plain without mountains or rapids, with no rocky ravines. Americans have inflicted such resettlements not only on Indians but also on Africans and now on Vietnamese and Laotian peasants. In our haste we have not recognized that such forced changes are also desecrations. They not only cause social trauma, they disembowel the gods and render whole civilizations incapable of coping with life. All people need symbols and stories for dealing with individual and corporate crises. But stories stem from particular places—this bush and that precipice. So when the bushes and precipices are left behind, the stories are sometimes forgotten. In this way a tribe can suffer something comparable to what in an individual we call a nervous breakdown.

What would have happened to Egyptian society, not only to its agriculture but to its government, religion and art, if for some reason the annual flooding of the Nile had ceased? Think of the impact of volcanic eruptions and glaciation on a Stone Age tribe's rudimentary religion. The experience of place is an important factor in the formation and change of religious vision.

One of the most remarkable features of the history of the people of Israel is that they responded to such jarring changes in geographical and political setting with such astonishing religious creativity. One reason for the persistence and universality of biblical faith is that, although it grew out of radically different experiences of space and time, it never forgot *particular* places. Rather it endowed specific locations with a universal meaning. Babylon now means any place of exile, and Jerusalem any city of home; Sodom is any den of wickedness, and Calvary any place of sacrifice and testing. At the same time these sites and scenes gave flesh and cartilage to the faith. Without their particularity it could not have had the widespread appeal it has.

City people have a different religion from others. Their faith comes in part from the past but also in part from their urban experiences of space. This has been true ever since the first city. But our time is different. Not only do many more people now live in cities, but many millions have had to make in one lifetime the shattering transition from rural to urban that in previous centuries were made over generations. Since I made that change, it has always been a part of my theology. Someone once wrote that the best literary descriptions of the Catholic Church are not written by "born Catholics" but by people who have either been converted to it or left it. One thinks for example of Graham Greene the convert and James Joyce the apostate. The same is true about the city. To be able to write about it one must probably have had to come to it or to have fled it, to have felt firsthand the difference it makes. During those first years in Philadelphia I was formed in my spirit and intellect as much by living in the city as I was by the lectures I heard and the books I read. Also, something else was happening, a kind of religious equivalent of a well-known biological phenomenon. Just as the tiny human foetus starts out with tail and gills, and recapitulates the evolutionary history of the species, so was I reliving in my own psyche the jarring religious and cultural pilgrimage of twentieth-century man. If more and more of my personal reality was defined by the dynamics of the city, that was also true for the whole human race. Thus *my* way of stating my own religious qualms and quests had become in one sense at least quite typical. As a theologian I could have some assurance that my own experience was not eccentric and that, although it was part of my own story, it was the story of a lot of other people as well.

But what is the nature of this crucial difference in the religion of urban man? First of all, cities draw to themselves a wide variety of people, so city man's faith must be capable of living in the midst of fractious pluralism. No religion that relies on cultural isolation or spatial insulation can long survive the close-packed density and daily conflict of a city. Again this was something I first experienced only when I began to live in cities. Even in fusty old Philadelphia there were not only Baptists, Nazarenes and Catholics; there were Jews and Buddhists and atheists and Communists. There were also pimps, panhandlers and con artists. My tolerance was put to the test. I not only discovered how much of a minority I was, I also learned that most people living in a cosmopolitan urban center eventually discover they are a minority too. During those years I became aware of a new kind of human being. I called him "secular man." I think now that was a misnomer. Perhaps what I should have called him was "cosmopolitan man" or "self-conscious man." I meant that person who knows at a very basic level of his being *his own story is only one among many*. The shock of this discovery may make him an agnostic. On the other hand he may reappropriate components of his religious heritage in an even more personal and conscious way. He may be totally taken in by the religions of the media, but he can never again be uncritically and unreflectively "religious" in the traditional sense again. He cannot go back to the tribe. The secular city man may still remember the old stories and symbols, but he recognizes them as such. This makes his religion, whatever it is, very different from the faith of the villager.

Besides being necessarily pluralistic and self-conscious, the urban person's way of articulating the religious question also differs in another way. He must test out his powers and come to terms with his limitations, not against nature but against the vast social and technological artifacts that frame and outline his life. Like human beings of all ages, his faith must help him find his own place within the cosmos, his proper role in history and his appropriate relationship to the holy. But the powers he contends with are different.

The difference between urban man and others is a matter of degree but an important one. For the preliterates, nature was always the first concern. It was powerful, unpredictable, beneficent and cruel. Their religion of taboo animals, fertility rituals, harvest feasts and rain dances related them in complex and imaginative ways not only to one another but also to these dark and whimsical natural forces. Later, during the rise of the so-called "higher religions," when nature seemed to be more often a friend than a foe, and when social structures were of a sufficiently modest scale that few felt overwhelmed by them, the compelling concerns had to do with what we now think of as "religious" questions: death, relations to the deity, final guilt and punishment. These issues have provided the principal focus of most of the major religions of the world since the disappearance, except for isolated survivors, of preliterate societies.

Ironically, urban man's contemporary religious quest is more like that of "primitive peoples" than it is like that of classical Christians and Jews. He too is more interested in finding his place in a cosmos which is also both beneficent and cruel. But that cosmos is no longer, in the first instance, nature. It is a society and a network of artifacts, both created by previous men. It is an asphalt jungle whose thunder comes from splintered sound barriers and whose plagues are caused by the poisons spewed forth by man's own inventions. But when the A & P shelves are empty he knows of no fertility dance that will fill them, and when he wants to gain favor from one of the powers that rule him he knows no prayer to say. The fascination we have today for primitive societies is understandable. We are more like them than we think. Our religious questions are similar. Who am I? Where do I fit in? But their questions were addressed to a very different world, so we cannot simply copy their answers. We must find our own.

Ecological writers who criticize Christianity and Judaism for their overwhelming emphasis on the relations between God, man and neighbor, with little emphasis on the rest of "nature," are partially right. These faiths emerged in history at a time when nature was no longer seen as such a terrible threat and the religious question focused on man and God. It was a time when human beings were going through that crucial evolutionary stage of understanding their uniqueness as creatures who, though clearly a part of "nature," also in some ways transcended it. So the critics have a point: "Nature" is not a crucial factor as such in biblical religion. History, not nature, is the place where a drama of choice and destiny, rebellion and reconciliation is played out.

But what the ecological critics of Christianity overlook is that our present crisis is not *primarily* one of our relations to "nature." It has to do with man, with whether we can begin to control the runaway growth of technology, redirect the use of energy to compassionate purposes, reorder our institutions to a more humane scale and design habitations that will not strangle or suffocate their inhabitants. It has to do with how we can devise an economic system which does not exist by creating false needs, using up non-renewable resources to assuage them, and poisoning the planet with the effluvium of the process. So this challenge to our survival obviously requires a faith that helps man deal not so much with "nature" but with choice, power, institutional corruption and corporate greed. Though our questions today are very much like primitive man's, it would merely hasten the disaster to emulate his answers. Our job is not to return to the forest but to turn around a juggernaut.

Christianity was born at just that period in history when the foundations for our present global-urban civilization were being laid. It sees the threat to man not in thunder and flood but in invasion, plunder and conquest. It sees the spirit of evil not in taboo trees but in armies, chariots and proud towers, in "spiritual wickedness in high places." Jesus is not Osiris. He is not sacrificed to assure the fertility of the soil. He is executed by a nervous imperial official who fears him as a threat to the political order. Christianity, in other words, centers mainly on man's powers and temptations in the personal and political realm. But I see this as a strength, not as a weakness, in facing the "ecological" crisis. No single religious tradition has the answers we need, and if urban man is to survive at all, his faith must surely include a symbolization of his place within nature. But we cannot find again our place in "nature" (a slippery concept in any case) unless we cope at the same time with the man-created practices, institutions, customs and goals that have now brought us to the brink of ecological disaster. Urban man's question about his place in reality *includes* nature, but it focuses specifically on his place in social reality: How much can he control it? How much must he be controlled by it? How much must he simply find a place within it?

How does the new urban pilgrim answer these questions? The classical myths often provided such answers in the past and still do today, albeit often in newly tailored costumes. Karl Marx saw himself and the spirit of nineteenth-century man best epitomized by the figure of Prometheus. Nietzsche, with his idea of the Übermensch, the superman, seemed to agree. As we saw in the last chapter, some recent writers believe it is just this Prometheus complex which has gotten us into all the trouble, and they call for a rebirth of "Epimethean Man," the quiet receiver, the unassertive husband of earth, the resigned and ironic refuser of power. But there is a special problem today. Whereas for the Greeks Prometheus and Epimetheus represented two separate role possibilities, city man today feels that he is both at the same time. This anomaly is understandable, since, ironically, modern urban life heightens both man's sense of possibility and his sense of powerlessness, both his anger and his acquiescence, his rage and his resignation. The contradiction is now worldwide. The city has its tenements and executive suites, its dominated groups and its ruling elites. It has produced a Jekyll-Hyde world-city denizen who combines the hubris of Prometheus with the resignation of Epimetheus. Sometimes he wants to plan and control everything, to program the whole universe, leaving nothing at all to chance or impulse. At other times he wants to resign it all, "let it be," allow nature to take its course. Furthermore the two contradicting selfviews prod and irritate each other. Defeated by the bad results of a spasm of controlling and dominating, man then sinks back into cynical acquiescence and indifference. But this too produces intolerable consequences, so he rushes forth to straighten things out again. It is a kind of manic-depressive syndrome. Can Christianity still contribute an alternative identity image?

Only if we first undo some previous mistakes. Christian theology, instead of holding human creativity and creatureliness together, has falsely emphasized the *contrast* between man's exercising power on the one side and his accepting the will of God on the other. As a result, the church has often viewed rebellion against any form of domination including tyranny as rebellion against God too. Or theology has counseled urgent activism, told man to subdue nature and build a new world, with no place given to enjoying what is here now, loving with the earth as a sister and conserving all the threads in the fragile web of nature. Christian theology has not itself used images of Prometheus (assertive activism) or Epimetheus (letting things be) very often, but it has perpetuated these styles with its own images. The frenzied soul saver and the frightened recluse represent Christianized versions of Prometheus and Epimetheus. The cool big-time operator and the cynical bench warmer are their secular equivalents. So cyclical spasms of getting things done alternate with seasons of bottomless despair. But these images just will not provide a viable story or a credible self-symbol for urban man. Instead of any of them I prefer another image: the biblical metaphor of the old and the new Adam, of man fallen and restored.

Metropolitan man's spiritual dilemma centers primarily on who he is, what his powers are and what his place is, and only indirectly on the character of God; therefore I believe the stories of Adam in Eden and Jesus and the New Jerusalem inform us better than the old Greek heroes or their modern stand-ins. Adam, who represents both man and woman, was made out of the muck and slush of earth and is therefore always a part of it. He is in nature, and nature is in him. Though his "ruach" or spirit came directly from God, he was not, like the Greek heroes, born from the amours of a demigod and a princess. He is fully human, and any pretensions of ever becoming a god are excluded. Adam becomes a steward of the world not as an act of adolescent rebellion but to fulfill the purpose of his creation. He is given the gratification of naming the animals and the responsibility of cultivating the garden. He enjoys these powers not through an act of *stealing* from the gods but as a prerogative granted by the Creator. He is expected to use his status to conserve the greenness of the planet, to shepherd its resources in service to his fellow man and to relish its fruits and bounty.

Man's "fall" in the old myth did not begin with his exceeding his limits. It began when he asked the snake to make the first decision he confronted, whether to snatch for the status of deity. His sin was not pilfering God's fire but abdicating his choice to a fork-tongued consultant, not so much pride as sloth. After that, of course, Adam panicked. He tried to become the omnipotent all-controlling deity. Instead of imaginatively fulfilling that part of the cosmos-tending he was well equipped to do, he plotted to become the Master Programmer, the Ultimate City Planner. This obsessive need to run everything led, according to the old biblical story, to exile, sorrow and fratricide. It still does.

The banishment from Eden, however, is now behind us. Most people in cities, especially poor people, do not suffer primarily a rebellious Promethean urge. They perceive themselves to be the limp marionettes of an invisible hand. The cities they live in throb and pulsate, grow and sprawl with no apparent reason or direction. Sudden death, unexpected joy, hilarity, violence and madness wander their streets. Somebody else decides if a skyscraper goes up or a neighborhood is torn down. For powerless people an automobile accident or an adequate apartment is a mere instance of statistical probability or of favors dispensed by faceless figures "up there."

But man's natural need to shape his world and order the chaos will not be stilled. If he can't find one way he'll find another. Sitting in a Detroit jail during the uprising of 1967, fifty young black men repeatedly asked their guards how the fires they had set were going: "Is it really burned down?" Tired of being the playthings of an invisible puppeteer, they had at last reached for the flame. Though locked in cells, they felt they had finally achieved *some* control over their own destinies. For a few glorious hours they had taken the strings in their own hands.

Since man sees his relationship to the modern city in this manic-depressive way, we are indeed exiled from Eden. Our cities are becoming progressively uninhabitable. Although some European capitals have so far escaped the worst dirt, muggings and din of their American counterparts, the cities of the Third World are becoming more and more like Los Angeles, vast carbon monoxide–clogged conglomerates where paranoia is the only reasonable posture.

There are many questions one might ask about the blighted technopolis of today. Mine has to do with the future of faith in the metropolis. If the city by its very ethos is forming the religious sensibility of millions of people, just as my spirit was sculpted by my early years in Malvern, what kind of spirit is it shaping?

My fear is that millions of people, most of them now children, will grow up feeling not like any god or hero at all, not even feeling like human beings but like rodents locked into a cage which is tended by someone else and in which there is no way to change anything. Their response to this plight will not, however, be pious resignation. Rather, as Stanley Kubrick has forecast so frighteningly in *A Clockwork Orange*, it will be sporadic, impulsive and ultimately useless violence undisciplined by any real hope. To some it seems that the curse God once breathed on Sodom and Gomorrah is now damning all cities, that fate has marked our cities and with them our urban civilization for either airless strangulation or instant nuclear death.

But let us recall once more the old myth. God's answer to Adam's depressive abdication of the human *locus* and his manic grasp at total control is *not* unending divine punishment. God does not, according to the biblical story, fetter Adam to a rock. Instead there is another chance. A Second Adam appears and initiates an impulse toward the restoration of man in his proper relation to nature and God. As the Second Adam or the New Person, however, Christ does not finish things completely. He is not a *deus ex machina*. Rather he begins something, then enlists people in the process of redeeming and rebuilding. The culmination will be, according to the promise, not another garden but a New City.

I do not believe the "fallen" men and women of our time, the power-mad controllers and deflated dropouts, can be restored to appropriate human powers by mere exhortation. They will be saved by a new corporate reality which, paradoxically, must be both a task and a gift. It will be a city they build and also simply receive, a result of combining the keenest human dexterity with that unpredictable input from elsewhere that still merits the term "grace."

Any credible theology of "The City" today must begin with the recognition that our actual cities are in deep, deep trouble. Refugees stream to the suburbs, possessions in hand, like the dazed survivors of a bombing. They return each day in platoons of cars to plunder, so smog and traffic thicken. Programs to mend, renew or improve cities follow one another into the dust-bin of disappointment. Meanwhile, as cities swell beyond any reasonable size, and gag on the mucus of their own infection, they have more and more diagnosticians but fewer and fewer friends. Not only do our terrestrial cities suffer under the siege laid on them by the times, they must also endure the active dislike of ecologists, poets and idealistic young people. Worst of all, the very idea of the city as a desirable form of human com-munity is now called into question. Anti-urbanism, always an alluring cause in America, has recently recruited a mixed crew of new champions. Revolutionary writers like Franz Fanon and Che Guevara, still popular among some young people, oppose the city because it harbors powerful oppressors and weakens the ardor of young rebels. The parents of the same young readers hate American cities because they are full of blacks, foreigners and welfare cheaters. Ironically, hatred for the city is probably the only element in the thinking of Che and Fanon with which the harassed parents of America can agree.

Despising the city produces strange bedfellows. The late Frank Lloyd Wright, America's most honored architect, disliked cities intensely, described them as a cancer, and wanted to disperse the entire population throughout the countryside on small plots of earth. But the Broadacre City he advocated was actually very close to what we now endure in suburbia. In America, as Morton and Lucia White have shown in *The Intellectual Versus the City*, our leading thinkers in all fields have always displayed an anti-urban animus. They might have added that our religious leaders have often been anti-urban as well, and many popular religious writers remain so today, although their reasons for opposing the city are diverse and often even contradictory. Two examples— one Protestant and one Catholic, one from several decades back, one contemporary—illustrate this puzzling agreement among the divines in detesting the city. Josiah Strong, the influential turn-of-the-century Protestant divine, feared that the city could well become the place of mob rule, and worse still mob rule by non-

Anglo-Saxons. "The city," Strong wrote, "has become a serious menace to our civilization." It contained, he said, such evils as "mammonism, materialism, luxuriousness, and congestion of wealth." Furthermore, the city was the home of the saloon and of socialism, but worst of all, "because our cities are so largely foreign, Romanism finds in them its chief strength."

The recently deceased Trappist monk and writer Thomas Merton, the most recent poetic prosecutor of the city, saw it not as a mob scene but as a technological monstrosity. By its very nature, Merton believed, the city prevents people from contemplating and thus from achieving any real relation to God. In his essay "Rain and the Rhinoceros" he contrasted the attitudes toward rain of country folk, who welcome the cloudburst as a refreshing gift of life, and city people, who rush to get out of it and view it as a vile interruption of their routine. Merton used "The City" as a dramatic symbol of the world without God. As a counter symbol he preferred "The Monastery," where men may pray and meditate without distraction.

Some of Merton's complaints about our cities are true and his vivid descriptions of New York, its "ceaseless motion of hot traffic, tired and angry people in a complex swirl of frustration," are often accurate. What worries me, however, not just about Merton but about other religious critics of the city, is their tendency to use the awful woes of earthly cities today as the excuse for making "The City" into a symbol of eternal metaphysical evil. One could certainly find corrupt monasteries, weed-infested gardens and shabby villages that would also cast some doubt on the serenity, beauty and simplicity of their religious analogues. But these places do retain symbolic power. Likewise with the city. The sad fact that it is now in such trouble seems to me a reason to stand by the ancient urban ideal, not to scuttle it. Anti-urbanism, in short, is too faddish and too popular to deserve the support of a person as rightly contemptuous of mere "trends" as Thomas Merton was.

Religiously inspired anti-urbanism appeals to people of many different theological viewpoints. There could hardly be two people of more contrasting spiritual temperaments than Josiah Strong and Thomas Merton. The reason for this disparity seems plain enough. Different people hark back to different experiences with the city, sometimes very contradictory ones; hence "The City" symbolizes diametrically opposed things for different people. For some it is the prime location of order and even of regimentation; they oppose it in the name of freedom. For others it is the den of deviation and licentiousness; they oppose it in the name of law and order. For some it is the place where innovation and novelty spring up; they oppose it in the name of continuity and tradition. For others it is where established routines weigh most heavily; they flee it for the unstructured simplicity of somewhere else. It is Babylon, Sodom, Gomorrah, the Harlot on the Seven Hills.

This religious anti-urbanism is deeply ironic. Christianity was born in a troubled provincial capital, flourished in the slums and ghettos of the ancient Mediterranean basin (Rome, Corinth, Ephesus) among an urban proletariat, spread through the settlements of Europe, spawned new cities in North and South America, and hymned its vision of destiny with the image of a New Jerusalem. What then can we say to these recurrent episodes of hatred for the city which Christianity still seems to produce?

I cannot reply to all the anti-city theologians at once. Some indeed hardly merit a reply. But there is one who undoubtedly does, the man who, of all the current religious rebukers of the city, is the most vigorous and relentless, namely the French Protestant lay theologian Jacques Ellul. I find myself stunned and angered by his recent anti-city manifesto, published under the title *The Meaning of the City*, but it commands attention if only because of its sweep and energy and because of Ellul's growing popularity.

Ellul believes that what is wrong with the city is in no way accidental or remediable, it is universal and essential. The city in short has been cursed. It is the incarnation of the venerable Calvinist doctrine of total depravity.

But surely what Ellul, as a good Calvinist, means by "cursed" is that in some sense every part of man and the entire panoply of human works are tainted by sin, that all men everywhere need grace? Wrong. In Ellul's eyes the malediction under which the city grovels is a special one. "This curse," he says, "is not only that is placed on the entire world, but is a special curse on the city, both as belonging to the world and in itself." There is nothing we can do to save it.

That sounds dire, and at this point readers who are not familiar with the sin-and-grace reverse loop Ellul is employing might be tempted to go watch TV instead. If there is really *nothing* to be done, then reading Ellul's remaining 200 pages seems pointless. Those who sniff out the gambit, however, perhaps tipped off as I am by deeply instilled childhood memories of Protestant sermon structure, can predict what is coming. Though sin abounds, we know grace abounds even more in the final reel. Meanwhile, however, the picture painted must be unrelievedly odious.

Grace does come eventually in Ellul, even for the cursed city, and is symbolized by the New Jerusalem. But something is missing. Ellul's grace doesn't quite *reach*. "Let there be no confusion," says Ellul. "There is no use expecting a new Jerusalem on earth. Jerusalem will be God's creation, absolutely free, unforeseeable, transcendent." Well then, does the New Jerusalem make *any* contact whatever with our cursed and smelly old Jerusalems here in history, our Tokyos, São Paulos, and L.A.s?

Apparently not. Ellul assures us that "as individuals with a life to live we are in contact with the condemned city and not with the New Jerusalem." This coming glorious city is a "revelation of God's grace" and we should resist the temptation, he warns us, to force it in any way "into the present course of things."

But it is a temptation, even for Ellul himself, who deftly draws some policy opinions from his *theologia negativa* of the *urbs*. For instance, he is against decentralizing cities. It would merely multiply average-sized cities, he says, and facilitate social control. He is very negative about building new cities, and he is against both reform and revolution in the old ones. In other words, if the promise of the coming New Jerusalem cannot be applied to the course of things here below, its very lack of relevance does suggest an occasional idea—always negative.

What then *are* we supposed to do? Ellul admits his advice sounds a little banal.

> . . . our job is to lead the life of the other inhabitants of the city. We are to build houses, marry, have children . . . And thus we are to continue from one generation to the next, assuring, it would seem, that very stability and depth which men were seeking when they built the cities. Are we to do nothing differently? There is one thing which is not asked of us, and that is to *build* the city. We are to live in the city already existing. [P. 74.]

This will surely come as good news to the average apathetic churchgoer, or more likely as no news at all. It is just what he always suspected the Bible had to say, about cities or anything else: nothing. We are supposed to dwell within the city but make no effort to change it, none whatever.

True, our average churchgoer may idly wonder about Jesus' attitude toward Jerusalem. Didn't he confront her rich with stinging rebukes, lash out at her lying lawyers and swindling tax collectors? Didn't he upset the tables of her religious racketeers, rouse her rabble and finally get himself arrested and executed by her power elite? It is here that even John Doe might wonder about Ellul's use of the Bible. "When [Jesus] speaks to the cities," Ellul says, "he never has anything but words of rejection and condemnation. He never proclaims grace for man's work. All he recognizes is its devilish quality, and his only reaction is to struggle against the power of the city trying to hinder his work." Does this interpretation describe the mixture of sorrow, love and anger that seems to color Jesus' words to Jerusalem in the famous passage in Matthew 23:37 where, after rebuking the city for killing the prophets, he then says, ". . . how often have I longed to gather your children around me, as a hen gathers her brood under her wings, but you refused"? Ellul sees only the condemnation. Jesus speaks to the city, he says (and he insists it is *all* cities), "only to curse her. Furthermore," he continues, "his words are not exactly spoken to the city, but are pronounced *against* her, and they do not establish a relation, but serve notice of a schism." Jerusalem as the ultimate city receives a kind of ultimate curse. But in receiving it she really stands for all cities. *No* city, Ellul insists, can escape God's condemnation.

By now we have begun to suspect, rightly as it turns out, that Ellul's chilling verdict has to do with something more basic than the city or its merely terrestrial miasma and muggings. He is really talking about something else. And it is only as we begin to grasp what else he means by "the city" that his sentence of death makes any sense at all.

I have already said that attitudes toward the city vary so basically because "The City" is a *symbol*. It means more to people, positively and negatively, than the sum of its parts. Ellul is no exception. For him the city is the most vivid and compelling symbol of man's stubborn pride and rebellious disorder. "The city is," he says, in a sentence reminiscent of St. Augustine's description of his wayward male member, "independent of its inhabitants." It seems to go its own way. It is not made just of bones and blood, nor of steel and concrete. It is principalities and powers or, as Ellul himself puts it, "a symbol and a spiritual power."

Ellul deals with "The City" in much the same way he discussed "*la technique*" in a book which appeared in English as *The Technological Society*. Like the city, technology for Ellul is a metaphysical reality. Like the erotic impulses that finally drove Augustine to chastity, technology is caught in a self-propelling autonomy. It is just here that Ellul's most original contribution comes, but it is also the point at which his thought can be most misleading. Ellul rightly sees man embedded in *structures* of sin and evil. In New Testament terms he is deeply impressed by the continuing might of the *exousia*, the demonic forces that constantly mock and spoil man's best intended projects. Here I agree with Ellul, though the idea is not a new one. The Pauline-Augustinian-Reformation tradition preserves a realistic respect for the uncanny if invisible power of systems. It also harbors a skepticism about the usefulness of mere good will or individual good deeds. This may explain why many radical students are deeply impressed with Ellul, a Calvinist biblical theologian. Why? They too gauge the depravity of our society precisely as total. They too doubt the efficacy of reform. They too believe in corporate structures of evil, "The System."

Old theological debates constantly recur in new guises. Pelagius (c. 355–425) argued, against St. Augustine, that man did not have to rely solely on grace for his salvation, that he was capable of achieving moral good. His teaching was condemned at the Council of Ephesus in A.D. 431. Jacobus Arminius (1560–1609) opposed Calvin on similar grounds. There is an element of "Pelagianism" about those people, usually designated as liberals, who fondly believe that such things as technology, the state and the city are merely neutral instruments, equally capable of use for either good or evil purposes. Ellul rightly scorns this liberal axiom completely. He sees what both Karl Marx and Sigmund Freud saw—that man is *not* simply a free moral actor, but that his consciousness is shaped by forgotten forces, deformed by cultural pressures, and falsified by social position and class interest. Therefore no technology can be "neutral," because every technology is the product of a human intention, and no human intention is untouched by greed, sloth or pride. Technologies are tainted and suffused with human meaning *fully* and *from the beginning*. They are involved in *original*, not accidental, sin. They cannot be redeemed even by the very best of human intentions. Like that notorious thing called "The System," which personifies metaphysical evil for today's young radicals, Ellul's "technique," as well as his "City," cannot be improved or upgraded. Both City and System resist all palliatives and programs. They are going to hell and they need salvation, not self-help schemes.

Here, of course, Ellul and his non-theological admirers part company. Ellul's solution for the mess is patience; theirs is revolution. Still a certain variety of Marxism coheres very well with a certain kind of Calvinism. The convergence keeps appearing time and again, even in people who would be surprised to be told about it. Both traditions teach that radical evil demands a radical solution.

But the problem with Ellul is analogous to the one created by certain forms of what might be called "revolution*ism*." Ellul's case for a corporate view of human evil is right. My argument with him is that he hoists grace to such a stratospheric altitude that it disappears out of sight, and the only reasonable human response is inertia if not resignation. So also with certain forms of revolutionary thought. If Joe Radical argues that nothing at all can be accomplished before the seizure of state power, that in fact anything else is a counterproductive sop, then he has a neat chic-radical excuse for doing nothing at all. He serves best who merely sits and bitches, or perhaps at best spreads the revolutionary word and shoots down any incremental step as "objectively reactionary."

Here is where Ellul and I part ways. Although his recognition of the irreducibly structural quality of evil is both theologically and politically accurate, he has been led astray by a flabby doctrine of grace. The best clue to Ellul's fatal flaw comes when he tells us that there is *no continuity* between the old terrestrial city and the New Jerusalem. The fact is that in Christianity there is always continuity between the old Jerusalem and the new. Creation is *not* destroyed by grace; rather it is transformed, deepened and purified. Ellul is right to point out that the relationship between Creation and Kingdom does not arise from some inner capacity for self-salvation. It is a gift. He is wrong, however, to see grace as *abrogating* the works of man in history. Though man's attempts to forge community are often self-deceptive, and are always infected by his greed and compulsiveness, they can nevertheless at times become signs of the Kingdom. This is the miracle of grace. The Kingdom of God breaks in upon us now and then, frequently when least expected. It is, as Jesus said, "in the midst of us." We can build human community, maybe even new cities, with some hope that grace will not cancel out our efforts completely.

It is surprising that Ellul, as a Calvinist, should turn out to be so undependable here. Unlike Calvin, he exhibits a curiously thin doctrine of creation when he says that "man's power is first of all the result of hardening his heart against God . . ." This is Prometheus, not Adam. According to the Genesis story, God endows man with powers and responsibilities before there is any hint of a fall. He is charged with the task of tilling the garden and is given dominion over the earth. Yes, he blows it. He "falls." But then there is grace. By grace man is not only once again *called* to his worldly responsibility, he is also *empowered* to assume it. The gods punish Prometheus by chaining him to a rock, rendering him totally powerless. God deals with Adam's mixture of despair and egomania not by depriving him of his powers but by restoring them in the Second Adam. The difference between the two myths is fundamental, but I think Ellul has missed it.

The nub of the issue is this: Can man use *any* of the *exousia*, the structures and systems, to serve his neighbor? I think the answer is yes. The "powers" are not only being defeated, according to St. Paul, they are also being *tamed* and *harnessed*. Christ, according to the apostle's striking metaphor, "takes captivity captive and gives gifts to men." Not only is the soul-destroying capacity of the principalities being taken from them, they are also being made servants of man. The trouble with Ellul is *not* his Pauline doctrine of corporate sin. On that he is right. The trouble is that his doctrine of radical evil is not matched by an equally powerful doctrine of *corporate* grace. One gets the feeling in reading Ellul that sin abounds, but grace doesn't abound quite as much. He holds a quasi-Promethean view of modern man's sin. This leads him to an Epimethean solution to the crisis—resignation and irony—rather than the one symbolized by the New Adam.

I think Ellul is wrong both in his theological diagnosis of the city and in his baleful prescriptions. Our culpability today, for

Ellul, stems not from dereliction but from trespass, not from sloth but from pride, not from the things we have left undone but from the things we have done.

I disagree. In my view, the disaster that seems about to overtake us springs not from our brash cocksureness but from our cynical suspicion that there is nothing we can possibly do about it. I am not arguing that man's sin is *solely* that of abdication, sloth and cowardice rather than pride and swagger. I am saying that our sin is a curious *admixture* of both. It mingles arrogance and timidity, rushing in and sneaking away, hubris and acedia. I would further contend that in today's world, for most people, fear and impotence and self-pity seem more central. But, in any case, Ellul's unilateral emphasis on arrogance certainly misses the mark widely.

There may even be a kind of elitist bias in Ellul's thought. His strictures may be necessary for that handful of people who bother to read books on the "crisis of the city" (among whom, admittedly, one finds an unusually high percentage of messiah complexes). But surely accusations of "bravado" and smugness are hardly relevant to the people who eke out a daily existence in the *favellas* of Brazil or who dive into the Asian mud to escape American bombers. Like the pope's well-intentioned exhortations to the rich that they should share with the poor, Ellul's book means nothing at all to the hostages of powerlessness and deprivation—whose masters have for generations enjoyed the support of theologians.

Ellul is right to remind us that our struggle is not just "against flesh and blood," but against "principalities and powers." But a *struggle* it is. And in order to struggle a man needs hope. Grace, or whatever word we can use to convey the content of that idea to postmodern man, must be real and accessible—the incalculable source of surprise and newness in a closed and jaded world. Otherwise the "Gospel" (Good News) is just more bad news. And there is enough of that already.

Ellul's radically corporate and stubbornly theological view of human evil is his most important insight. If it were matched by an equally robust view of man's possibilities under grace, Ellul would be one of the most significant Christian thinkers on the scene today. Unfortunately it is not, and perhaps that is too much to ask anyway. We should be thankful for what Ellul does give us: an interpretation of our present plight that makes us suspicious of jim-dandy answers.

It is also a shame that for reasons that stem no doubt from his own life experiences Ellul has picked "The City" as his target. I wonder what lies at the base of my difference from him in our feeling for what the city symbolizes? Was he wounded by the endless humdrum of the Paris suburbs, the glacial immobility of the French bureaucracy, the traffic on the Champs? In any case, his wrath would be so much more justified if he aimed it at, for example, the sovereign state as he does in *The Political Illusion.* The city, after all, is one of the oldest and most persistent forms of corporate human existence. Unlike what Ellul believes, urban civilization cannot be blamed for inventing warfare. On the contrary, many of the early cities emerged when people huddled close to protect themselves from the marauders who rode in from the country. Lewis Mumford is closer to the truth when he sees cities as expressions of man's instinctual desire to share life intimately with numbers of his fellows.

I believe Mumford is right. Even in the midst of imperial decay the Greeks knew that they had reached their apex in the age of the polis. Biblical religion celebrates the vision of a city as man's ultimate destination.

Not only is this a City of Light, one where war and exploitation are abolished, it is a festive New Jerusalem where even mourning and death are seen no more. Man's destiny is not to return as a drop to the great sea but to find himself and his fellow man in a New City.

The urban image will not go away. St. Augustine combines his Platonic and Christian sides in an ecstatic description of the City of God. Bunyan's Pilgrim is sustained throughout his trials by his ultimate goal: The Celestial City. Most important of all, however, is the fact that during the many centuries in which this hope has been cherished Western man has also decided that he need not wait for heaven to taste the fruits of the New Jerusalem. As Étienne Gilson writes, the very existence of the *Civitas Dei* was enough to inspire men to build, in the image and likeness of the Heavenly City, an earthly society which would be "temporal like the earthly city, yet just in a temporal way." Motivated by this hope, men have persistently striven to build the Just City on earth. The very names of some of our American cities (Nazareth, Concord, Providence, Bethlehem) remind us of these "holy experiments." And of course *my* first city, Philadelphia, was the most explicit holy experiment of all.

It is all too easy to point out how badly these holy experiments went. Churches, schools, families and uncounted other human efforts have often gone bad too. But the failure to achieve a vision does not discredit the vision itself. Nor does it detract from the people who were trying to construct at least certain rudiments of the *Civitas Dei* on the stubborn soil of earth. The failure of many of these cities even to approximate the ideal did not kill the dream. People kept trying.

If energy and spiritual imagination are to be directed again in our time to the building of the Just City, then we must know what has gone wrong with the cities we have. For one thing, cities today are built not to incarnate a vision but to make a profit. Religion has been diverted into internecine bickering and has failed to keep alive the image of a New City. Christianity has contented itself mostly with churchly aggrandizement, individual soul saving, or influencing the big power structures. Neither the priest nor the promoter seems interested in envisioning or building the Just City. The separation between spiritual vision and city building has widened into a divorce, and the divorce has resulted in a theological poverty in the whole concept of the city. I think this theological poverty has a lot to do with why today's cities are such a mess.

How can we begin to restore vision and give cities a new lease on life? In my own efforts to find such a vision I have been greatly helped by the urban fantasies of two people I know personally. Both have theologically well grounded views of how cities have gone wrong and how we can do better, though neither one is himself a theologian. One is Richard Sennett, a young sociologist and student of cities; the other is that "urban prophet in the desert," Paolo Soleri.

Richard Sennett bases his diagnosis of the city on a modern equivalent of the doctrine of original sin. Our cities today, he believes, are victims of oppressive overplanning. By overplanning he means the megalomaniacal compulsion to chart and guide every segment of urban life, as described in his book *The Uses of Disorder*. Sennett traces this obsession back to Baron Haussmann, who rebuilt Paris under Napolean III in the 1860s and whose grandiose ideas have influenced social planners ever since. At the heart of these ideas, says Sennett, is the notion that nothing be out of control, that The Plan include everything. No room must be left for the unpredictable, wayward, sporadic or random. That would mar the model. The city is viewed "as a whole," and its parts must contribute to the whole.

But this parts-make-the-whole-go idea, argues Sennett, is a machine-inspired model, not one appropriate to a community of human beings where the whole should contribute to the health of the parts. In a machine, if a part deviates, it is repaired or replaced. The machine is never wrong. But in a city, the opposite should be the case, so what Sennett wants is a new kind of city where the parts-persons (neighborhoods, racial and ethnic groups) rather than the whole are seen as the ultimate benefactors of planning. How could this be done?

Such a city could be planned, Sennett insists, by not only "allowing for" but *promoting* a significant degree of decentralization, density and disorder. At the same time the impingement of bureaucratic structures should be lessened. People should be left much more on their own, having to deal constantly with diverse and unpredictable elements, and thus growing toward what he sees as "adulthood."

Sennett's dense, disorderly city is the exact opposite of
Wright's Broadacre City. It is therefore also the counterpole of
contemporary suburbia, where life is overordered, sectored, never
dense, carefully zoned, and designed to *prevent* anything unpredictable. If questioned as to whether his city would not increase
incidents of violence by admixing people with too many conflicting temperaments and traditions, Sennett would answer that our
present panicky efforts to seal such people off from one another
is what in fact leads to violence, since it does not allow for
situations where people must deal with such conflicts every day on
a human level. Without such daily opportunities, hatred and
suspicion store up and smolder. Eventually they are bound to
erupt. Sennett's city would change this by giving its residents the
chance to live with conflict and express it, and to learn that expressing negative feelings need not lead to violence.

Sennett's proposal may seem farfetched to some, but there is
evidence that in a very few years his ideas could be quite work-
able. One bit of evidence is the constant reports we hear from
suburbanites of the boredom and banality of their lives, and their
growing hunger for risk and diversity. Sennett's tumultuous new
city would surely cure monotony.

Whatever one might think of the details of his city, Sennett's
diagnosis of the bacillus which infects many city planners is in
my opinion his main contribution. I would call it the "omnipotence syndrome," and I believe it can also be detected in numerous other realms of society. How many well-intentioned
deans, doctors, ministers, social workers and business executives
does it accurately characterize? But what Sennett probably does
not realize is that he has restated the biblical idea of sin in secular
terms. The world is too complex and unpredictable, he says, for
anyone to try to control it completely. Still we try. We reach for
the apple of omnipotence. But when that impulse to control is
defeated (as it invariably is), not man himself is defeated, "only
his belief in his own omnipotence is." The urge he describes is the
urge "to be all powerful, to control the meaning of experience

before encounter." It is a "godlike presumption about other people's lives." Eat of this fruit and you shall be as gods.

But Sennett does not want us to resign from planning cities. In fact, he argues, we can only begin to plan cities that will not end in disaster when we do forgo our illusions of grandeur and think of cities as places of welcome instability and a certain amount of healthy disorganization. Sennett's diagnosis is biblical, not Greek. He does not want to fasten even the most compulsively totalistic planner like Prometheus to a desert rock. Rather he wants all of us to repent, to stop trying to be gods, and to accept the excitement and satisfaction of doing the proper work of human beings, including the building of cities. Furthermore, he believes we *can* repent. We are not fated. In terms of an earlier part of this book, he believes that the signaling institutions of the society, when cut down to appropriate size and returned to their proper role, *can* aid and undergird those more fragile groupings where spontaneous activity and storytelling occur.

Richard Sennett's diagnosis of the city's ills is a secular restatement of the myth of Adam's fall, the human desire for omnipotence. There is another diagnosis, also clearly theological, that grows not from a doctrine of the fall but from a religious vision of humankind's destiny. Paolo Soleri is a man whose ideas contrast markedly with Sennett's but who is equally bold both in his rejection of today's cities and in his hope for the city of the future.

Although I had read Soleri's theories and looked at his drawings some years before, I first met him personally only in 1972. Meeting him, a shy and diffident man with piercing black eyes and a gentle smile, made the difference. I have been fascinated by him ever since. Soleri's theological premises are more explicit than Sennett's. Basing his thought on the great Catholic theologian Pierre Teilhard de Chardin, Soleri sees humanity as part of a vast evolutionary process moving ineluctably toward further complexity and deeper self-consciousness. As the process unfolds, drawn by a cosmic Christ-reality in the future, certain nodal events occur. Life itself emerges from inert matter; consciousness appears in life, then self-consciousness. According to Soleri, again following Teilhard, humanity has just come through a long period of fragmentation and is now headed for a kind of "quantum leap" in which a new nodal point will appear.

It is this newly emergent nodal point which poses the challenge for the city planner, Soleri believes, because it will result in a new form of consciousness, a corporate and collective form as different from present individuated consciousness as present consciousness is different from brute instinct. But Soleri believes that this new consciousness has no chance of appearing unless human beings first devise a "shell" or structure to facilitate its actualization. The city of the future, for Soleri, is this as yet unseen superorganism, and its shell will be supplied by the colossal single-structure cities he is now designing and has even begun constructing in the desert near Scottsdale, Arizona.

Soleri calls his stupendous design structures, some of them over a mile high and designed to hold a million people, "arcologies." The term is derived from "architecture" and "ecology." It suggests that Soleri, more than most urban planners I know of, including Sennett, is deeply worried about the ecological crisis. His tightly packed future cities would help ease that threat, he says, in several ways. First, since they soar far, far up instead of spreading out, they would not devour as much land. Even at that, Soleri is building his first one in the Arizona desert so as to use even less arable ground. Second, people will move from one section of the arcology to another by walking or by gravity-operated elevators, hence there will be no cars, and arcologies will make only minimal use of oil and other vanishing energy resources. Still they will not coop people up. Because of their unprecedented height, density and miniaturization, arcologies will save open spaces and actually make grass, trees, hills and wilderness more immediately available to their residents than most cities do today.

But for Soleri the heart of his project consists in the new corporate consciousness, the "quantum leap" he believes the arcology will make possible. Like most prophets and visionaries, Soleri is not very tolerant about other possible views of the future city. He sees no point in renewing or rebuilding old cities, but believes we must start entirely afresh. Though a pleasant, warm man, he judges all other approaches to the city as "doing wrong better," and therefore misled.

When I first saw Soleri's drawings and models—grotesquely high towers that would dwarf the Empire State Building—I admit I was shocked and staggered. They seemed so cold and lifeless. Also their unprecedented density bothered me. Wouldn't the people living in them always feel crowded? But then I remembered how "dense" it often is at an intimate party, on a dance floor or on a large ocean liner, without a feeling of being overcrowded. On the ship it is partly because of the vast surrounding sea. In the other situations it depends entirely on what mood seems to prevail. As Soleri says, there is "good crowding" and "bad crowding." Also I wonder what the alternative could be in a world of burgeoning population and diminishing resources. One thing is sure. We cannot continue to bulldoze orange groves and wheat fields indefinitely to make room for the spread of megalopolis. Our present urban areas cost too much both in land and in the fuels used to get from place to place. The cities of the future cannot be infinite replications of Los Angeles.

Besides, Soleri impresses me personally. Though I cannot accept the arcology notion *in toto*, I must concede that Soleri is not just writing *about* a new city, he is building one. Our best response to him, I think, is not to carp at his ideas but to begin putting flesh on our own.

Some critics of the city, like Ellul and Merton, have little hope for it. They loathe it as somehow essentially and irrevocably evil. Others, like Sennett and Soleri, criticize many characteristics of our present cities but do not reject the city as such. I agree with the second group, and for that reason I believe the time has come to stop merely talking about new cities and to begin actually building them. Consequently I have been working off and on for two years now with a group of friends and colleagues to

design and plan a whole new city. The team, which meets under
the auspices of The Cambridge Institute, an independent research-
action center, includes architects, economists, sociologists, urban
planners and a host of ordinary people who refuse to surrender
the idea of the New City as a viable human goal. It also includes a
significant number of young people who want to live in a community where a more cooperative and communal life style will
not only be tolerated but encouraged. Together we have carefully studied previous efforts, both here and abroad, to build new
cities, such as Columbia (Maryland), Reston (Virginia) and
Irvine (California). We believe these attempts, though they have
succeeded physically, have largely failed in human terms. They
have flopped mainly because of too much focus on designing new
buildings and plazas and not enough attention to new, more
participatory institutions. They have succeeded mainly in trans-
porting the problems of the old cities to nifty new quarters. And
that is no success at all.

Some of our friends think that our idea of building a whole
new city is eccentric or even a little mad. I disagree. Admittedly
we cannot go much beyond the planning stage yet because the
funds and the land for a new city are not easy to come by, but no
one really expected them to fall into our hands right away.
Within the next thirty years dozens of new cities will have to be
built in America, so we are proceeding on the assumption that we
will eventually find land and money somewhere. Meanwhile we
are thinking about what kind of city we want—what kinds of
schools, if any, what sorts of cultural, religious, economic institutions. We all agree that the institutions of the new city must be
far more decentralized, must place far more power in the hands
of more people at more levels of organization than is now the
practice in any city we know about. Most of all, however, we are
trying to find ways to involve as many of the future inhabitants
as we can in the actual planning and design of the city. This provi-
sion for participatory planning is the most significant difference
between this new city and any other one I've ever heard of.

When people eventually move in, it will be to a city they themselves have helped to plan and construct.

Working on this new city was a big step for me. As a writer of books and articles about "religion and the city" I felt a little like the musicologist who is suddenly asked to compose a symphony or the film critic who is handed a camera. I have also had to ask myself, "What does a theologian contribute, among all the other specialists, to the planning of a city?" In addition all of us working on the new city have had to ask whether, when the moment comes, we will be ready to pull up stakes, say goodbye to Harvard Square, and step aboard our equivalent of the *Mayflower* to start a new life. I have not answered any of these questions satisfactorily yet.

In the meantime I have become convinced that religious groups ought to be among those planning and constructing new communities and cities today. Churches should be at it even now. There should be hundreds of such cities, different in piety, theology and ethics, but each incarnating an identifiable life style. But why do we need a variety of types of new cities, and why should religious groups become involved in building them?

First, we need a new kind of city because only a completely unprecedented new pattern of rural-urban relationship can save us from the ecological disaster that urban-industrial society is headed for. Our human species is courting extinction today not only by depleting nonrenewable resources and poisoning the air and sea, but also by its accelerated movement toward a single unified interdependent system. The survival of any species depends on preserving options and maintaining diversity, on not putting all its eggs in one basket. From this perspective, our race is in a much more precarious condition now than it was two hundred years ago before industrialization spread its unifying sinews around the globe. Now, if industrial civilization fails, hardly anyone will be left to perpetuate the species. Ultimately we must invent a new system that returns all resources for use again and again, but we do not know how to do this under modern conditions. So we need thousands of social experiments trying to do it in as many different ways as possible. Religious groups should contribute to this process because the future existence of mankind is at stake.

But there is another reason why religious groups in particular should be devising such new rural-urban communities: The market mentality has failed. It has proven that it can no longer provide us with our values the way it has in the West for the past four centuries. What else could? In their surveys of cultures that have remained ecologically stable and successful, ecologists have discovered that what held most of them together was not the market but religion. Although they have markets, ecologically sound societies do not define the value of life in terms of producing, consuming and accumulating. We need a non-market value system, but we cannot simply import the value system of these other cultures the way we have their oil and sugar and lumber. We could never just convert our whole Western society to Buddhism, which may or may not have a less destructive stance toward nature. Nor could we all decide by fiat to become Central Australian bushmen or African spiritists. What we need to replace our market-determined value system is an alternative that is accessible enough to our own history to be available but different enough from the market economy to save us from its devastation. What would it be?

We must begin our search for a new value system at that point in our own Western history before our religion was perverted by the worship of acquisitiveness, competition and performance. This means retracing our steps and extricating what we can of the Christianity that informed Western culture before the rise of mercantilism, capitalism or industrialization. Naturally this could not be done, at least at first, on a civilization-wide scale. So what we need are thousands of social models, large enough to make the experiment worthwhile but small enough to keep it cohesive, where various types of communities based on different religious values could be tried. We need a rebirth of the monastic movement in which the monasteries are co-ed and are also cities.

At first this idea sounds completely implausible. Religion does not have the hold it had on people before the market began to dominate. Christianity is weakened by divisions, challenged by myriad secular faiths and other world religions. All this is true. Such new communities could not require adherence to an orthodox creed. But if churches founded communities explicitly based on their own rites and ethics, and welcomed people who would also live accordingly, even if they had doubts about the underlying theology, I think untold thousands of people would be attracted. There is a widespread hunger today for some form of community that is not based on the market. I do not think the new monastery cities would fail for lack of applicants.

The human race is now at a perilous juncture. It is becoming dangerously unitary and must *rediversify* in order to survive. Churches and other religious groups could contribute to this survival strategy by sponsoring and supporting new community enterprises. They are in an excellent position to do so. Both the Catholic and the Protestant traditions are replete with examples of new cities and alternative forms of human community inspired and built by faith. This would not be an unprecedented thing for churches to be doing. Remember Cluny, Monte Cassino, Iona, Philadelphia, Oneida, New Harmony? Also, the programs that denominations have developed in recent years are eliciting less enthusiasm. Still, denominations often have large skilled staffs and executives with considerable experience in the fields of housing, communities for the elderly, social action, urban mission, new church financing and education. It would be natural for them to move toward the planning of whole new rural-urban communities that would become the experiments we need in diversification, ecological balance, and alternative belief systems. The ecologist Garrett Hardin has written in *Nature and Man's Fate*,

> To the biologist it is clear that the best chances for man's long-time survival depend on the fragmentation of the species into well-separated populations. But it would be foolhardy to say what form the separation should take. It might be a matter of nations, as we know them; or some sort of caste

system that would permit genetic isolation with geographic
unity; or—far more likely—some new kind of communities
that are neither nation nor caste nor anything that has yet
been conceived of.

I hope everyone agrees that whatever our new human assemblages turn out to be, they should by all means *not* be castes or
nations. What "new kind of communities" that are not "anything
that has yet been conceived" might they be? Again we hear the
echo of the "religious question." Only this time we ask it not just
for the spiritual health of those who will live in the new communities. Something much more substantial is at stake, the physical
survival of the whole human species.

When I boarded the dark red cars with peeling gold letters of
the old Paoli local to return, tired and satiated, after a Christmas
outing in Philadelphia with my father and brother, I did not
know that I had spent a day in what a very earnest group of
people in the late 1600s hoped would become a new and just city,
a city of brotherly love. I did not even know that the broad-
hatted man whose statue stood atop City Hall, William Penn,
believed that The City could be the most concrete and viable
expression of the realm of the spirit on earth. I learned all that
only years later, and maybe, given the fate of Philadelphia, it is
misguided to bring it up now. But I do not think so. We cannot
abandon our hope for a just city without becoming cynics or
nihilists.

The City remains our existential polity. It exists at that crucial
level of life, somewhere between the circle of family and friends
on the one hand and the *imperium* of mankind on the other, the
level where life must be made civil as well as livable. "Civility" in
fact is just what I hope any new city will offer. "Civility," in its
valuable archaic sense, is a virtue that combines two dimensions
of life that our age, to its detriment, has surrendered: authentic
intimacy and political maturity. Today encounter groups seek
the first while reformers and activists seek the second. I believe

that these separated virtues can be reunited only in a city that will be in effect a federation of small neighborhoods, a city whose institutions and design invite the continuous exchange of feeling at the face-to-face level and genuine popular participation in its larger life.

But *polis* and *imperium* must not oppose each other. The idea of a new city cannot be an escape from the present woes of urban life. It cannot be an Arcadia or a space platform. We need a new city whose quality will catalyze changes in existing cities and inspire innovations in the cities of the future. I know we cannot just conjure the Just City into existence by moral incantation. Building a city requires an enormously wide range of technical skills, a vast store of patience and at least an adequate supply of that most earthly of resources, money. I believe, most of the time, that all of these essential ingredients can eventually be assembled. But all these earthly means will falter, in whatever supply we find them, unless those who eventually *inhabit* the New City share in its shaping, participate fully in its governance, and expend their spirits in an undertaking that is unapologetically visionary. When churches begin to tackle a job like this there will be many who will call them mad, but I am finding a surprising number of people who are willing to be mad with them.

My father died in 1956. He was only fifty-five. He died before I could ever really thank him properly for those holiday sorties into the city. He had no way of knowing how much those trips meant to me, how huge a part the image of the just and joyful city has come to play in my imagination. I wish he could have lived long enough for me to tell him, perhaps even to describe the New City.

Maybe we will never build any new cities. I know that full well in my saner moments. Certainly if we do build them, they will not live up to all our expectations. Even if they did, our grandchildren will want to build yet other new communities because their hopes will transcend ours. But what I know for sure is that I cannot go back to the tribal village to live. It's too late for that now. Nor can I be satisfied with the present anti-cities in which the natural environment is pulverized and man dominates man in a vicious caricature of civility. We can debate about whether the new cities will emerge from the ashes of the old, spring up on their edges, or appear elsewhere; whether they will look like lively hodgepodges or the soaring shells of a new consciousness. I'm uncertain about that myself. But of one thing I am sure: If there is no hope for a human city—somehow, somewhere—then there is no hope at all.

CHAPTER THREE

The House of Intellect

I am sure that an age will come when our present devotion to history, and scrupulous care for what men have done before us merely as fact, will seem incomprehensible; when acquaintance with books will be no duty, but a pleasure for odd individuals; when Emerson's philosophy will be in our bones, not our dramatic imaginations.
—William James

ANYONE WHO has grown up in the religious atmosphere of Protestant pietism knows what "giving a testimony" means. It means getting to your feet in a room full of people and telling what the experience of God has meant to you, how His grace has touched your life, and maybe the circumstances of your conversion. In my own small church we did not have testimonies very often. I remember them only when an unusually zealous visiting preacher came or when our youth group would visit some more devout congregation.

I was glad we did not do it much, because I was always terrified at the prospect of having to give a testimony. It wasn't that I did not know what you were supposed to say. I had heard lots of testimonies. But that was just the problem: I knew exactly what I was supposed to say, but I also knew I didn't feel that way inside. My own "conversion," such as it was, had not been a very dramatic affair. There were times when I wanted very badly to know God, to experience the love of Christ, perfect assurance, the joy of salvation, and all the things people who gave testimonies talked about. More often, though, I felt that someday I would like to be saved, but not until I had done a lot of things I heard sinners did before they were saved and I had not gotten around to yet. I knew that anything I would say in a testimony would sound patently insincere. I had just not felt what others said they had. So when folks began giving testimonies, my back stiffened and my stomach tightened. I listened attentively, but I dreaded having to speak. I knew I could not bring myself to say what was expected.

Years later I came upon two classical religious texts during the same week of reading, both of which in their own way helped me to understand better my boyhood trauma about testimonies. One comes from St. Augustine's *Confessions*. It is the famous line in which the great saint tells about how he had once prayed, "Save me, O Lord, but not yet!" I knew just how he felt, and I also understood those medieval heretics called the Cathari who waited until their deathbeds to receive the sacrament of baptism because they believed it washed them clean but could only be used once. I still carry a little of the Augustine-Cathari syndrome. My yearnings for spiritual perfection is tempered by the recognition that it might require my giving up some things I would rather not surrender.

The second helpful text I came across is a classic fourteenth-century mystical treatise called *The Cloud of Unknowing*. The anonymous author of this work helped me, years after the fact, to understand why I had trembled with fear when I was asked to put my experience of God or lack of it into words. The experience of the holy, he says, is in its very essence one of darkness and emptiness, always beyond the capacity of language to express. This is how he puts it:

> . . . thou findest but a darkness and as it were a kind of unknowing, thou knowest not what, saving that thou feelest in thy will a naked intent unto God . . . thou mayest neither see him clearly by light of understanding in thy reason, nor feel him in sweetness of love in thy affection . . . if ever thou shalt see him or feel him . . . it must always be in this cloud and in this darkness.

Soon after reading *The Cloud of Unknowing* I discovered the other great mystics and found that my boyhood discomfort was not unusual. St. John of the Cross, the sixteenth-century Spanish Carmelite, also convinced me that I was not as odd as I had once thought. That confusion and emptiness, that thirst for a feeling I wanted to have but could not, he refers to as the "dark night of the soul," and teaches that it is itself a profound spiritual experience. Thus reassured by a much broader spiritual tradition that I was not the outsider I had once feared, it became easy for me to dismiss my boyhood embarrassment by marking down the testimony meeting as a cruelly coercive setting. At times I even become angry, in restrospect, at the well-intentioned church people for seeming to expect me to talk about something so inherently resistant to speech.

But that dismissal was a little too easy. There is a terribly subtle connection between personal spiritual experience and the community of faith. After all, St. Augustine and St. John of the Cross did write books. Many of the great mystics and contemplatives did struggle to *describe* their interior pilgrimages, and I had profited from what they wrote. They too were in a sense giving testimonies. True, that does not excuse these meetings I sat in, shivering and fearful, while other people spoke so easily, it seemed to me, about such awesome things. Since reading more religious history, I have come to realize that the meetings I was exposed to encouraged a somewhat corrupted form of testifying. Those attending them were often merely repeating standard phrases that for their forebears had been on fire. I was probably right to be anxious and angry. Still, the *idea* of testimony itself remains powerful and essential: to try to give voice and word to what is so patently interior, to stammer at its unspeakableness, to try so hard to be honest to your inner reality, to know when it is over that you have failed but that the failure itself was necessary.

The mystics and contemplatives have served as the guardians and explorers of that uniquely human realm called "interiority." I think we need them today, perhaps more than we ever have, precisely because authentic personal life is now so fatally threatened by an intrusive technical world. This may explain why we are seeing around us a spectacular rebirth of interest in meditation, Zen, Yoga and the classical contemplative disciplines. It is a renaissance of interiority, and it represents an instinct for survival by the jostled modern spirit. We are so relentlessly pounded today by messages and stimuli from without that we need support from any source whatever to learn again to listen to what comes from within. There is even good clinical evidence that these ancient spiritual practices help us "deautomatize" ourselves and teach us how to tune down our overdeveloped capacity for responding to external signals from the media and elsewhere. Learning to meditate is like lowering the volume on an ear-blasting stereo; it makes us more capable of hearing ourselves and one another. Nothing could be more important. An automaton is a machine that lights up instantly to every cue relayed to it from the control board. A human being on the other hand selects, digests, orders, decides, responds—all on the basis of an interchange between his own interior life and the culture. The difference between the robot and person is interiority.

"Interiority" may be another word for what Kierkegaard called "subjectivity" or for what an older tradition simply called the "soul." In any case, these different words all remind us that men and women are more than the sum total of all the social, economic and other forces that influence them. This in turn suggests, however, that the old religious fear, that somehow I can "lose my soul," is not as silly as we once supposed. I lose my soul if I become merely the sum total of all the external inputs. There is more than one way to lose one's soul, but there is also more than one way to try to save it. During a single week as I was writing this book I kept a record of the lectures, sessions, labs and workshops that occurred in the greater Boston area featuring one or another of the classical spiritual disciplines. After I had gotten up to thirty or forty I lost count. There were the regular Yoga sessions in several church halls and community centers. Yoga is also being taught now in some college gym classes. There were the weekly gatherings of the followers of the

Maharshi Mahesh Yogi, passing on his wisdom about "transcendental meditation." There were the Hare Krishna dancers chanting near the subway stop, and the members of the Church of the Final Judgment inviting people to their meditation and chant evenings. Posters announced the arrival of a Sufi drummer who also led chants and dances. (The Sufis began as a sect of Islam but have now spread around the world. Their specialty is a finely calibrated use of key chant words and bodily movements that put most people rather quickly into alternate states of consciousness. The storied "whirling dervishes" described in Western travelers' reports of their voyages to Arab lands were probably Sufi holy men utilizing bodily movements to affect their own consciousness.) There was a formal lecture on Tantric Yoga, a demonstration session on Zen, a contemplation retreat sponsored by a Roman Catholic order, a discussion group on the *Egyptian Book of the Dead*, an experimental encounter group using replicas of old African masks, and a healing service at an Episcopal church. There was also a small notice informing all Capricorns who wanted to meet other Capricorns that a star-crossed rendezvous could be arranged by dialing a certain number.

Of all the re-emergent spiritual disciplines, the ones that seem to attract the most attention are those that teach people how to meditate. Since in recent years I have begun to learn how to meditate, an art which takes a lifetime to perfect, I think I know why it is becoming so popular. But I think I also sense its limitations. Through meditation, or another of these venerable traditions, we learn to turn down the quantity of the outside "noise" of pictures, words, sounds, and to attune ourselves to the fragile silence within. But too many meditators leave it at that, and it is just not enough. Inner silence is a welcome change from outer clangor. But who would want to live in a world of beings who, however rich and deep their inner lives, did not enjoy and cherish one another? If it quakes under so-called "outer oppression," a world of inner peace falls short of the world we want. The renewed quest for interiority is a way of fighting the violation of our marrow we experience in an acquiring-consuming-

competing society. But *human* interiority cannot stop with ecstasy. It requires love and community: gesture, touch, movement
and sooner or later speech. Eventually we give our testimonies
and listen to the testimonies of others, however broken and
inadequate they may be.

The movement from recovered interiority to renewed community is a perilous one. For some reason we have endless
stratagems to avoid it. When I remember my terror during the
testimony meetings, I also recall that everyone knew two ways to
escape the tension, other than by mere physical flight. One was
just to remain silent. That could be very good, as it often is
during the silent periods of a Quaker meeting. But I always felt
that even the powerful silence of such gatherings is incomplete.
The Quakers sense this too. In their meetings if someone is
moved by the spirit, he or she may speak. The other way people
escaped the tension at testimony meetings was to lapse into a kind
of talk that was general, abstract, maybe even *interesting*, but not
testimony—not trying to say out what was inside. That often felt
good too. It relieved the pressure and helped everyone relax. But
you could tell when it happened that we all knew we had just
stepped back from a painfully promising frontier.

Testimony, like everything else, is susceptible to debasement
and trivialization. But in its essence testimony is the primal human act. It breaks the barrier we erect between the "inner" and
the "outer" worlds. Telling my story is the way I dissolve this
artificial distinction and create a lived and shared world. I do
not abolish the chasm, either by surrendering my interiority to
the outer or by keeping it entirely to myself. I break out by
claiming the world as my own, weaving its stories into my story,
and making it *our* world. My interiority, instead of being swal-
lowed by the world or retreating to a well-guarded citadel,
widens out to include the worlds of others in itself.

Testimony means the telling and retelling of my story. This is
not a merely marginal human need. Some psychologists believe
it is an utterly central one. If people cannot tell and retell their
story, they go mad. This is one reason why I have gotten in-

terested recently in autobiography as the spiritual genre most needed in our time. I surely value the hallowed silence of the wise old sage who knows that to speak would be to lie and so remains speechless. I admire the well-wrought work of the theologians, whose sysems can provide a home for the mind. Both the mystic and the metaphysician contribute to the richness of the whole. But testimony goes beyond both silence and system. It is that form of speech that saves me from the isolation of silence and the triviality of talk. In the law, I am wisely permitted to "testify" only about something I have experienced myself, not to opinion, conjecture, theory or hearsay. Here, at least, the law is wise. It knows that in those matters that concern us most, only words that spurt from experience have any real truth.

Testimony is me telling my story in a world of people with stories to tell. It is an effort to construct a common world that fuses authentic interiority with genuine community. Mostly the attempt fails, or at least does not succeed completely. But we never stop trying.

Since the autumn of 1966 I have been a member of the Harvard faculty, teaching as a professor in the Divinity School. Harvard University was founded in 1636 as a school to train ministers, so the faculty I belong to is one of the oldest in the United States. It was at our school that Ralph Waldo Emerson over a century ago, in 1838, gave one of his most famous lectures. In that lecture he excoriated the mere passing on of doctrines and dogmas and pleaded with both the faculty and the students to learn about religion in the experience of the transcendent itself. Emerson was deeply suspicious of taking anybody else's word for anything, especially if that person was not reporting on his own experience. I think he would have understood the current renaissance of interest in seeking the holy through old spiritual disciplines. I also think he would have understood the importance of testimony as a form of religious discourse.

But the testimonial form is not in particularly good standing today. It has always been a disappointment to me that so little of it comes through in most of the theology I read. What was happening to Paul Tillich, for example, when he wrote *The Courage to Be*, a book which, when I read it in 1952, seemed to lift me into a whole new orbit? Was he himself troubled by atheism, alienation or "existential anxiety," the themes he wrote about so eloquently? If so, what were the historical circumstances, the people and events that contributed to his trek? Only those privy to his personal life have any clue. We know a little of why Reinhold Niebuhr tackled issues like corporate greed and religious hypocrisy in his theology, because he has left us an energetically written early book entitled *Leaves from the Notebook of a Tamed Cynic*. It recounts some of the things he lived through during his turbulent years as a pastor in Detroit. But later, perhaps when he became an academician, Niebuhr became more reluctant to let us in on his personal struggles, so we are left to guess. About many other important recent theological writers we have even less autobiographical data. Their books and articles seem to float on a cushion of ideas like a Hovercraft on the *Zeitgeist*, disjoined from the places their writers inhabit or the people they contend with.

Why this lack of interiority? Many of the most influential theologians in the past have not displayed such reticence. St. Augustine gives us a tumultuous account of his inner and outer struggles in his *Confessions*. Newman's semi-autobiographical *Apologia Pro Vita Sua* is also in some ways his best theology. Both John Wesley and Søren Kierkegaard left us their journals. Gandhi gave us his *Story of My Experiments with Truth*. But all we have from many of our contemporary theologians are hasty autobiographical introductions to collections of their works and an occasional short piece on "How My Mind Has Changed."

I think this is insufficient. We teach our students to look into the intellectual currents affecting a theologian's age and how he was influenced by them. Sometimes we show them how to analyze the class structure, economic influences, and other factors that will help them grasp various theologians better. We may publish writers' letters to their intellectual correspondents and speculate on the significance of their friendships. On some occasions we assay the influence of wives and lovers, if we know anything about them. But what we do *not* know, unless the writer tells us, is what was going on inside his head. We only know on rare occasions how a lover might have influenced his theology more by spurning him than by passing on a lucid theological insight. Religious writers fall in love, work and die too. How do their own feelings about death, losing a job, not getting a book finished, moving to a new city, being passed over for a promotion, being sick or depressed or elated, relate to what they write, and even to which issues they choose to ignore or to write about? For most theologians (as for most economists, philosophers, sociologists) we just don't know.

Still, it could be argued, that is just as well. After all, they have given us their books and articles, and that should be enough. They have a right to their privacy. Anyway, if we knew what was happening to them in their own lives we might be tempted to judge their theology on that basis instead of on its intrinsic merit.

I don't think this objection holds water. Of course everyone, theological writers included, has a right to privacy. I am not pleading for a theological version of *True Confessions*. What I do wish we could have is a reinstatement of the personal dimension *among* the others. It might combat the massive demotion of interiority that curses our age and correct the false impression that theology is written by sophisticated data processors.

We are used to including the personal factor in much of what we say to one another in ordinary conversation. Why should our books expunge it? Our daily talk is studded by such phrases as "After I lost that job, I suddenly realized that . . ." or "When I came back from the Service and found she'd married someone else I . . ." Whatever the endings to these sentences might turn out to be, we neither accept them at face value nor reject them just because we know something about the situation out of which they arose. Rather we have more access to their significance for the person uttering them. Consequently we can identify with him or her more imaginatively and thus bring our own experience to bear on the idea. We may still ultimately disagree, but now we can make a little more room for the other person's world.

The notion that when we read a book or evaluate an idea we do so only with our heads is itself a misleading idea. Our reception of ideas is a much more subtle process. It always involves our own life histories in some way. Why not the writer's too? Thinking is not merely the rationalization of instinctual impulses. Nor is it just putting in words the grunts and roars of our furry prehominoid ancestors. There is such a thing as a well-reasoned argument; and the ability to weigh the evidence advanced for competing claims is a good skill to develop. But reasoning is so infused with the peculiarities of life history that to separate them from each other is impossible. Furthermore it is also undesirable. It is true that we must learn not to be *misled* by our experience. But we learn to do this not by severing reasoning from feelings; we do it by becoming aware of our feelings and learning how to allow them to enliven and broaden our understanding of any situation. Our objective is what H. Richard Niebuhr once called "the informed heart."

For me the best example of what we mean by the informed heart is the person who is a "good judge." A good judge of anything can weigh evidence. He or she is also, however, a person whose richness of experience and accumulation of wisdom catch the subtleties in a complex case. A good judge is not swayed by mere facts.

When the life experience dimension is excluded nowadays people feel cheated. When I ask my students to read something for a class, they want to know *why*. And when they ask why, they want me to tell them about the person who wrote it, why he wrote it and, most of all, why *I* find it important. They want especially to know what in *my* experience leads me to think they should bother to read it.

Students will not sit still any more while I argue that anyone who wants to be familiar with the "field" should know this book. They are drowning in things they "ought to know," as we all are. They sense already what it took me years to discover—that they will *never* know all the things somebody thinks they ought to know. Like me, they stagger under the daily surfeit of words we call the "information overload crisis." They wisely suspect that much of what they are supposed to "know" is useless information that has been magically transformed into awesome lore by those who control educational institutions and career advancement. But they do not want lore, they want testimony.

Although most students would not recognize it, their demand that the esoteric lore of the academy be personalized before they spend time on it has a sound theological basis. During the first centuries of its life Christianity wrestled with a pervasive religious movement we now call Gnosticism. The root word *gnosis* also gives us our word "knowledge." Gnosticism was a complex set of cultural currents, but one thing most Gnostics agreed on was that humankind could only be saved by knowledge. Further, the knowledge required was hidden, esoteric and available only from those who possessed the secret key.

Against this cult of secret esoteric knowledge, Christianity insisted that, mainly because of Jesus, all anyone would ever need for salvation had been made openly available to everyone. The cabalic code had been broken. The big secret was out, they claimed, and no one could now control it. Also the early Christians claimed that by its very nature "truth" is not something that can be stored or hoarded. It is "incarnate," they said, expressed through human fleshly existence and passed on by example linked with word. Christianity bitterly opposed the idea that truth is in the possession of those with special access or is transmitted secretly or can best be grasped by shedding the fetters of flesh as the Gnostics often taught. In other words, the earliest Christians were saying, in their own way, that any "knowledge" that is not both equally available to everyone and integrally united with life history is not knowledge at all but error and ignorance. Christianity is testimony, not lore. When Theodore Roszak calls for the dismantling of science in his *Where the Wasteland Ends*, and advises a return to the "Old Gnosis," I can sympathize with his critique of the pseudo-objective, overspecialized way knowledge is defined in the modern West. But gnosis, old or new, is not the answer. It simply removes us from the grip of one group of specialists to put us under the aegis of another.

The sad truth is that the modern Western university has already fallen into a kind of Gnostic heresy. It has chosen to pursue a type of knowledge which becomes progressively less available except to initiates, a type of "gnosis" that is controlled by specialists and is stored and distributed with no reference whatever to the fleshly eccentricities of either teachers or students. But something has happened. Students and others who have never heard of Gnosticism are rejecting the Gnostic version of knowledge. They are demanding a more incarnational approach to learning. I think they are doing it as a matter of psychological survival. Faced with a roaring avalanche of data, people know instinctively they need a *selection device* to keep from being buried alive. My generation had such a device. We called it "specialization." We organized all knowledge, both in storage and in production, into fields, subfields and sub-subfields. We had the Dewey decimal system and the partitioned edifices of university departments, professional societies and college catalogue divisions. We coded the lore of the different fields on discrete computer tapes, on different library shelves, in separate bibliographies and in ever more esoteric journals. Then we restricted ourselves to trying to keep "abreast of the field" in our own specialty. Even then we often felt the stones and clods of the data landslide sweeping over us.

It is a discouraging business. I used to try to "keep abreast" of the books and articles in my "field." Then I dropped back to "keeping abreast" of the *reviews* of the books and the *titles* of the articles. Now even that seems like too much. But then I have always been a secret sinner against the orthodoxy of specialization, even falling into transgression as a graduate student when presumably I should have been exploiting every moment to prepare for my comprehensive exams. I was weak. I simply could not prevent myself, while walking through the massive alluring stacks of Widener Library in search of a book in my field, from stealing sidelong glances at the titles in a section I happened to be walking past. Venial turned to mortal sin as I first stopped, made sure no one was watching, then reached out for a book far afield from any exam I would ever face, to squander sometimes a whole hour or two on it. I now confess that there were more than one of these secret trysts; that I loitered, dallied and frittered many such afternoons away—and that the books I stealthily savored were drawn from such a chaotic variety of stacks and floors that no one could possibly relate them to any one "discipline." These were flagrantly *un*disciplined acts of impulsive self-indulgence. But I do not repent.

Still I know people who have pummeled themselves into avoiding the temptation to which I so readily yielded. The "specialist," not the *uomo universale*, is the ideal personality type in most universities. And he must be a self-denying ascetic, able to quell fugitive intellectual whims and choke back unseemly curiosity. He must realize that such habits lead inevitably to out-and-out academic vagrancy.

The specialist does possess one advantage most people lack. In handling the information avalanche, he may ignore whatever is not in his field. If that still doesn't reduce the landslide to a manageable quantity he simply narrows his specialty again. But it never quite works, so he exhibits the same original sin I have discussed in previous chapters, the admixture of a compulsion to master and a tendency to criminal negligence. He must master his own subfield, but he can neglect everything else. The trouble is no subfield is ever small enough to master completely, so he is constantly anxious and ill at ease about it. Also, leaving everything else to others invariably allows people he distrusts and despises to make the big decisions. And he feels bad about that too. We need another principle of selection. What my students are saying, sometimes incoherently, is "I don't want to master a field, nor do I want to leave all the decisions to experts and pros. What will help me survive, choose, fight back, grow, learn, keep alive? That I'll read or think about; anything else can wait."

The sentiments are not those of mere intellectual vagabonds growing up to be dilettantes. We are evolving a new way of organizing the life of the mind, and contrary to the criticisms, it does have a principle of selection and order. These students want to learn whatever will help them make sense of the world as they experience it and enable them to work for the changes they believe are needed. They will also gladly read something they know has made a real difference to someone they respect, be he faculty, student or anyone else.

There is another reason why specialization is a dangerous way to handle the information overload crisis: It is inimical to a free society. I realize that those who do defend specialization, especially in such areas as medical science, seem to have a strong case. Do we want to do without the fruits of specialization—penicillin, Salk vaccine and X rays? What the defenses leave out, however, is an accounting of the political and psychological price we have paid for such benefits. How many of the diseases we now cure by such methods are themselves the by-products of the superspecialized society? People whose lives are narrowed and blighted by fragmentation, anxiety and structural segregation continue to spawn new diseases that in turn require new remedies. Superspecialization is psychologically—and therefore physiologically—pathogenic. It is a vicious circle. To find "cures" for cancers and cardiacs we further intensify the social sickness that causes them. Specialization is politically dangerous because when it is carried to the point we now have, it creates what I call the "specialist mentality." According to this mentality, there is always someone more competent to deal with any question "outside the field," especially political questions which it finds upsetting or bewildering. The specialist becomes the delegator *par excellence*. He is not, however, the coordinating-overseeing delegator prized by theorists of administration. Rather he becomes the abdicating delegator who can be a patsy for rule from above and moral irresponsibility. Adolf Eichmann always claimed he was *not* in charge of killing Jews. That was not his field. He was merely in charge of arranging transportation. To have interested himself in who was being transported or to what destination would have constituted an overstepping of his competency.

We who live in ever more complex and specialized societies forget that this is not the only way either society or knowledge can be organized. And we ignore the pitfalls of doing it this way, for example the fact that the infinite multiplication of specializations requires ever more complex systems of coordination, and that the sheer magnitude of such a system guarantees the ever-increasing distance of the individual from the levers of coordination and rule. Specialization necessitates hierarchy, bureaucracy and vertical authority. That much seems clear. But the question even the most critical specialists rarely ask today is Why? What factors pushed our age toward more specialization and less democratic participation? Eichmann is not the only personification of disaster by delegation. The sorry role so many American intellectuals and academics have played in the Indochinese war was made possible in part by the fact that each was only doing a small "bit"—inventing Napalm, designing rocket systems, predicting enemy responses to American moves by game theory—and each one thought someone else was keeping an eye on where it was all heading. Significantly, Project Manhattan, the program for developing the atomic bomb, probably represents the greatest triumph of coordinated specialization ever devised. Only those at the top knew what it was all about.

All societies in history have evolved some form of division of labor. I doubt that any future society can or should avoid such division entirely. But in our society specialization is running amok. The sickness it induces—mastery of the minutiae and neglect of the momentous—now imperils the existence of our species. For this reason some pioneer forms of social organization in this century have consciously rejected the idea of specialization as their organizing principle. In some Israeli kibbutzim, for example, nearly all tasks are systematically rotated. The same is true in many communes.

Specialization in the academic world is not an isolated fact. It simply reflects, even caricatures, the splintering, echeloning and efficient irrationality of the entire society. In academia the cardinal rule is never to question the competence of someone in another field. Further, the coordination of the two fields, if any, is left to a third specialist whose specialty is different from the first two. As for the tricky question of the *use* of the articles one writes or the data one turns up or the weapons one makes, that is again decided by someone else. Like other people, academics are hesitant to stray from fields where they feel they are more or less masters into questions on which they would have to give up any pretense to omniscience: original sin again, and not correctable by self-improvement schemes. Only when people are freed from the need to control and master can they run the risk of admitting they are not omnipotent. I wonder if such people would suffer fewer heart attacks and nervous breakdowns.

How do we move beyond a society that organizes ideas and people on the basis of specialization and therefore requires a top-down signal-coordinated form of political rule? Again the answer to this question must be both political and personal. Politically we should oppose those groups who profit by vertical control patterns and who therefore fear and oppose popular participation in making social decisions. At the same time we can personally refuse to be sorted and sifted into the niches society has marked out for us. In teaching, this means to respectfully decline to restrict oneself to the issues, sources, language, methods and approaches as defined by the "discipline." Even the word "discipline" has now come to mean something different from what it did. It once meant one *way* to approach a total whole. Now it is often used to designate a kind of province or fiefdom whose major concern with other disciplines centers on boundary disputes.

There is a religious dimension to all this too. Historically the subdividing of human knowledge into cubicled cells arose not just because of the increased amount of data but also because of the erosion of any persuasive picture of how it all goes together. The "story" no longer seemed convincing. Consequently in the long run we will not be able to dismantle the castle of overspecialization before a new and compelling vision of the whole emerges. Until then, however, we should minimize as best we can the most fatal danger of our present arrangement, the tendency it induces in people to identify themselves with their specialized functions. It is bad enough when would-be omnipotent politicians and planners inflict the machine model on us. It is much worse when we then begin to think of ourselves as replaceable pistons and gears. We do *not*, however, adopt this mechanical identity only because the signal system tells us to. All outward oppression is built on an inner need. People fit too easily into a cog box because they need some story to make sense of what they do every day. And when their own daily experience and personal interiority begin to dissolve, when they lose touch with their own story, then their tiny place in the big system provides the only personal story they have. With it they can at least make some sense out of the multitudinous messages that descend on them every day.

Because the current arrangement does meet a real human need, the mere substitution of testimony for specialization as a way of selecting data and giving it coherence will not suffice. It will not supply a unifying vision nor will it change the society that requires such specialization. But it is a survival technique, an interim strategy; and if a unifying vision does appear, it will come because enough people have kept in touch with themselves and with one another and are sufficiently suspicious of the standard signals to make it happen.

I want to restore the element of testimony to theological writing. When we neglect it, even inadvertently, we promulgate a kind of Gnostic theology. We imply that divinity can be severed from flesh, that religious truth need not leap from one life story to another, that revelation can be registered and retrieved like units in a data bank. Even worse, when we imply to our readers that our own life histories are irrelevant, we cannot avoid conveying the impression that their autobiographies are also unimportant. Consequently readers begin to neglect their own life history. They repress any attention to interiority. They slip further into the sundering of inner from outer life. The evacuation of personal existence spreads a little more and the anesthesia of mankind deepens.

This is not a pleasant process to watch. It could result in a world population so alienated from its inner impulses as to be vulnerable to total control by indoctrination through the mass media. Some of our most prescient modern writers have sketched out the prospect of what such a world would be like. Their scenarios are even more depressing than those of the vampire films I referred to earlier, because in the newest versions the vampires' victims do not even resist. They don't hang wolfsbane or brandish crucifixes. They seem to *like* being hapless pawns. Remember the tear in the eye of the lobotomized anti-hero in Orwell's *1984* when he hears Big Brother's voice over the loudspeaker and knows Big Brother loves him? Or the alphas and betas in Huxley's *Brave New World* who go through life chanting, "I'm glad I'm a beta," because that message had been beamed at them from egg cell on? This loss of soul could never happen in a world where interiority and psychic depth are cultivated.

A horror movie I especially appreciate is a 1950s thriller called *The Invasion of the Body Snatchers.* No ordinary sci-fi feature, it is a classic of its kind. It tells the story of an American town where a dreadful species of extraterrestrial life is gradually transforming the whole populace into a race of "pods," people who look and sound exactly like human beings but who totally lack any capacity for feeling. In the last scene a young doctor and his girlfriend are hiding in a cave from their friends and neighbors, all of whom have turned into pods and who want them to become walking vegetables too. The doctor leaves his sweetheart momentarily. When he returns he takes her in his arms to kiss her, but her limp embrace and glassy stare make him recoil. She too has become a pod.

True, horror movies often epitomize the worst offscourings and sensationalism of the mass media. But like everything else, they have to appeal to *something* or they would not work. I think they appeal to an instinctive but soundly based fear present in the collective consciousness of our age. This is especially true of the films that feature living persons reduced to soulless zombies. We feel something or someone is illegitimately invading our inner psychic citadels. We associate that invasion with a kind of living death. We know that somehow it must be resisted. In all of these instincts we are right.

The Gnostics were the "body snatchers" of their time. They wanted to "departicularize" people, encourage them to disavow the flesh, lead them into a truth that canceled out all the messy tuggings of being a specific person at a certain time, that is, of having a body. I have been suspicious of Gnosticism ever since I first read about the Gnostics in college. I am just as opposed to the twentieth-century successors of the Gnostics, the body snatchers. Also I am sufficiently haunted by the dystopias pictured by Orwell and Huxley and by such films as *The Invasion of the Body Snatchers* that I have promised myself to resist the invasion as best I can. "My God, Jenkins, they've surrounded us. There's only one way out."

The decision to make interiority—my own life story and that of my students—a part of the mysterious exchange we call "teaching" has made a difference in the way my classes proceed. Last year, for example, I taught a seminar course for Harvard and Radcliffe freshmen called *Theology and Autobiography*. It was the first course I have given in which I applied in full measure my decision to encourage interiority, resist the body snatchers and challenge the reign of specialization.

Each Monday afternoon I pedaled down Massachusetts Avenue, past the Midget Restaurant (scene of the young lovers' first date in *Love Story*), turned right on Shepherd Street and proceeded out to Hilles, Radcliffe's new library-classroom, where I locked my dilapidated old bicycle in a rusty metal bike rack and went in to meet the fourteen students in the class. I could only take fourteen because of the rules of the freshman seminar program, so I had to select these fourteen from the written applications of a hundred and eight people. The selection job was awfully hard. I did it partly at random and partly to get diversity of region, sex, ethnicity, and religious background. I especially wanted people who found themselves in differing relations to their own traditions: still closely attached, puzzled, questioning, angry, rejecting, or searching.

It worked beautifully. The class included a loquacious young woman from Spanish Harlem, a wide-eyed liberated girl from Southern California, a highly verbal Jewish boy from a huge suburb on the North Shore of Long Island, an understandably paranoid Unitarian from the Bible Belt, and two second-generation Irish Catholics, one of whom wanted to be a Jesuit while the other (she says) had "thrown the whole mess out" and was looking for something else. Each week we read and discussed an autobiography (loosely defined to include journals, diaries and letters), which they helped to select from a list I gave them when the seminar started. We started out reading Nikos Kazantzakis' *Report to Greco*, Elie Wiesel's *Legends for Our Time*, Thomas Merton's *The Seven Storey Mountain* (which on rereading this year I found disgustingly triumphalist and even arrogant), and Sam Keen's *To a Dancing God*. Later on we read Simone Weil's *Waiting for God*, Bonhoeffer's *Letters and Papers from Prison*, *The Autobiography of Malcolm X* and a book called *Black Elk Speaks*, which is alleged to be the stenographically recorded self-told story of a Sioux holy man. I'm still looking for other autobiographies of people outside the Jewish and Christian traditions, but I have not found many good ones yet.

More important than the books was the way we went about the discussion. I asked the students to look for the incidents in the books that reverberated most clearly with something in their own experience (for example, the death of someone close, first brush with romantic love, turmoil over religious belief). Then I asked them to focus on the incidents which seemed strangest or most remote from their own lives. I also encouraged them to keep their own journals (not for handing in) and to use parts of the class period to explore one another's emerging autobiographies.

The course is over now. As I think about it, I do not care very much how many facts they remember in ten years about Merton or Bonhoeffer. What I hope they did "learn" is that their own personal lives, as well as those of Wiesel and Kazantzakis, are enormously significant, utterly unique and endlessly intriguing. I want them to honor and attend to that life (as I was never really taught to do in my own schooling). I hope they learned that anyone who in any future course, or anywhere else, asks them to deny their own inner reality is asking something wholly unacceptable. I hope they learned to fight off the invasion of the body snatchers, never to have their tears and love snared away by any Big Brother. I hope they learned how to keep so closely in touch with their own stories that no one can force them into some role required by a new world, brave or otherwise.

The battle to regain and deepen our sense of interiority will not be easy. In the modern world, where we tend to define all problems politically, we forget that the interior life needs more than freedom from overt oppression in order to develop; it also requires its own kind of nurture and sustenance or it will atrophy. Also, authentic interiority can be destroyed even more easily by subtle cajoling and neglect than it can by the rack and the inquisitor's fires. At least in an overtly oppressive society the lines are clear. Our society is overtly repressive with some groups, which may explain why Malcolm X and George Jackson, two black men, produced two of our period's most moving diary-autobiographies. It is also sporadically repressive with everyone. But by and large it manages to accomplish the abolition of interiority by a much more subtle method. First it excludes almost all opportunity for cultivating or expressing the idiosyncratic element of life history from the educational curriculum. The curriculum is more or less uniform, despite its apparent variety, and its cornerstones are standard achievement tests, uniform lesson books, and dossiers filled with grades, ratings and scores, most of which locate the person with

reference to one or another abstract norm. Then it fills the
vacuum created by the evacuation of interiority with a ready-
made supply of preassembled identities, self-images, feelings and
fantasies.

This is why I think it is so important to provide places and
times in the lives of young people (and others too) where they
can listen to their own inner voices, recall their deepest feelings
and learn how to cultivate an authentically interior life. This is
why not only in the course I just described but in my other
courses and seminars as well I proceed on the premise that education, especially in religion, is not principally the imparting of
skills and information. It is the enlistment of other people, with
experiences and competencies that complement mine, in the
continuous development of our own communities of psychic
survival and our own lived autobiographies. I believe that people
who begin not only to write their own autobiographies but to
live them provide unlikely candidates for citizenship in some
Brave New World or *1984*. They will sense it instantly when
their lives are being stolen from them. They will kick and scream
and fight back. They will demand the space and the time to be
themselves and a society that provides that space and time for
everyone.

Teaching is the shared appreciation of the anger, ennui, delight
and exasperation that comes with the exploration of texts and
ideas, images and connection, insights and errors. I want to see
students as colleagues and my colleagues as teachers (and students). I want to confound the previously fixed points on the
compass so that they begin to slide into one another and everybody begins teaching and learning at the same time. Only this kind
of tonic can restore the red cells and white cells of the learning
process to the balance from which they have so dangerously
departed.

PART TWO

PEOPLE'S RELIGION

When wilt thou save the people?
O God of mercy, when?
Not kings and lords, but nations,
Not thrones and crowns, but men.
Flowers of Thy heart, O God, are they:
Let them not pass, like weeds, away:
Their heritage a sunless day;
God save the people.

Shall crime bring crime forever,
Strength aiding still the strong?
Is it Thy will, O Father,
That man shall toil for wrong?
"No," say Thy mountains; "No," Thy skies;
Man's clouded sun shall brightly rise,
And songs ascend instead of sighs:
God save the people.
    —Hymn by Ebenezer Elliott
    (1781–1849)

CHAPTER FOUR

Viva Jesús, Quetzalcoatl and Zapata!

Religious distress is at the same time the expression of real distress and the *protest* against real distress. Religion is the sigh of the oppressed creature, the heart of a heartless world, just as it is the spirit of a spiritless situation. It is the *opium* of the people.
—Karl Marx, *Toward the Critique of Hegel's Philosophy of Right*

I DO not remember when I first became aware of the importance of "people's religion." The recognition that whole peoples as well as individuals have a "testimony" probably grew slowly. So did my realization that when a group loses its corporate autobiography it can quickly disintegrate into an amorphous aggregate in which all personal interiority also disappears. For years I had lamented the nostrums and delusions inherent in the faith of impoverished and defeated peoples. Only recently have I begun to see that the religions of the oppressed are also their guarantors of psychic survival, inner dignity and persistent hope.

I say I do not recall when I first became conscious of the positive significance of people's religion. I do, however, remember one turning point in the process. It happened a couple of years ago when I was visiting a friend in Santa Fe, New Mexico. It was also then that I first saw how little preparation my academic training had given me to appreciate the meaning of people's religion, and I started to make amends.

The moment came just after our rusted Chevy sedan turned out of the main section of town and headed into Santa Fe's barrio, where the houses are smaller, the roads are bumpy and pocked and the signs are in Spanish. After a few blocks we stopped at the corner of Dolores and San Francisco streets at a Chicano-run community center. Looking out the car window, my eyes were instantly overwhelmed by the mural on the white stucco wall, newly painted there by the people of the barrio when they took the center over. Splashed exuberantly across the whole front of the building, its gleaming pastel colors seemed to say, "This is ours." I climbed from the car without taking my eyes away from it. Who were these figures staring powerfully down at me from the mural?

I shaded my brow and looked. There on the right, his huge sombrero framing his drooping mustachios and cartridge belt, was Emiliano Zapata, the martyred hero of the landless peons of Morelos province. Treacherous rivals killed him in 1919, but his demand for "Land and Liberty" still stirs the blood a half a century later. Just above Zapata and a little to the left was Jesus Christ, his head gashed by the crown of thorns, scarlet drops of blood coagulated thickly on his brow. Next to Christ stood Our Lady of Guadalupe, the earth mother and protectress of Mexico's poor, the most recent reincarnation of the Aztecs' feminine goddess, Tontin, the mother of Christ and patroness of all Mexico. A trace of a smile played ironically at the corner of her lips. Around her head the stars shone, under her feet the moon reclined. Further over but close to Our Lady appeared Che Guevara, and the guerrilla priest Camillo Torres. And near the base, shining ferociously in the New Mexico sun, leered the terrible Quetzalcoatl, the deity of the Toltecs, his bonnet bedecked with the plumed serpent.

The mural was eloquent. The people of the barrio had already told me almost all I needed to know about their hopes and memories before I had even entered the center. The mural was their testimony.

The rest of the day I could not stop thinking what a master stroke of people's religion and imaginative syncretism that mural was. Its outspoken colors, its saints and heroes told me more than a million words could about the pride, the resiliency and the integrity of an angry, oppressed people The mural included nearly everything Chicanos feel is important to them in their history. It was a kind of autobiography, a story they live as well as paint.

Later, as I left the Center, I remembered the Black Pentecostals I once spent a hot Sunday night with in South Chicago. They had been singing about Moses and Ezekiel and remembering Martin and Malcolm—feeling again all that pain and rage and hope, and nurturing it. Their mural was painted in song, but it was just as vivid. And I remembered the St. Anthony festival I watched in Boston's North End, and the gaunt tobacco-chewing Appalachian folk I visited in Tennessee, stitching blue and white quilts and singing "The Old Rugged Cross" and "Bright Morning Star" as they gathered to march against the strip miners.

What is people's religion? Carl Jung coined the term "collective unconscious." I know its existence is still in dispute. But what about a "collective conscious" or better still a "collective interiority"? Of its existence I have no doubt whatever, for the religion of any human group is its corporate testimony, its stated claim to identity and dignity. It is a people's way of crying and remembering and aspiring. Sometimes it becomes an embattled folk's only way of fighting back. Without it they would be hollow, unable to resist or survive. A people's religion is one way it saves its soul.

Religion is more than autobiography. True the testimonial mode does seem eminently natural for religion. Shamans tell their wide-eyed tribesmen of uncanny midnight flights. Saints recount their heavenly visions. Saved sinners testify about how they found grace. But religion is more than the sum of all these personal stories, it is also *collective* remembrance, group consciousness and common hope. It is the corporate autobiography of a people. It is their own story, told and retold, altered and amplified, passed on from parent to child. I once wrote, in *The Feast of*

Fools, that religion is to a civilization what fantasy is to an individual. I would want to enlarge that now. A people's religion includes not just fantasy and hope but also memory and nostalgia. It is a living compilation of the songs and ceremonies a people accumulates through its history, a fund of remembrances without which there could be no future at all.

In celebrating the significance and survival value of the religions of the poor it is important to avoid romanticizing. Like all other natural instincts, our human impulse to pray and our need for fables and myths can easily be used against us. Invaders, oppressors, developers and other kinds of conquerors and self-appointed helpers have invented more than one way of managing the piety of their vassals. They know that if a people's piety persists in its original form, it can prevent the complete control the dominator always wants. One need not exterminate the victim's religion if it can be used against him.

I call this misuse of faith "the seduction of the spirit." Whether it is done by churches or mass media, and whether individuals or groups are seduced, the process is pathetically the same: the seducer twists authentic inner impulses into instruments of domination. Vulnerable persons and powerless peoples are maneuvered into seeing themselves through images thrust upon them by the distorting mirror of the managers. People's needs and hopes are cleverly parlayed into debilitating dependencies. Their gods and heroes are captured. Their own rituals are twisted and used to keep them in line. The timeless stories they have lived by are incorporated into a set of meanings supplied by the conqueror. Soon, as a people, they become what they are expected to be; expected, that is, by someone else.

The seduction of the spirit is a "religious" process. Both the individual and the group are led to depend on symbols laid upon them by their betters. But ironically, their defense against this fourflushery is also religious. In their inner spirits the victims know something is wrong and they continue, in furtive prayer, group memory and millennial fantasy, to be something other than what the dominating culture demands. Captive and defeated peoples convene in secret, preserve the cultural shards of a former time, whisper the songs they dare not sing aloud, and pass on the stories to their young. They nourish the hope that one day they can win their full liberation, so they may celebrate openly what they must now remember in secret: "Let my people go that they might worship me."

The differences between oppressive and liberating religion, between self-sustaining faith and the devotions decreed by higher-ups, is often hard to discern at first glance. Any single religious phenomenon can be partly the symbolic outpouring of rage and joy and at the same time partly a potent means of social control and psychological manipulation. The problem is complex. Though some analysts try to understand religion merely as the symbolization of a people's experience, they never quite succeed. Such analyses leave out the cruel fact that religion is often a sedative administered without consent, that conquistadors of all eras have used elements from the religions of vanquished peoples against them. The Spanish could hardly have defeated the Aztecs without exploiting the Aztec belief in the return of Quetzalcoatl. But neither is religion always and everywhere an opiate of the masses. Religion is also sometimes the only way a defeated culture can preserve its history and its hopes in the evil day.

Religion is often the only tie that keeps a people knitted to their inner impulses and historical memories during periods when violent rebellion would result in corporate extinction. The religious history of black people is a good example. Though many writers have seen in the black Christianity of America only a cruel hoax foisted on the slaves to keep them in line with promises of happiness beyond Jordan, that is only part of the story. Any subjected people must first survive before it can fight back. Black theologians are demonstrating today how the slaves staved off both extinction and absorption in part because of their religion. Their inventive adaptation of the distorted Christianity to which they were subjected by the masters helped keep them from falling into pieces psychologically and culturally despite the efforts of whites to make that happen.

The red people of America were not as successful as the blacks. When they found themselves pressed against the oceans and the canyon wall by the white man's insatiable expansion across the plains, they turned to the peyote cult and the Ghost Dance. The peyote pipe may have helped them behold again the fleeting shades of their tortured ancestors, but at the price of acquiescence to white hegemony of the outer world. The Ghost Dance stoked one last warpath fire of rage and revenge against the usurpers. But it ended in the bloody snow of Wounded Knee. Usually it is concluded that both these religious expressions of the Indian soul failed. But I am not so sure. In recent years the title holders of pre-Columbian North America have begun to awaken out of the coma their forefathers were bludgeoned into during the centuries-long invasion that robbed them not only of their hills and their hunting grounds but also of their gods. Was their religion an opiate?

Only the most vacuous observer could say it would have been better for the Choctaws and Modocs if they had thrown out their wood spirits, their medicine men and campfire rituals and employed every ounce of energy to fight the U.S. Cavalry everywhere to the last man. Sad to say, the Cavalry would probably still have won, but they might have exterminated the race completely instead of only partially. The result would have been almost as bad if the red people had managed to survive physically but only at the price of abandoning their gods, tales and ceremonies. Even if such cultural self-mutilation had somehow enabled them to stave off extinction, which is doubtful, it would have left them without any spiritual weapons for resisting absorption or genocide at some later time. The religions of the Indians united them to the bison and the prairie with mystical bonds. Their faith in a Great Spirit also linked the Indians to one another. The present reassertion of native American dignity and rights is rooted in that ancestral religion, as is amply demonstrated by the statements of native American spokesmen collected in T. C. McLuhan's *Touch the Earth*. The red renaissance is not *just* a rejection of the culture and religion imposed by the

Cavalry and the society it represented, it is also a revival of Indian "soul."

I have often wondered what the religion of the Indians might have been if history had permitted them to fuse Christian and aboriginal elements as Africans have done. Maybe we will now see, and possibly some American Indian version of Christianity, marked by the Indian's intuitive awareness of the terrible delicacy of man's concordat with nature, will help us find our way to the new view of man and nature our ecological mess now requires. If aspects of Christianity find a place in the emergent consciousness of red people, it will not be surprising. Few faiths ever escape modification when they collide or interact with others. Most profit from such encounters. Every religion is like Peer Gynt's famous onion. If you tried to peel away all they have absorbed from other faiths, which are in turn already conglomerates, you would find only more and more layers underneath. Christianity is an onion made up of striations, first from the ancient Hebrew faith, which itself had already absorbed Canaanite and Babylonian elements, then from Near Eastern mystery cults, assorted pieces of classical culture and a grab bag of other elements. I am not saying that Christianity and Navajo religion and other faiths have no "uniqueness." They do, as does every living religion. But the genius of a faith is found more in its characteristic way of combining things than in some induplicable inner essence. The distinctiveness of a tradition can be traced in the way it unites the peculiar experiences *one* people has in history with the primordial realities *any* people must contend with regardless of where or when it lives. But ultimately a people's religion, no matter how it has been composed, becomes that people's own "soul." Whatever inner contradictions it houses, it serves an essential purpose for those whose collective consciousness it represents. When the "soul" departs, as mortals have known since the beginning of time, the body soon dies too.

For me to be able to utter an inward "amen" to the religious vitality of a Chicano mural in Santa Fe came as the culmination of a long process of change. In ten years I had come almost full circle in my attitude toward religion and its significance for poor and oppressed peoples. A decade before I might have viewed that mural and the faith it depicted largely as opiate of the masses. But now I could detect in it the inner core of a people's identity and the fuel of their fight for dignity and survival. This section of the present book traces some of the steps that led me in one decade from "secular Christianity" to people's religion.

CHAPTER FIVE

Beyond Bonhoeffer

We are moving toward a completely religionless time . . .
a complete absence of religion . . . then what is a religionless Christianity?
—Dietrich Bonhoeffer, *Letters and Papers from Prison*

In August of 1962 an unexpected invitation came to me to live
and work for a year in Berlin. I was immediately excited by the
prospect. It was just after I had finished my Ph.D. at Harvard and
the letter asked me to come to Berlin to do some work in the first
stages of what was even then beginning to be called the "Marxist-
Christian Dialogue." I was intrigued by the assignment itself. But
to be honest, the lure of adventure in a divided city, the escape
from the U.S.A., and a change from seminars and term papers
probably motivated me even more. After talking it over for one
day with my wife Nancy, we decided to go.

Berlin in 1962 was an armed camp. East German jets still
buzzed airliners now and then. Columns of American tanks rolled
over the cobblestone streets with an ear-splitting clatter you
could hear ten blocks away. The city had already been split in two
by the wall for a year when we arrived that August afternoon
at Tempelhof airport. Nancy and I took an apartment on a noisy
thoroughfare called Bundesallee in the district of West Berlin
known as Friedenau. Through an arrangement made by the
World Council of Churches I became an "ecumenical fraternal
worker" in a center for adult education across the barricade in
Communist East Berlin named for Johannes Gossner, a nine-

teenth-century German church leader. My own church, the American Baptist, sent us a small check each month and I've always been grateful, because it was an utterly formative year for everything I've done since.

Life in Berlin was complicated. About four times per week I traveled from West Berlin to East Berlin and back, using the elevated S-Bahn or walking past both the American and the East German guards at the famous Checkpoint Charley on the Friedrichstrasse. I was allowed to do that because Berlin was still officially controlled by the four victorious powers of World War II. Although most Germans were not allowed through the wall, I could cross back and forth subject only to the delay and harassment any other foreigner had to undergo. Three times during the year I was detained on the East Berlin side and interrogated by the gray-and-green-uniformed Volkspolizei. But each time I was eventually released on the same day. For a whole year I lived as a man between two worlds, or really between more worlds than that. Not only was I trying to provide a link between East and West Berlin, I was also trying to be a part of the embryonic conversations just beginning between Christians and Marxists inside East Germany. Also I was laboring under the adjustment any foreigner makes during his first year abroad, discovering that as different as East and West Germany were from each other, both were very different from the America I had temporarily left behind.

I grew up a lot during that icy, gray winter. In a bomb-pocked badly heated old apartment in the Alexanderplatz section of East Berlin I met every other Thursday evening with a group of schoolteachers who were determined not to leave East Germany but to stay and work on the Christian-Marxist conversation at the grass roots. They had a particularly good opportunity, since the Communists were at that time lavishing much attention on curriculum and school policy. I met with groups of ministers, college students and ordinary church people. I ate more boiled potatoes and *Wurst* than I had ever seen. I also gave lectures and led discussions at the Gossner center on theology, ethics and sociology. The students were remarkably patient with my German, which was painfully weak at first. It improved markedly by the end of the year. Nancy and I drank in play after play by Bertolt Brecht as they were staged in four-week runs at the theater on Schiffsbauerdamm in East Berlin where Brecht himself had worked. We saw not only *The Threepenny Opera* but also *The Rise of Arturo Ui, Schweik in the Second World War, Mother Courage* and *The Caucasian Chalk Circle.* Nancy visited rehearsals there on afternoons occasionally and once even met Helena Weigel, Brecht's widow.

It was during that year in Berlin that I fell most decisively under the influence of the theology of Dietrich Bonhoeffer. I had read some of Bonhoeffer before and had been put off by his earlier, seemingly sticky pietism, but I was greatly attracted by his later works written while he was resisting the Nazis. In Berlin, Bonhoeffer suddenly seemed enormously right. After all, Berlin had been Bonhoeffer's own home town. I frequently rode past the somber walls of Tegel prison where he had been held during part of the two years of captivity before his execution by the Nazis. I met and worked with people who had known him, studied with him, and some who at least claimed to have been a part of the Twentieth of July Movement (Die Zwanzigsten Juli), the underground anti-Nazi political group in which he worked. His spirit still seemed very alive during those tense cold war days. But what seemed especially right about Bonhoeffer for me in Berlin was his idea of a "non-religious interpretation" of the Gospel.

We don't hear much at all nowadays about a non-religious interpretation of Christianity. In fact the whole idea has been pretty much discarded by most theologians recently as an anomaly. But in 1962 it was no anomaly. In fact it seemed then like a crucially important concept if the dialogue between Christians and Marxists, at least the ones I was talking to, was ever going to go anywhere. It seemed to us then, quite simply, that Marx had been largely right about religion. It was a stage in human history that would eventually be left behind. And by some stroke of

Providence, Bonhoeffer seemed to believe the same thing. It was the famous 30 April 1944 letter to Bethge from his *Letters and Papers from Prison* that was then our key text, almost our manifesto. The heart of that letter goes like this:

> 30 April 1944
>
> You would be surprised, and perhaps even worried, by my theological thoughts and the conclusions that they lead to; and this is where I miss you most of all, because I don't know whom else I could so well discuss them with, so as to have my thinking clarified. What is bothering me incessantly is the question what Christianity really is, or indeed who Christ really is, for us today. The time when people could be told everything by means of words, whether theological or pious, is over, and so is the time of inwardness and conscience—and that means the time of religion in general. We are moving toward a completely religionless time; people as they are now simply cannot be religious any more . . . Our whole nineteen-hundred-year-old Christian preaching and theology rest on the "religious *a priori*" of mankind. "Christianity" has always been a form—perhaps the true form—of "religion." But if one day it becomes clear that this *a priori* does not exist at all, but was a historically conditioned and transient form of human self-expression, and if therefore man becomes radically religionless—and I think that that is already more or less the case . . . what does that mean for "Christianity"?

At this point most theologians might have begun to reply to their own questions. But Bonhoeffer does not, instead of answering he goes on to make the question even more difficult.

> . . . if our final judgment must be that the western form of Christianity, too, was only a preliminary stage to a complete absence of religion, what kind of situation emerges for us, for the Church? How can Christ become the Lord of the religionless as well? Are there religionless Christians? If religion is only a garment of Christianity—and even this garment has looked very different at different times—then what is a religionless Christianity? . . . What do a church, a community, a sermon, a liturgy, a Christian life mean in a

religionless world? How do we speak of God—without religion, i. e., without the temporally conditioned presuppositions of metaphysics, inwardness, and so on? How do we
speak (or perhaps we cannot now even "speak" as we used
to) in a "secular" way about "God"?

That is still a powerful passage. Just rereading it today speeds
my pulse, especially when I remember how and where Bonhoeffer wrote it, locked in a Gestapo cell and becoming more
aware every day that he would never get out alive. But it is also
an important text for me because I have never felt I was a particularly "religious" person. I had never had many of the feelings,
experiences or even beliefs most people associate with being religious. I wanted a non-religious interpretation of Christianity not
just for the Marxists. I needed it myself.

In Berlin the passage took on importance for still another
reason. The challenge that presented itself to me and to many
young East German churchmen at the time was how to affirm
socialism and remain Christian at the same time. In almost any
other setting, Britain or France for example, this would not seem
to have been such an overwhelming challenge. Those countries
both have old traditions of mixing Christianity with different
brands of socialism. But Germany never did have such a tradition, at least at the popular level, and in the East Germany of 1962,
where the reigning form of socialism was Walter Ulbricht's rigid
brand of Stalinist Leninism, the problem seemed even more difficult. It was not that any of us liked Ulbricht. Almost everybody I
met in East Germany despised him, but for different reasons. The
conservatives hated him as the traitorous turncoat who helped
Bolshevism conquer the Fatherland. My friends loathed him as an
enemy of socialism posing as its protector, a third-echelon party
hack who had come to power solely because of his unswerving
loyalty to the Kremlin. But Ulbricht himself was not the issue.
Regardless of how state socialism had come to East Germany, it
was undeniably there, and the question came down to this: If
someone is to live as a Christian in a Communist society, where
"religion" is slated to disappear, how can he do it? The answer

came out of *Letters and Papers from Prison*—by developing a "non-religious interpretation" of Christianity.

The problem was of course that no one really knew what a "non-religious Christianity" would be like. Bonhoeffer certainly did not. Would it be merely ethical? Political? Intellectual? Would it involve, as Bonhoeffer hinted, an "arcane discipline" (a secret personal life style not visible to the public)? We didn't know, but we talked about it a lot, and some did a lot more than talk. I remember meeting one young East German pastor who had left his parish to work as a crane operator with a construction crew. He believed the only way to build a Christian community was "in solidarity with the working people where they work." A remarkable man, he still did an hour of Bible study in the original Greek or Hebrew every day after he came home from the building site. He was one of a small group of pastors I met who reminded me to some extent of the Catholic "worker priests" in postwar France. Both were searching for a radically alternative Christian life style, something that would clearly distinguish them from the socially reactionary and one-sidedly cultic religion they associated with the Christianity of the past.

After my return from Berlin, still mightily influenced by my year there and by the new insights into America that my absence and re-entry had given me, I wrote *The Secular City*. Much of that book represents my attempt to do for the American scene what Bonhoeffer had done for his. But as I wrote it, and during the years after it appeared, I saw that a new direction was needed. And I also noticed that "religion" had slowly edged its way back into my thinking as an inescapable part of any conceivable kind of Christianity.

Since then I have never rejected the core of Bonhoeffer. I never will. He was looking for a this-worldly, politically viable, life-affirming expression of Christianity. For him this meant a new form which would leave behind most of what he associated with "religion." He was, and remains, right in his search, mistaken only in his terminology.

"Religion" had a negative ring for us in the Berlin of 1962, in part because it stood for everything we saw about Christianity that was wrong and repressive. What we didn't realize was that in the negative judgment we made we were not being as radical as we thought. We were merely perpetuating the conventional intellectual wisdom of the day, common to both East and West. It is a bit of conventional wisdom many people, including myself, are now setting aside.

The idea that religion is inherently incompatible with human emancipation comes to us not only in its Marxist form, with which we were most familiar in Berlin. It also has a Freudian face. In fact Freud and Marx, possibly also with Nietzsche, remain the principal progenitors of the most popular intellectual critiques of religion still alive today. Despite hundreds of refutations, persuasive and not so persuasive, their ideas still color current judgments about religion. People suspect religion as a tool of injustice and social control (Marx) or as a symptom of neurosis and personal immaturity (Freud) or usually as a little of each. What would a world without religion be like? Neither Marx nor Freud was much given to speculation about that question, but both allowed themselves the luxury of prediction occasionally and those rare passages are interesting ones. Marx foresaw a world without alienation in which work would be more like play, but he held that religion would persist so long as class domination blurred men's consciousness, that it would direct them to a hope for heaven, since what they needed obviously wasn't going to be theirs on earth. Marx started out his career as an angry young atheist, penning fiery denunciations of religion. He soon decided, however, that direct attacks on religion were a waste of ink. Religion would last until man's mind was liberated through the abolition of classes, therefore he urged people to forget the anti-religious propaganda and get on with the revolution.

Freud's conclusion seems to have been more fatalistic. He saw religion as a kind of corporate neurosis, occasioned by the repression of instinctual drives which is required by all civilizations. Although he allowed that evolution might one day alleviate the crisis, he did not seem to anticipate much change in the foreseeable future. The conclusion of his major statement on this issue, *The Future of an Illusion*, is that although religion is an illusion it does probably have a future. Man would not be fully reasonable and fully free, however, until the religious illusion too had been outgrown. So although they did not agree with each other on the character of the liberated world of the future, both Freud and Marx did agree that it would never be a fully emancipated world until it was a world "without religion." In 1944, in his own way, Bonhoeffer would have agreed.

Until very recently, most Western "intellectuals" believed something like the Marxist or the Freudian diagnosis of religion, or held to some vague admixture of the two. So did I. But while my mind has been changing, so, apparently, have some other minds. One reason for the change is that both Marxist and psychoanalytic thought have gone considerably beyond the ideas of their founders. Another is that Christian theology and the phenomenology of religion have also changed markedly. Underlying both these changes is the sheer fact that the world of ordinary experience has not borne out the thesis that religion holds men in servile acquiescence and cowed immaturity. In short, the question of the future of religion is open again. We don't know what the future will be, but we do know that the nineteenth- and early twentieth-century judgments no longer seem plausible to us. Let me turn first to the Marxist and then to the Freudian critiques of religion and see where they stand today.

The inherited Marxist notion that religion is the tool of the oppressor cannot be sustained by the empirical evidence today. Religious ideas, and persons inspired by religious beliefs, have made a distinctive contribution to the emancipation movements of our time. Gandhi is the clearest example. But there is also the Buddhist resistance to French and American colonialism in Southeast Asia. There are the energetic anti-colonial nativist churches of Africa, and the late Eduardo Mondlane, the assassinated Christian leader of the Mozambique National Liberation Front. Malcolm X and Martin Luther King were both, in their own ways, very religious men. Dom Helder Camara, Bishop of Recife and Olinda, is the spokesman and symbol of the nonviolent movement of poor people demanding social change in Brazil. Indeed one exiled Brazilian political leader told me last year that when the present military junta seized control in Brazil, four Catholics were imprisoned for every one Communist. In Latin America, and in many places in the world, the rich and powerful can no longer look to the Church as a servile ally.

Also, in the U.S., writers today frequently remark that neither the student radicals nor the counterculture displays the anti-religious animus that characterized either left wingers or bohemians thirty-five years ago. Indeed some new culture apologists like Theodore Roszak seem almost promiscuously "religious." In any case, those who seek emancipation from psychic alienation and political exploitation today, though they have their doubts about established churches, do not reject all religion out of hand as The Enemy. They often see it either as an ally or a potential ally. An honest appraisal of the evidence suggests they are right. Religion has often been allied with tyranny and still is, but religion cannot simply be *equated* with oppression, and everyone knows there are grotesque forms of oppression that are secular, rational and anti-religious. The picture has become much more complex.

We are also learning as we get further and further away from the era of Stalin that the Marxist attitude toward religion was never as monolithic or as negative as was once thought. To a remarkable extent Marxist thinkers have reflected in their writing about religion the varying religious atmospheres in which they themselves grew up. Lenin's tough, superficial attitude exactly mirrors the cynical caesaropapism of Czarist Russia. Antonio Gramsci, the brilliant founder of the Italian Communist Party, never shared Lenin's perspective, because he grew up surrounded by organic Italian anti-clerical folk Catholicism. He realized that religion spoke to human needs that would still be present after any Communist revolution in Italy. Palmiro Togliatti, Gramsci's successor as the leader of Italian Communism, took that idea one step further. In his famous *Political Testament* he called for a whole new Communist attitude toward religion and angrily rejected the idea that Catholics cannot be revolutionaries. Recent changes and softenings in the Marxist view of religion are not as new as their heralds proclaim. They often merely pick up and carry on ideas articulated by Marxists whose influence was lost or laid aside during the chilly night of Stalinism.

All in all it has become clear to me that my Berlin year led me to a somewhat uncritical fascination with one narrow Marxist view of religion. Thus my attempt to combine it with a hasty reading of Bonhoeffer was bound to run out of steam. Even the best of the German Marxists could see that. As a young Marxist philosopher conceded to me one cold night after a few glasses of cognac in an East Berlin café, "religion may disappear, but it will probably be around for a couple of thousand more years; so we Marxists better learn to live with it." Maybe we theologians had better learn to live with it too.

What is true about the alleged connection between religion and social oppression is also true of religion and personal repression. A new generation of therapists is much less willing to cast religion in the villain's role, or to see it only as the enemy of ego strength and self-expression. Some even say that the characteristic neurosis of our time is not repression and guilt at all, but anomie and meaninglessness, caused in part by the erosion of ecstasy, the thinning out of archetypes, the drying up of ritual, the dissolution of religious metaphors in life.

Some of this "softer" attitude toward religion comes from the increased popularity in recent years of Freud's deviant disciple Carl Gustav Jung, whose view of religion was often so uncritical as to be useless. But not all the softening to religion comes from the Jungians. Erik Erikson and Rollo May are typical of the non-Jungian but post-Freudian re-evaluation of religion. Erikson's classic studies of Gandhi and Luther demonstrated how religious symbols nurtured intensely creative people. In other essays Erikson explores the positive significance of faith in the life of an emotionally healthy person. His studies have led him to believe that religion is born when the infant learns there is someone outside itself who cares about its needs for nourishment, fondling and holding. This early experience provides the first step toward confidence in the universe and hope for the future, which for Erikson are the rudiments of all religious faith.

There is a host of other writers, informed in one way or another by Freud, who have left behind his rather one-sided identification of religion with repression. Rollo May's thorough and thoughtful critique of psychoanalysis in *Love and Will* is based in part on the theological ideas of Paul Tillich, especially Tillich's insight that religious symbols link man to the most powerful impulses in life, both the destructive and the creative ones. Volumes of material have appeared in recent years on the détente between psychology and religion. Rather than try to summarize this flood of writing, however, which in any case I am in no position to do, I would rather remain true to my "testimonial" format by focusing on two evolving therapies with which I have had direct involvement, those of Fritz Perls and Ira Progoff.

What interests me about the work of Progoff and Perls, though they differ widely from each other, is that both try to help people reappropriate the religious and mythological layers of their psyches *without* "decoding" them. They keep myth as myth, symbol as symbol. They are not looking for a psychological equivalent of a non-religious gospel. Their form of therapy thus takes a long stride beyond the theories of Freud and Jung. Both those great masters wanted clients to be able to understand the frightening images and bewildering symbols that rampaged through their dreams and fantasies, but both sometimes forgot that the very process of analysis itself can rob images of their symbolic potency. In the new therapies, people are helped to open the gate and allow these images to make their impact *as symbols*. They are not viewed, as Freud saw them, as impulses which, because of cultural repression, had to be disguised in dissembling masks. Nor are they seen only as universal archetypes deriving from a group unconscious. The new approaches put into operation something which has been known by mystics and holy men for eons and in the academic community since the work of Ernst Cassirer and Susanne Langer, namely that symbolic communication has a meaning of its own. A symbol is not just a confused form of "rational" speech awaiting explication or decoding. It is a compact, highly charged mode of communication which is inevitably diluted or falsified when it is translated into another medium.

The older therapists were correct in detecting their clients' estrangement from the subrational dimensions of life. They were right in trying to help people "get back in touch" with these dimensions. They were wrong, however, in thinking that this reintegration could be usefully accomplished mainly by helping people to recognize, understand and interpret their dreams and fantasies. It is a classic case of dissection. It is killing something in order to understand it, the major contradiction in those versions of science tinged with the prejudices of the Enlightenment—as Freud was.

A dream symbol is a concentrated compound of feeling, idea, association and maybe even residues of ancient species history. It can be horrible, beautiful, puzzling or terrifying. But whatever it is, the new therapies say, it is a part of me, and the way to absorb a symbol back to my conscious life is *not* to desymbolize it. Rather I must allow myself to become capable again of symbolic action and mythical thought. This requires, first of all, not changing the symbol but changing me; not "decoding" the message but getting me back on its wavelength. So the therapeutic process is turned inside out. The narrowed modern neurotic, only vaguely aware of his seething psychic depths, is still seen to be in need of therapy. But instead of decoding the symbols so he can deal with them like any reasonable man should, he is helped to enlarge and deepen his emotional and symbolic life so that the symbols need not be gutted in order to be understood. The whole process sounds very much like Jesus' words to Nicodemus, when he asked the master how to find the kingdom of God he was told that he had to be "born again."

It should quickly be added that so far there are no sure-fire therapeutic techniques for doing this. I have had some brief exposure to the therapeutic approaches of the two men I have mentioned, Fritz Perls and Ira Progoff; but I would not consider either of their approaches to be highly refined yet. Still, those exposures did have important theological implications for me, and both helped me reappropriate the idea of "religion" as a vital one for theology.

I met the late Fritz Perls in California in 1967 at a Gestalt therapy weekend he was leading. By then he was already a storybook figure, a balding, bearded old codger, usually dressed in a shabby sweater and torn slacks. During the weekend he lived alone in a small cottage atop a hill at the edge of the ocean, but he was given to shuffling around the grounds with a cigarette dangling from his lower lip, looking directly through you and greeting the most attractive female guests with a long kiss and an encompassing hug. Sometimes it seemed to me he was determined to be the walking embodiment of the "dirty old man" stereotype. He looked like a mixture of Hebrew prophet, Bowery bum and Puck.

When leading therapy groups, Perls was always unabashedly in control, no non-directive hanky-panky. He had a way of placing each person in the center and working with him individually, for however long it took, while the rest of the group sat in a circle on the floor and watched. He could cut through someone's resistance very quickly—and he was tough and direct about it. The main point he always made was that what is happening *now* is what is important. His therapeutic goal was not to get someone to understand why he was acting as he was, linking it to some childhood situation or the like, but to help the person become fully aware of everything happening now. For Perls, that was really all that was needed.

Those who have been in therapy groups with Perls know about the way he encouraged people in the group to act out recent dreams. The client became a one-man theater. He portrayed not only his own role in the dream but those of the other people and objects in the dream also. Perls explained that all the ingredients in the dream, whether ships or animals or food or other people, represented alienated parts of oneself anyway, so by acting them out one reclaimed them as his own instead of seeing them as "out there." It was basically a dealienation process, getting back to oneself what is one's own.

In my group there was a tall broad-shouldered young social worker with bushy hair who told about a recurrent dream of his in which a pillbox with a cannon similar to the ones along the old Maginot Line appeared. Then in the dream a large alligator would slither out of the water and up to the fortress. Perls had him act out the dream by *being* first the fortress, then *being* the cannon, then *being* the alligator, then *being* the water. The man did it all, including booming, slithering and sloshing. Later on he told me that even before he had finished acting all that out, he felt he had already pulled a lot of symbols back into his life—without dreading them or intellectualizing about them. He had *become* them, or better still they had once more become him.

Later the same year I visited a group of young people who had been trained by Perls and who were living together in a kind of kibbutz. Perls had now put them on their own, and they started each morning not only by acting out their dreams from the night before, the way I've just described, but also by inviting one another to extend and elaborate the dreams. They did it through movement, gesture and non-verbal communication. I will never forget the fascination I felt as I watched these men and women reach, crawl, shake and jump, to help one another find again those vital dimensions of the self that have been lost to so many of us, lost so fundamentally, I fear, that most of us don't even know we are missing them. What fascinated me most about the process, however, was not just that they were constructing a bridge to the lost symbolic unconscious of the species but that they were doing it *as a community*. I felt in some ways as though I might be witnessing the birth of a new church. They were breaking out of isolation and solipsism at a level that would scare most people away instantly. They were living out one another's dreams.

Suddenly, as I watched the dream sharing and acting out, something strange happened. I had an intense sense of *déja vu*. I sat there remembering vaguely something I had seen somewhere before, but for a long time I could not remember what it was. Then suddenly I did recall. It was a long movie I had once viewed in an anthropology class, a film showing the tribal rituals of some primal African or perhaps Australian aboriginal group. In the movie the tribesmen, never very far out of touch with their dream life or with the legends of their forebears, were dancing and miming it all by the flickering light of the village fire. They flourished spears, pursued one another with exaggerated phallic objects, ate, leaped, chanted and groaned. It was all part of a ritual, repeated periodically, which brought the scattered units of the clan back together, assured everyone of his place, and probably did more for the dancers in one evening than most people today get from a year of psychotherapy.

After thinking about the movie, I looked more closely at the boys and girls writhing and gesticulating in that mountain retreat. What I was seeing had crossed a kind of border. It was no longer merely "group therapy." It was now the re-emergence, centuries after its decline and decades after its alleged disappearance, of an ancient form of religious ritual. As I watched I remembered the passage from Hermann Hesse's novel *Demian* in which Pistorius tells the young hero that "we bear everything in our soul that once was alive in the soul of men." There is no god or devil, he says, be it Greek or Zulu, that does not still lurk somewhere within us "as latent possibilities, as wishes, as alternatives." I also wondered vaguely, amidst the crying and the hugging, what Freud, that very strait-laced doctor from Vienna, the distant progenitor of this revival, would have said about it.

I am not as familiar with the theories and therapies of Ira Progoff and have taken part only once in a group he has led. Progoff is no bewhiskered Levite or saffron-draped bonze, but a clean-shaven conventionally dressed shrink. What captivated me about that brief afternoon, however, was that Progoff went even further than Perls did in leading us into our own psychic recesses. By means of a kind of guided fantasy he introduced forms of mythic material—stories, legendary figures like knights, monks and dragons, ascents and descents, dialogues—designed to help us delve to levels of being that had not yet surfaced even in our own dreams. Progoff does this by using vivid images, by helping people to invent fantasied conversations with archetypal figures (alienated aspects of the self and the species) and by a bold use of the client's own imagination.

In the session I had with Progoff, which included nearly a hundred of my students, he helped us to fancy ourselves descending deeper and deeper down a very long spiral staircase toward a small dimly lit room far down in the depths of a castle where hooded monks are chanting. This imaginative descent, which requires several minutes, helps the person become quiet and reach for hidden levels of his mind. Upon arriving at the room, still guided by the therapist's softly worded suggestions, one encounters, in imagination, a sympathetic but faceless robed personage. He seems to be the leader of the monks. One listens, and eventually the figure speaks. At least it did to me. The "message" may be something the person has been trying to hear for a long time, maybe not. In any case, many people who take the time to learn the discipline required by this sort of imagination therapy testify to its extraordinary significance for them.

If Perls in his Gestaltist therapy was in fact using a long-mislaid ritual approach, Progoff is utilizing elements of what were once called guided contemplation and spiritual discipline, maybe even prayer. His therapy approach bears a distinct resemblance to *The Spiritual Exercises* of St. Ignatius Loyola and to *The Tibetan Book of the Dead*, which have helped generations of Jesuits and Buddhist monks sense sectors of themselves—and possibly of something or someone else—from which they have been living in separation.

No one knows in what directions psychotherapy will move in

the future. Already there are more forms of therapy than anyone can keep straight. The children and grandchildren of old Uncle Sigmund have become too many to enumerate. Therapies using reinforcement technologies or the primal scream compete with others emphasizing movement, dance, masks or sex surrogates. Whatever happens, however, it seems clear that the conventional intellectual wisdom of a few years back about religion as neurosis now seems somewhat quaint.

Perhaps one should be cautious when psychotherapists begin to sidle up to religion. The next step might be a bear hug combined with a kiss of death. Also in some cases the secular myths and rituals invented by these latter-day confessors and shamans are at least as questionable as the old religious ones they displace. I mention the changing psychological evaluation of religion not to embrace the psychiatrists but to document the fact that the religious question is open again. We may awake someday to find that psychotherapy has become entirely *too* religious. Indeed, with some of the newer therapies I sometimes think that time is here already. Maybe we need a new curmudgeonly figure, like Uncle Sigmund, to take up the cudgels for atheism again.

There is another reason why the classical Freudian identification of religion with repression is currently being set aside. Freud himself turns out to have been more "religious" in one sense than he would admit. As David Bakan has shown in *Sigmund Freud and the Jewish Mystical Tradition*, the father of psychoanalysis springs from a tradition of Hasidic piety that shows up time and again in his method and theory. This is especially ironic when one recognizes that Freud's own knowledge of religion was somewhat limited. Although he read a few field studies of primitive religions, there is little in his own writings (except for *Moses and Monotheism*) that reflects more than the narrow bourgeois religion that thrived in the Vienna of his time. Any student of religious history knows that religion begins just as much in orgy as in order. I mean by "orgy" not a midnight debauch but a socially approved occasion for "excessive" forms of behavior. Religion is expressive as well as repressive.

I think people need regular periods in which conventional norms are relaxed and elements usually repressed in the individual and group psyche are expressed directly rather than through devious sublimation. This is what I wrote about in *The Feast of Fools*. The fiesta, after all, is just as much a religious occasion as is the Mass. The tendency to see religion as repressive stems in part from a scholarly prejudice which has led us to study mostly clerically dominated religion. We have analyzed the Mass and forgotten the fiesta. But even if it were true that clerically led religious rites are repressive, which is clearly not always the case, most expressions of "people's religion" are not.

Prayer was always the hardest problem for any proponent of a "non-religious" interpretation of Christianity to deal with. Among psychotherapists, it has usually been viewed with deep suspicion. No wonder. To any reasonable person, the aspect of someone talking to an alleged "other" who is just not there looks, quite simply, like a delusion. So prayer and worship, along with most forms of contemplation and ecstasy, have often been seen by psychologists as examples of regression, the temporary return of the individual to previous stages in the development of his personality. Although Freud had spoken about "regression in service of the ego," still worship and prayer appeared to most therapists to be immature, perhaps even obsessive or neurotic forms of behavior.

Now, however, we can see that such periods of temporary regression may be not only useful but essential for the healthy person. They allow one to experience again aspects of his own life history, often at a level of intense feeling, that he might otherwise lose touch with completely. Prayer, as I explained in *The Feast of Fools*, can be understood as an exercise in religious imagination. The "other" we speak to or listen for may indeed be a forgotten part of the self or the species, but that in no sense excludes the possibility that the holy touches us at these points.

Psychologists are now less sure about all this than they once thought. Many no longer view glossalalia (speaking in tongues), eating and drinking the symbols of the god, singing and chanting, trances, mysticism, ecstasy, and other forms of extraordinary experience with the disdain they once felt. After all, psychotherapy itself consists in part in helping the client restore some lost communication with buried dimensions of his psyche. So, apparently, do some forms of ritual.

From this perspective, the so-called "liberated" person who is unable to listen to the lost layers of his psyche, or who cannot allow himself to taste the transport of the heightened affective states associated with religious ritual, may not be healthy or emancipated at all. On the contrary, he is limited to a narrow range of ways to explore and inhabit his world. He may need to be "born again." Just because it draws on those affective and preconscious aspects, for which it has so long been derogated, religion could supply such a person with a means of enlarging and enlivening his experience. What both Freud and Marx resolutely exposed was the demonic perversion of religion, not religion itself.

"Religion" is a much more polyglot phenomenon than either its critics or its defenders of the past century supposed, more complex than I thought during the height of my Bonhoeffer days. Not only is it more complex, it is also more persistent. Although certain dated expressions have passed into oblivion, and many churches exert less direct control than they once did, religion itself shows little sign of disappearing. To the puzzlement of orthodox Marxists, it has not disappeared from the countries of Eastern Europe or from the U.S.S.R. There are undeniable signs of a growing fascination with religion among Russian intellectuals such as Alexander Solzhenitsyn. Several of the young Soviet poets have begun to use Christian ideas and Orthodox images in their poetry. In Africa the so-called "independent" churches, which joyfully utilize drums and dance and spectacle, are spreading with incalculable rapidity. The same is true in Brazil of such movements as Condomblé, Umbanda and Macumba, the Afro-Catholic religious movements that feature spirit possession.

What does this unexpected late twentieth-century upsurge of religion, and indeed of unconventional forms of Christianity, suggest for the future role of theology? Certainly theology's task now cannot be to elaborate some "non-religious" expression of the faith. Nor can it focus on what is happening within the conventional churches. Such churches cannot be ignored. They are part of the picture even if they are not at its center. But a theology which focuses mainly on them will fail miserably in its task. It will not notice most of what is religiously significant today and will therefore fail to grapple, respond and struggle with it.

Theologians cannot fulfill their function if they fail to examine, criticize, ponder and even "evaluate" religion. Admittedly, what it means to "evaluate" in this context is not easy to define. I will return to that problem in the next chapter. But, as a bit of testimony, I must concede here that I now feel my avid search for a "non-religious" interpretation of Christianity, inspired by Bonhoeffer and born in Berlin, was probably doomed to failure from the outset. I do not regret the search and the struggle. I do not think any less of the colleagues and comrades with whom I worked. We were right in our intention. We wanted to dissolve the ancient alliance between throne and altar. We wanted to endorse the thrust toward breaking bonds we could sense all over the world, so we opposed "Gospel" to "religion," found the first liberating and the second enslaving. But we were mistaken. By cutting the world that way, we not only separated ourselves from non-Christians who, though on our side in the struggle, could never affirm our "Gospel." We also excluded many Christians who, along with that Gospel, would want to enjoy a little, maybe even a lot, of religion.

I have been back to Berlin only once since I left in 1963, and that was the following summer. I have not been there since. I am not sure why I avoid it. One reason is that after the Russian invasion of Czechoslovakia in August 1968 I learned that many of my friends in East Germany had disagreed bitterly with one another over what to say or do about it. I heard that people who had been close to one another hardly spoke, that groups I had been in were split. I knew it would be hard for me to go back and face that.

But I also knew I had changed too, both personally and theologically, and that my present direction might not be understood. Like Bonhoeffer in 1944, albeit from an incomparably safer vantage point, I could also write, "You would be surprised, and perhaps even worried, by my theological thoughts and the conclusions that they lead to . . . ." One of those conclusions would be a much less haughty attitude toward "religion." Still, as the years go by, the tug of that year in Berlin does not diminish. I know that soon, maybe very soon, I'll be ready to visit again. Maybe when I go I'll find that my friends, the ones who remain, have changed too, and that my present gropings may be better understood and appreciated than I once thought.

CHAPTER SIX

Learning from People's Religion

It was obvious to me then that my apprenticeship had been only the beginning of a very long road. And the strenuous experiences I had undergone, which were so overwhelming to me, were but a very small fragment of a system of logical thought from which Don Juan drew meaningful inferences for his day to day life, a vastly complex system of beliefs in which inquiry was an experience leading to exultation.
  —Carlos Castaneda, *The Teachings of Don Juan: a Yaqui Way of Knowledge*

DISCOVERING PEOPLE'S religion put me into a difficult dilemma. As the focus of my work began shifting from the study of "theology" in the traditional sense to an interest in "religion" in a broad sense, I noticed I was neither academically nor spiritually prepared for the change. How does one "study" people's religion? During my long formal training as a theologian I was taught, and taught very well, how to interpret the meanings of sacred scriptures and religious texts, some of them in their original languages. But no one ever taught me how to interpret living religion, especially the religious actions of ordinary people. I regret this lapse in my training, because in the final analysis it is always just such people who are the real bearers of religion. Scriptures are the residues. Even when texts inspire and create continuing movements as the Koran and the Bible and other holy books have done, it is people who are inspired and brought together, and it was people who wrote and passed on the texts. To understand people's religion we have to interpret people.

Admittedly this is hard to do for the past. From most periods in religious history we have only texts (plus a little archeological data) to help us find out how people served the gods. But in the present world we have live human beings of every possible religious bent, praying, meditating, dancing, crying and singing to more gods than we can number. Nonetheless, theologians have mostly ignored this carnival of the spirit and left its investigation to anthropologists and psychologists. These secular investigators in turn have not, until relatively recently, looked upon the religions of ordinary people as something they could learn from or as a story they needed to hear. At best they examined them with sympathetic curiosity, at worst with mild contempt. Only in the past few years have anthropologists themselves been able to see that religions do not reveal themselves to detached documenters, that even "mere observing" changes what is observed, and that therefore their endeavors, just as much as those of missionaries, were a part of the larger history of Western condescension to the ways of "less civilized" folk. Also, only recently have they conceded that, given the crisis of our own civilization, we must now begin to *learn* from the experiences of ordinary people and from other cultures, not just to satisfy scholarly curiosity but to discover ways of life that can enlarge and enliven the one we now live.

In seeking to understand people's religion it is essential always to keep one crucial distinction in mind. It is the difference between *"investigating"* and *"learning from."* I am convinced that people's religion is not something we can "study" or do research about in the old sense, for that approach betrayed a cavalier premise from the start. We turn to people's religion now not because we want to study it but because we want people to *teach us.* We want to learn from their lives. This requires shedding the role of the investigator and learning to be a seeker.

In my search for a new way of learning from the religions of ordinary people I was helped enormously by reading Carlos Castaneda's *The Teachings of Don Juan.* Castaneda, a young anthropologist studying Yaqui Indian religion, met and became friends with Don Juan, a Yaqui medicine man. The wise old sorcerer took such a liking to the young scholar that he allowed him to become his apprentice and to learn "from the inside" the mysteries of his calling. In becoming an apprentice, Castaneda quickly found that he could no longer simply "study" his master-tutor. He had to struggle with him, fight against him, argue with him. In the process he not only learned more about Yaqui religion than any previous anthropologist, he also learned to abandon many of the academic prejudices he had brought with him to the relationship. But he did not discard *all* his previous skills. That in fact is the strength of the book. In writing it, Castaneda *combined* the personal knowledge he gained from his apprenticeship to Don Juan with the best elements in the anthropological training he had brought to it. In order to learn from people's religion we must use our heads, but we must also be willing to become "apprentices" to whoever will teach us the lore, discipline us, upbraid us, nurture us and wrestle with us the way the wizened old Don Juan did with his young protégé.

Now the question is *how* do we become apprentices and seekers? How do we approach present-day religions (in both the narrow and the broader sense of the word) not just to accumulate data about them but to hear the inner story they tell? In the past couple of years I have been trying out two theological approaches that allow me to learn from the thing itself rather than from derivative reports about it, detached observations of it, or theories of how it should be. I call these two approaches "participant hermeneutics" and "experimental liturgics."

Participant hermeneutics combines elements of the venerable theological science of hermeneutics with the social scientific method called "participant observation." "Hermeneutics" comes from the name of the Greek god Hermes (Mercury, in the West), whose main job was to carry messages among the gods and from the gods to men. Hermeneutics is the study of messages or, more exactly, the study of how one interprets the meaning of texts. It is generally used in relation to documents stemming from a different historical period. My question, however, is how can we have a hermeneutics not of the past but of the present, not of texts but of people? How can we learn to read the message of a Pentecostal revival in Chile, a Kimbangoist church parade through the streets of an African village, a group of shaved monks chanting on a Burmese hillside, a Yaqui medicine man, or a midnight Mass at a church in Cambridge? I am not asking here for a method of finding out what the original writers of the songs, chants, stories or Bible verses used at these occasions *intended*, which is the question standard hermeneutics would ask. I am asking what it all *means* to the people now involved.

Obviously this method is only in the earliest stages of its evolution. I do not pretend it is ready to be emulated. However, it has been enormously useful to me when I have tried on occasion to become an "apprentice," if only for a few hours. So I list its four components here in the hope that someone else who is also intrigued by what the gods may be saying to us through the piety of everyday people might be able to use them and enlarge upon them. The parts of the approach are 1) a careful effort to discover the *prehistory* of the event or phenomenon now being studied; 2) an equally rigorous attempt to learn about the larger setting within which the present activity takes place; 3) a thorough observation of the phenomenon itself in all its many details; and 4) a meticulous awareness of the meaning it all has for *me*, the interpreter-observer-participant.

The first two parts of this method need little comment. Prehistory is important because it is impossible to understand any present phenomenon, religious or otherwise, without knowing something about where it came from and how it developed. This is true of a sacred text, a mural painting, a priest's robe or a song. Becoming familiar with the larger setting is also obviously crucial because in order to learn from one event we have to be aware of the *whole* life of the people involved—what they do the rest of the time, what stresses they face, what place this event occupies for them in their total routine. These initial steps correspond to what we learned in the older hermeneutics about locating a particular text in a larger work and in the other literature of its period, as we do with a passage from the Bible or the Church Fathers. Though these two parts of the method seem almost self-evident upon first hearing, it is important to keep them in mind. We can be seriously misled by a narrow or hasty exposure, because no aspect of the people's religion can be properly understood in isolation from its place in the history and total setting of the people. Castaneda could learn more from Don Juan because he had done his home-work on the Yaqui Indians beforehand.

The third step in the process, careful observation, also re-sembles the way we were taught to read a text, but here it is applied to a person, event, liturgy, procession or whatever. It de-mands a rigorous attention to subtle detail—pace, mood and the minutiae of expression—for which few theologians have been trained. In fact it demands the kind of skills a therapist may develop only after years of practice. Like therapy, it proceeds on the assumption that *nothing is trivial.* How and where people enter, sit, stand; how the furniture is arranged; who participates and how; costume and gesture—everything *counts* as a significant datum. All this demands well-developed powers of attention and a capacity for listening, observing, remembering.

But the fourth part of the method, asking about the meaning it has for *me*, is both the most important and the most unorthodox. It means that *how I feel*, throughout my whole participation, is not irrelevant. It is an indispensable component in understanding the thing itself. This is difficult. To learn how to do it, the ap-prentice-observer-interpreter must often *unlearn* most of what he has heard in his previous education about "keeping your own feelings out." Consequently, for example, when we are going to attend a ritual, I try to teach my students, and try myself, to be fully aware of how we feel before the experience (apprehensive, eager?), during its several stages (bored, elated, frightened?) and after it.

There are two reasons for insisting so strenuously on this self-awareness aspect of participant hermeneutics. First, being atten-tive to one's own feelings in the midst of a new experience deepens one's awareness of his own interiority and thus makes him more capable of appreciating the inner meaning of another person's actions. Second, since religion has at least as much to do with feeling as with ideas, people who are aware of how they are feeling participate more fully in the event, even though their own feelings may at many points be very different from the ones the other people around them seem to be experiencing. A person who knows what he is feeling can detect the inner recesses of another's state, even if it is a different one, better than someone who is determined to remain the cool, distant observer.

Within this four-stage framework of participant hermeneutics a wide variety of techniques can be used. Books and articles are essential in order to know anything about prehistory. Interviews, community studies and surveys can help establish the larger picture. The key to the whole thing, however, lies in the successful combination of all the parts. Even then only half the work is done, because one who really wants to *learn from* a living religion cannot simply retire when the descriptive phase is complete. He will eventually let the story he has heard meet his own story. He will appropriate, question, reject and accept aspects of what he has seen. He may change his own story in view of what he has learned. Most importantly, however, he will always respond and evaluate *provisionally*. No *final* judgments are made. Also, no evaluation at all is made until the question of what it meant to everyone involved, including the observer, is answered.

At some point, however, an authentic human response to someone else's faith entails some kind of "reply," some yes or no, usually a combination of the two. This is where the going gets difficult. We have all been taught, from high school social studies on, that we should be "objective" about other people's values, beliefs and practices. We should neither praise nor condemn. This is admittedly a valid *stage* in any learning. We should listen before we speak. But we are dealing here with the faith of actual persons, and the only way I can allow a person to make a difference to me or permit his faith to touch my actual existence is to move from detachment to involvement, from listening to speaking, from observation to response. And response always involves bringing my own values and beliefs to bear on the matter at hand. Castaneda learned this. His anthropological approach had to be tempered by a more "religious" way of learning. I think his insight is an invaluable one. The person who embraces or wrestles with the one he is learning from treats him with incalculably more respect than does the person who merely examines. In the process he also learns incalculably more. So in order to avoid the coolly clinical connotation of "evaluate," let us say instead that a theologian must ultimately *respond* to the religious phenomenon he is "studying." This response will inevitably express his own beliefs and values, and will always produce *some* change in both the teacher and the learner.

Theology then is a form of critical, informed and sympathetic response to "religion" in the broadest sense of the word. Like literary criticism, theology is a derivative discipline. It does not create religion. Religion comes first, theology second. Theologians try to understand religion. But their work is not merely descriptive. Since theology (unlike, say, sociology of religion) works within an explicit community of faith, it takes sides, says yes and no, makes judgments. The theologian is more music critic than musicologist. He enjoys music, but he also "evaluates" it both in the light of a tradition and in terms of his own sensibility.

Does its responsive posture condemn theology to narrowness and provincialism? This accusation has often been made in the past, but I do not accept its validity. Theology's norms are at least explicit, not hidden behind the rhetoric of "objective" analysis that for so long obscured from Western social science its own unnoticed provincialism. Having explicit sources, goals and presuppositions does not make theology narrow. It can make it more self-critical. It could even serve in part as an example of how a humane science should operate.

But how can a theologian avoid being provincial? He always responds, at least in part, from a perspective produced by a particular religious community. His stance is Christian or Buddhist or Moslem or humanist—all traditions with their own coloration. Must he not then always be unavoidably narrow? There are five or six major living religious traditions in the world, to say nothing of the smaller ones and the innumerable sects and subdivisions. Can a theologian, operating within one of these, do justice to the others?

Theologians recognize today a kind of universal religious consciousness which assumes disparate if overlapping forms. They see that although a theologian, like any human being, brings his own history and that of a people into any situation, he can no longer think and write exclusively in terms of one community of faith. This would confine him to a preplanetary past. The Christian must consciously respond to Moslems and Hindus—to a larger, highly diverse, indeed world-wide family of faith. A Buddhist can no longer write as though he were isolated from Christianity or Islam. He must in some way relate his thinking to other specific traditions that impinge on it, and eventually to the religiousness of the entire human family. Some of the most forceful religious pioneers of our century would not have made the impact they did if they had not crossed over and drawn heavily on another tradition. Gandhi's use of Christianity and Martin Luther King's of Hinduism exemplify this borrowing process.

The borrowing we need today, however, should not mean that the historical particularity of a living religion is dissolved in some universal pabulum. Theology should discard both the ideal of an abstract universal science and that of a global religion unsullied by the stain of concrete history. Religion at its best is one of the guardians of human eccentricity. So theology must move back and forth between the particular tradition in which it arises and the heterogeneous religious consciousness of mankind. Theology today is "opening out" both in its sources and in its focus of attention. But it remains *responsive* instead of merely *descriptive*. It seeks not just to describe the spirits but to "test them to see if they be of God." I accept this developing role of theology and try to do that kind of theology myself. The problem is that once one begins sifting and responding, not just describing, one must make his or her basis for doing so as clear and explicit as possible. The observer need not reveal himself. The responder invariably does.

For me, the touchstone by which I respond to religious phenomena is summed up by the single word "liberation." Liberation, on the cultural, social and personal levels, as the plumb line
by which theology assesses religion, was first used most widely
by radical Catholic theologians in Latin America. Its use as a
controlling norm is still not fully refined, but it is beginning to
provide a criterion for making judgments among religious phenomena and religious movements, for saying yes and no, for
testing the spirits. This criterion of human liberation is the same
one which under a different label once led me to look, with
Bonhoeffer, for a non-religious interpretation of Christianity.
Now, however, it prompts me to sort out the wheat from the
chaff in a wide variety of religious movements, to register my
response not according to their degree of religiousness but according to whether they contribute to human liberation. But
how do we define "liberation"?

Like every theologian today I am learning to move back and
forth between the two poles supplied by 1) the religious tradition
within which I came to consciousness and 2) the variegated but
universal religious consciousness of mankind. Both have something
to say about liberation.

1) One of the two poles within which I operate is my own
Christian tradition. Within this tradition there are in turn two
principal foci, Exodus and Easter. But liberation is the common
theme in both. The Hebrews were peons in Egypt who gained
their national liberation, and for them that historic event became
the point where the Creator had revealed who He was and what
He was up to in the world. Exodus points to the emancipation of
man from political and economic bondage. Easter, the resurrection of Christ, is the Christian parallel of the Exodus. It suggests
that not even death can nullify the significance of human life.
Easter in the New Testament faith celebrates the liberation of all
men and women from "sin and death." "Sin" is understood as
whatever chains people to the past, and "death" as whatever
terrifies them about the future. The early Christians thus saw
Easter as a kind of continuation and enlargement of the Exodus. I

suggest that Exodus and Easter add up to a vision of "God" as whatever it is within the vast spectacle of cosmic evolution which inspires and supports the endless struggle for liberation, not just from tyranny but from all bondages. "God" is that power which despite all setbacks never admits to final defeat.

If the liberation of humankind is seen as the *purpose* of Christianity, and if theology is to serve the purpose of the faith, then theology too must be directed toward human liberation. This means its questions and its methods must change also. Some theologians have already turned away from the nineteenth century's fascination with the "essence" of Christianity. They now more frequently ask about its influence and its impact. They see that the meaning of Christianity is not to be found in some timeless essence. Rather, its "essence" is seen in how it actually operates within history, in the conflicts and clashes of earth. So the critical question theologians should ask now, about any religious idea or image or institution, is: How does it actually operate, what does it do for or against liberation? The truth of a doctrine should not be determined merely by its agreement with past formulations but by its contribution to deliverance from bondage (Exodus) and to new life (Easter), a process which is never completed.

If liberation is the issue, then a lot of things become clear. No matter how neatly a present rite or teaching may cohere with an orthodox past, if it locks people in stupefied bondage it must be questioned, for it no longer carries the spirit of Exodus and Easter. It is "heretical." Similarly, this liberation theology makes room for innovation, but it is not a fad-mongering modernism. When new religious ideas and practices appear, they are weighed according to the Exodus-Easter axis: Do they contribute to the fuller consciousness, the joy, the maturation and the emancipation of man? When the question is put this way, neither newness nor oldness is itself a value. Something which at first seemed archaic or obsolete can assume a liberating function. An ancient chant breaks the power of technical jargon. Forgotten spiritual disciplines unlock neglected recesses of the psyche. A rediscovered utopian vision undercuts the dull blueprints of social engineers. Even "otherworldly" spirituals keep dignity alive until history makes rebellion possible.

The theology of liberation has several advantages. It makes Christian theology less provincial, less elitist and less ecclesiastical. It is less *provincial*, since the Exodus-Easter aspects of *any* religious tradition can be evaluated, not just those appearing in Christianity. For although Christianity, Judaism and Islam make more of the Exodus than do other faiths, at least rhetorically, none of them holds any monopoly on the reality of liberation and new life. In fact the Exodus-Easter reality can often be discovered totally outside the boundaries of these traditions, or of any consciously held religious tradition at all. "Liberation theology" thus helps save Christian theology from provincialism. Also it guards theology against *elitism*. If the actual impact of a religious idea on people is what is crucial, then the focus of theology cannot be merely on what is written, preached or taught. The experience of ordinary lay people in all religious movements becomes just as important as the teachings of the stated authorities. Theology of liberation also saves theology from *ecclesiasticism*. The evolving self-consciousness and full liberation of the human species are what are at issue. These are obviously neither enhanced nor retarded only within "religious" settings in the narrow sense. They transcend church boundaries.

2) So much for the "particularistic pole," the biblical tradition. Now what about its other pole, the global but fragmented religious consciousness of mankind? How does the second pole influence theological thinking about liberation?

Here the question at stake is what human liberation is anyway. The term "liberation" or something close to it appears among Buddhists, Hindus, Christians and others; but there is considerable disagreement about what human liberation means. In fact dramatically diverse images of freedom vie with one another. It can mean liberation from bondage, from earthly needs, from the desires of the flesh, from the wheel of birth. Still there is not *only* disagreement. There are important elements of consensus, complementary insights, areas of convergence, and valuable correctives. One urgent task of any twentieth-century theologian is to uncover both the correctives and the convergences. When one begins this work of locating areas of convergence, he will quickly make an important discovery: Writers from nearly every religion are more and more trying to bring their traditions into the service of human fulfillment here on earth. Less and less does a hereafter or some future age of bliss totally overshadow the needs of here and now. In this sense most of the world's faiths are moving not toward secularization but toward what I would call "terrestrialization"; that is, they are becoming alternative ways of deepening and symbolizing human existence on earth, not varied modes of escaping it. I doubt, however, that these changes will ever create some syncretistic world church. I hope not, for in religion as in everything else both truth and survival are better served by heterogeneity and variegation than by unification and uniformity. But the current "liberation" movements in the world religions will assuredly provide a point for dialogue and for mutual conversation. This planetary pole reminds the theologian whose particular pole is Christianity that his own ideas of liberation are in no sense ultimate, that they have arisen within a particular cultural climate whose overtones they carry.

But our universalism must be critical too. Some theologians give way to a temptation to be critics of religion in general with no personal base from which to think or respond. I think this is a mistake. No responsible theologian should "go universal" to escape his roots. The particularistic pole is important too. Without it a theologian sloshes around in an oozing swamp of a vague global religiosity, just as without the universal pole he sits locked into a stifling provincialism. Like the juxtaposition of different melodies, the two poles keep theology attuned and attentive. No future theology can avoid moving between both poles, especially if it is to serve the genuine liberation of homo sapiens, not just of Western man.

The second approach I have evolved for learning how faith actually functions I call "*experimental liturgics.*" It draws on that branch of theology known as "liturgics" which studies the history and structure of ritual. But it also uses the social experiment or trial model method of modern science.

The best way I know to flesh out what I mean by experimental liturgics is to describe an actual event I helped plan and conduct. Two years ago a group of friends and students joined me to organize a celebration of what we called Byzantine Easter in a huge discothèque called The Boston Tea Party. We had already learned a lot from participating in traditional rites and festivals. We now wanted to move on to plan something of our own. We wanted to surround the colorful Byzantine (Eastern style) Mass with participatory liturgical dance (versus the spectator kind), with light-and-music collages, with physical encounter movements—and also somehow to bring those powerful old Christian symbols of New Life and shared bread more directly into the service of human liberation.

We selected the Byzantine date for Easter partly because the Eastern Christian tradition has preserved a more gloriously festive Easter liturgy. But we also chose it because we wanted to emphasize the link between Easter and Passover and between Exodus and Resurrection and between Jews and Christians. The dating of Eastern Easter does that. It comes at the end of Passover week, so deliverance from political bondage in Egypt or anywhere else is linked with liberation from sin and death. We wanted to celebrate all these things at once. We scheduled the occasion for four in the morning and suggested that those who came should bring a loaf of bread to share.

The publicity was very modest. Several people told me they thought the idea was great but the hour was wrong, that only insomniacs and speed freaks would come to something at four A.M. They were mistaken. By three-thirty A.M. the discothèque was already teeming with people, heavy on youth but spanning the alleged generation gap. We had placed a huge table in the middle of the dance floor as an altar. As people arrived they heaped it high with pumpernickel, cinnamon buns, doughnuts, twinkies, long French loaves, matzos, scones, heavy black bread and raisin tarts. People painted Z's (for "He lives," from the movie that was popular at the time), peace signs, fishes, crosses, and assorted graffiti on one another's faces and bodies. Some fashioned tiaras out of silver foil and crowned one another or painted pictures on long strips of paper taped to the walls. By four there were nearly two thousand people present, creating their own cathedral and costuming one another for the rite.

At four-thirty the Passion Week portion of the evening-morning began. Everyone grew serious as a multiscreen light-and-music collage transformed the Tea Party into a contemporary Via Crucis, with scenes of war, death, cruelty, loneliness and racism. People watched and listened intently, singing with the music when they knew it. Then an extraordinary group of free-wheeling liturgical dancers dressed in black and white leotards began to move among the multitudes enticing them into sacred gesture and ritual motion. People who had never danced in their lives before stretched out arms and flexed legs and torsos. The lithe solemnity of the movements made me think we should get rid of pews in churches forever.

After the dancing, people came together in small groups to prepare for the ceremony of the Mass. Hands reached out and clots of people, from three to fifteen, formed. The human clusters swayed, hugged, moaned and clung together as people lifted each other and reached out toward the flickering pictures on the walls. In one group a teeny began humming "Jesus Loves Me," and soon her whole arm-and-leg-enmeshed group began to hum with her. Then from the sound system poured forth the recitatives and choruses of Bach's St. Matthew Passion. Again people clasped and unclasped in embraces; arms reached up and out. "He was wounded for our iniquities . . ." The whole crowd seemed to be participating imaginatively in the crucifixion, and in man's perpetual crucifixion of his neighbor.

Then came silence. Then a brief reading from the Gospel of Luke: "Why seek ye the living among the dead? He is not here, but is risen." Then Handel's "Hallelujah" chorus.

It was the high point. Most people have always secretly longed for a chance to sing the "Hallelujah" chorus, booming out the bass or soprano with full fortissimo. But in our spectator-performer style churches they have mostly had to bite their lips and listen. Here everyone joined in: "And he shall reign forever and ever . . ." Not only did they sing, they jumped, danced, applauded. As the last Amen of the chorus faded, the procession entered. It included not only the officiants but a line of fruit and bread and wine bearers, censers and a crucifer, accompanied by the march music from Z. Slowly it wound through the crowd to the bread-bedecked table. Candles flickered, vestments glistened and clouds of incense wafted through the air. The celebrants included an Episcopal priest, two United Church of Christ ministers, one of them a woman, a Catholic priest of the Melchite rite, and a Roman Catholic priest. And myself, acting out, as one friend put it, the alter ego of my Baptist boyhood, expressing my repressed fantasies of icons and chants and liturgical splendor.

As the ecumenical communion began, an alert quiet crept over the crowd. They joined in the chanting of the Kyrie eleison; they responded to the reading of the prophesy of God's judgment on Babylon with shouts and applause; they hummed a long "Om" during the epiklesis. Then the celebrants lit the enormous Easter Candle, holding it aloft to the four corners of the earth, blessed the mounds of bread, and invited people to take it "for free" and share it with their neighbors.

After the benediction we greeted one another with the Kiss of Peace. Again the discothèque swayed and sang. A Resurrection light collage leaped onto the walls. Since the hall is equipped with twenty-six projectors, the effect was like moving in an instant from a dim cave into a cathedral of luminous windows. Just as the collage was reaching its apex with the Beatles singing "Here Comes the Sun," someone threw open the back door. By some miracle of celestial timing, the sun was just beginning to peek over the Boston extension of the Massachusetts Turnpike.

But like everything else in this uncertain life, even a Byzantine Easter must cope with the custodians of convention. Just after sunrise someone called me into the discothèque's main office, where I was awaited by two very formidable Boston policemen who did not seem to be experiencing the empyrean ecstasy of Resurrection.

"You told us this was going to be a religious service," one of them said, "but it looks to me like a debauch." I wondered what a limited experience of debauches he must have had, but I kept quiet and listened.

"Furthermore," he went on, "the people are dancing in there and the music does not sound religious to me." He brandished in my face an empty wine jug we had used earlier for communion and asked if this sort of thing ordinarily went on at a religious service. I thought of quoting those lines from Acts of the Apostles to the effect that these people were "not filled with new wine but with the spirit." I doubted, however, that the reference would be appreciated, so I saved it. The officer's final complaint was that he smelled marijuana. I assured him that what his vigilant nostrils detected was a particularly fragrant variety of Oriental incense. He seemed unconvinced.

The police insisted that the celebration be halted. We were coming toward the end anyway, but still I wanted desperately to refuse. At that moment another section of the St. Matthew Passion was playing, and hundreds of people were moving to it in gentle undulating waves. At the edge of the turnpike a group was bowing and chanting to the sun. If I had said no and gotten arrested, I thought, it might touch off the Scopes Trial of the 1970s: Can the police stop a worship service because they don't think it seems religious? But the discothèque staff members were looking at me with silent, pleading eyes: Don't ruffle the fuzz.

So I nodded and ambled over to the microphone. I announced to the saints that the celebration was over. At least for now. We turned the lights on and the music off. In fifteen minutes everyone was gone, streaming out into the sunlight humming the "Hallelujah" chorus. A few stragglers helped with the sweeping up. The upholders of law and order slammed the doors on their patrol car and drove away unsmiling.

Later on, as I climbed into the car to drive home, I felt a little sorry. But then, as I glanced down to where my hands rested on the steering wheel I noticed something I had almost forgotten. On the backs of my hands, earlier in the evening, someone had painted a Z ("He lives") and a peace sign. I turned on the ignition and smiled. I knew that, for that moment at least, I believed in the Resurrection.

During the next few weeks we thoroughly relived and evaluated Byzantine Easter. Those who had planned it conducted interviews with many of the people who attended, asking a series of questions we had prepared before. The planning group spent a whole day at a country inn rehashing what we had done and how we had felt.

We didn't concur on everything, of course, but we did on many aspects. We unanimously agreed, for example, that the milkman hour was indeed right. One of the group remembered his "special" feelings as a boy when he had gotten up while it was still dark for one of those chilly hillside Easter sunrise services where the hymns came out in clouds of visible water vapor from your mouth, but everyone felt fine because they knew the service was followed by coffee and piles of eggs and flapjacks in the cozy basement of a nearby church. Other people recalled midnight Masses, prayer vigils and even the heightened anticipation caused by getting up early to go fishing or leave for a trip. There is probably a physiological basis, we speculated, why people feel unusually "up" for such occasions. Interrupted from its normal routine, the body itself is not as dependent on habitual cycles and is more receptive to new sensations. People had actually arrived for the celebration, we noticed, already in a different state of consciousness, a kind of heightened expectation.

We also agreed that the unusual length of the celebration had been important. We began to see why Eastern Orthodox liturgies often go on for hours, and services in black Protestant churches frequently last twice as long as comparable white services. We all felt that most normal Catholic and Protestant services simply don't last long enough to allow for anything of significance to happen. Maybe, someone suggested, instead of an hour once a week, five hours once a month would provide a better calendrical rhythm for liturgical events.

One of the people in the planning group was a shapely dancer with no denominational label but with what she described as a "third eye for things of the spirit." She had wanted all along to hold Byzantine Easter in a church, where, as she said, "the vibes would be better." I had insisted on the discothèque. I did so out of a strong conviction derived from my own observation as well as from my reading of various communications theorists. The conviction is that *juxtaposing* event and environment greatly enhances our powers of perception and that the psychological *setting* within which someone perceives a symbol accounts for at least half of what it means. It all has to do with contrast. We are so used to bread and wine and vestments and altars in churches that we often hardly notice them. There is no "counterenvironment" to set them off, no field against which their profiles are sharpened. So they often fade into the milieu.

But even conventional religious symbols seem to take on a newly vivid quality in a strange setting. It is a little like tethering elephants in hotel lobbies or otherwise admixing objects we never see adjacent to each other in life. The juxtaposition of figure and field dislocates our normal perceptual sets. We must look again, and we see more. Like an assemblage of found objects or an imaginatively contrived collage, the unexpected configuration can shake the beholder into a new way of experiencing.

After the Byzantine Easter the three-eyed Terpsichore who had debated with me on this point conceded that the Tea Party had been right, at least this time. Still she thought that next time we should "try it in a church." She may be right. Leotarded clairvoyants sometimes are, and many of my students have planned comparable events, though on a much smaller scale, for churches. But in a church, where the "vibes" are admittedly very different from those of a rock emporium, the elements of the juxtaposition should be reversed. In a setting replete with crosses, dossals, founts and stained glass, it would be necessary to utilize very "secular"-looking and -sounding elements to create the same contrast of figure and field. Ironically, the more "secular" the setting, the more "religious" the content can be without simply disappearing into the environs. People "see" dancers in churches and Masses in dance halls more than vice versa.

My own criticism of Byzantine Easter draws on this principle of contrast and juxtaposition. I think the event itself could have used *more* identifiable "religious" symbolism. For example, the thousands of slide transparencies we flashed on the walls and the music that accompanied them movingly carried the temper first of crucifixion and later of new life. They did so, however, mainly by means of secular themes. For the crucifixion we used pictures of bombing, loneliness, garbage and waste, ruined rivers, racial injustice and faces full of fear. The Resurrection élan was carried by joyous folk and rock sounds and by the visualization of natural vitalities such as flowers bursting into bloom, splatches of color, and joyful people's faces. The dancers helped conjure the different tonalities of the crucifixion and the Resurrection episodes, in both cases inviting the guests into their movements.

Surprisingly, however, most of the people we questioned later on, although they spoke positively about these "non-religious interpretations" of Good Friday and Easter, still said the high point for them had been the Mass itself and the "Hallelujah" chorus. This confirmed my hunch that in the discothèque setting we should have used more conventional visual depictions of the Passion, drawn perhaps from classical art, and more identifiable "religious" music. If we had held the celebration in a church, however, I would have argued the other way, for less traditionally "religious" content in all the media.

The power and flexibility of the old Byzantine rite came as a pleasant surprise to all of us. Its subtle admixture of color, spirit and movement was a relief both from the overly moralistic interpretations of Easter the Protestants were used to, and from the more doctrinally specific Roman Catholic ones. In the Eastern Mass, for example, there is no single moment, punctuated by a *hoc est,* in which the bread wafer, held aloft by a priest, is suddenly transformed into the body of Christ. Rather, in the Eastern version, the Spirit of Christ is believed to suffuse the entire congregation; the epiklesis (calling on the Spirit) makes the bread the focus and vehicle for a spiritual reality that is believed to be already present in the people. We maintained this diffuse, non-cognitive, spirit-guided atmosphere throughout Byzantine Easter. There was no sermon, people fed the communion elements to one another, and the Kiss of Peace was not just a discreet peck on the cheek.

I personally believe that the Eastern Mass itself set the tone for the entire event of Byzantine Easter more than we expected it could. Maybe in the next decades the various kinds of "Eastern" Christianity—with their distrust of centralized church government, their synthesis of Oriental and Western ingredients, their emphasis on God's *presence* rather than on His command, their less exacting view of doctrinal specificity, together with the incomparable splendor of their worship services—will provide hospitality for far more than one homeless modern soul. I think Eastern Christianity could make such a contribution. It brilliantly fuses the main symbols we already know in Western Christianity with the incandescent spirituality we associate with the East. It is relatively uninfected by the moralism that plagues much of Protestantism and the rationalism that curses Rome. It has no pope, no work ethic and little real estate. Its ethos inspired Dostoevsky and Berdyayev and even such disobedient sons as Tolstoy and Kazantzakis. Its music is superb and its art is incomparable. It honors holy men more than theologians and is the only Christian tradition I know in which holy fools have been beatified as saints.

But paradoxically Orthodoxy, which has retained much of its spiritual wealth by a certain resistance to change, will be able to share its riches now only if it changes drastically. It must give up seeing itself solely as the religion of particular national and ethnic groups. It must deregionalize and "de-ethnicize" if its invaluable spirituality is ever to reach the people who need it most today. It must also surrender its male monopoly on priesthood.

The stories and symbols of Christianity are still powerful if they are removed from contexts people associate with prudery and top-down control. Byzantine Easter was "successful" in large measure because of the non-authoritarian participatory quality both of the planning and the event itself. We began imagining several weeks ahead with five or six people, quickly enlarged to a dozen and eventually enlisted seventy or eighty. More importantly, we resolved all our disputes by discussing them until we reached a consensus. At the celebration itself the participants not only prepared the environment, "vested" one another, contrived their own dance movements and fed one another the sacraments, they were also responsible for pace and timing. We had designed an overall contour, but what happened within it, and when, was largely up to the people who attended. We had no "schedule," no printed Order of Service. The guests could have moved in any number of directions. Furthermore no one paid admission, contributed money or signed up or joined anything. Our planning was designed not to channel anything but to facilitate spontaneity and even a little chaos.

Many people, I discovered, feel vaguely or even deeply uncomfortable in such a setting. One of the priests who helped with the Mass told me later that he had been very worried because he just did not feel "in control of things." He was terrified most of the evening, he said, that people might get out of hand, take their clothes off or rush out and break windows, or that something awful would happen. Nothing did. There were no fights, and with nearly two thousand people occupying a space designed for far fewer, there were not even any reports of arguments or incidents.

Byzantine Easter proved again a point I have advanced throughout this book: that most of us today feel cramped, overly controlled, planned for, registered, scheduled and channeled. We feel this way not only about our churches but about our schools, places of work, cities and families. Although we may be uneasy at first when the clasps and buckles of routine are removed, we soon begin to savor the foretaste of another way of life. As more and more people glimpse this new possibility, it is bound to make a dramatic difference. We will demand more freedom of movement at the micro level, and structures at the macro level that insure and encourage such freedom. Byzantine Easter might have been the parable for a new world. And we need parables.

When reports about Byzantine Easter were published in the Boston papers and in some national news magazines, readers by the score who had not been a part of the planning or of the celebration itself wrote or phoned me about it. Some were so shocked and angry that no assurance from me would have helped. Others raised thoughtful questions. For example one man agreed that we need new parables but asked whether we could afford to create them at the price of "tampering" with age-old liturgies? Others thought such events as Byzantine Easter were a heartless way of manipulating and misusing people for questionable ends.

I know that liturgical experiment is risky and can be misused. But it need not be. Even the Roman Catholic and Episcopal churches have sanctioned provisional changes in their liturgies on a "trial" basis. Liturgies have never been static. If you study their histories you know they change, grow and develop. If they do not, they die. I agree that some of what passes today for "experimental liturgy" is tasteless and gimmicky. But an experimental approach to liturgy will inevitably produce many failures. The question is how do we know when an experiment has failed? And what could it mean that a liturgy was "successful"? The students and others with whom I have been working in recent years on these questions have developed only quite provisional answers. We have no grid or checklist. We do believe, however, that no liturgy which proceeds entirely as planned is "successful." It succeeds only when something unexpected happens. Also, no liturgy is "successful" unless it is a people's liturgy, one that the worshipers themselves help to shape. No one can invent liturgies for someone else.

There are other provisional principles of evaluation too. Since Homo sapiens is a many-millennia-old species and has accumulated important archetypes during that period of evolution, liturgies should tap into these symbolic traditions, not cut people off from them. But at the same time, liturgy should by its very nature invite and attract "outsiders," not exclude them. There are other clues. But the core question for me is always whether or not a liturgy elicits and encourages genuine participation. A performance or a spectacle, however well executed, is not a liturgy.

An "experimental liturgy" when it is planned with care and carried out with respect and sensitivity will not be manipulative. At the same time, conventional or inherited liturgies can be coercive and authoritarian. In any case we should not stop trying to deepen and broaden our cultic life as human beings because of real or imagined dangers in the process. The Catholic Mass was at one time an innovation. So were all other existing forms of worship. Those faiths that resisted the psychic growth of the species and refused to guide and undergird religious evolution have passed from the scene. Students of religious history are familiar with the liturgical equivalents of the brontosaurus and the pterodactyl, forms that became extinct because they were incapable of adaptive change. In religion, as in everything else, survival is assured only by change.

The inexorable evolution of our species suggests another reason liturgical experimentation is not merely frivolous or manipulative: We need new liturgies to express the emergent religious reality. Our inherited rituals, although they preserve indispensable elements we can use and enjoy, do not by themselves suffice. This is partly because they come from a less pluralistic and less global period of history. Our spiritual needs are different today. Where are the marriage services that permit lovers from different traditions to plight their troth? Are there any that do not perpetuate the subservience of women? Where do we turn for rituals that will enable people from disparate faiths not only to marry each other, but to celebrate the birth of children, observe the days and seasons, and mourn the dead without feeling like strangers or guests in another's liturgical house? My interest in fashioning new liturgies is not just a scholarly gambit to uncover the elements of ritual and find out how it changes and grows. It is motivated by my desire to respond to pressing human needs. And I do it also because *I* need new rituals, rites that will neither cut me off from my friends nor uproot me from my past nor force me to renounce the symbolic dimension of my own life.

What I call "people's religion" includes both folk religion and popular religion insofar as they are expressions of a group identity, inherited or emergent. Though they might appear to differ from each other, the folk religion of a Pueblo village or a saint's day parade in an Italian section of New York City have much in common with a novel rock Mass celebrated by a group about to go on a peace march. Despite the difference in the forms of people's religion, what they all share is intensity of participation and a deeply felt sense of community. Because the two do have this in common, I am not surprised that those who search for new liturgies and more full-bodied religious rituals today are drawn to the songs and rites of preliterate, poor and powerless peoples. Such peoples sometimes have what so many searchers want, a religion that expresses the undisguised feelings of the people themselves. So folk religion and popular religion are finding each other. The evidence for the convergence is considerable: the use of dance, masks, exorcisms and other "primitive" elements in the new liturgies, the popularity of folk hymns like "Amazing Grace," the use of new instruments and pop tunes by older groups, and the incorporation of the drums and sitars of other cultures into contemporary liturgies. The result of this confluence will be enormously significant not just for religion but for American society as a whole. It augurs the breakdown of the barriers that have separated the youth-hippie-rock culture from the rural-pietistic-gospel song culture as each discovers its kinship with the other and with the ethnics, rednecks, Indians, black militants and other marginated groups who have retained a sense of joy and resistance in face of the homogenizing pressures of the larger society. As this happens, each group will discover that although their songs and stories differ from one another, what they have in common is their mutual opposition to being overwhelmed by structures and signals. Though people's religions differ from one another, they agree in their shared suspicion of the top-down imposed religion of the signalers. We all have much to learn from people's religions, and they have much to learn from one another. But the learning has only just begun.

CHAPTER SEVEN

People's Religion and Radical Theology

To be radical means to go to the root, but the root of the matter is man.
—Karl Marx

EVER SINCE the movement called "radical theology" appeared in the 1960s, marked by the publication of books by Bishop Robinson, the so-called "death of God" theologians, and myself, I have been uneasy about my relationship to it. For one thing I tend to be a loner and am not a very good member of any movement. For another, the writers who described the movement, as well as the people within it, frequently disagreed on whether I really belonged. The confusion was always rife. During the late 1960s a book appeared in Spanish which devoted a whole chapter to me as a "death of God theologian," which I never was; at the same time another writer placed me on the "right wing" of the radical movement. Both descriptions annoyed me and confounded the muddle further.

Although I dislike labels, I suppose it is accurate to describe me as a "radical" theologian, though I would want to reserve the right to define the term myself. As for the idea of the "death of God," I do not think it is a particularly radical one. Above all I do not think "radical" and "death of God" should be equated. What then does it mean to me to consider myself a radical theologian? The answer has a lot to do with what I have been calling "people's religion."

To be radical in any sense today means to be in touch with

those people who are ordinarily seen as "losers." It means to be touched by the pain and hope of the poor. To be a radical *theologian* today must mean, at least, to listen to the singing and the sobbing in the religions of the poor. But learning from losers' religion, from the faith of the poor, has never become a serious part of so-called "radical theology." Its premises are still culture-bound and even elitist. The emerging "Third World consciousness," in my view the most important religious and cultural event of our century, still barely affects Western theological writing. Radical theology has also failed so far to fulfill the hopes of many of its early admirers that it would be able to break out of Western Christian categories and enter into fruitful conversation with the non-Western religious traditions. Although radical theologians are generally more receptive to non-Western religious themes than other theologians, none has probed the significance of the *political* radicalization of Buddhism documented in a book like D. C. Vijayavardhara's *Revolt in the Temple*. Had we been more aware of this movement we would not have been so surprised at the appearance of "Buddhist socialism" in Burma, or at the self-immolation of monks or the activism of Buddhist leaders in opposing the American invasion of Vietnam. The neo-Christian "nativist" movements of Africa have also failed so far to attract our attention as theologically significant. We see them as exotic or quaint. We remain, when all is said and done, very provincial.

Being provincial is always bad, in theology or in anything else. But in the case of white Western theologians today, remaining provincial is a disaster. It is a disaster because our thinking always expresses in part at least the internalized consciousness of our own culture, and this makes it virtually impossible for us to grasp the emergent cultural awakening (and therefore the religious consciousness) of the Third World. The impossibility stems from the fact that we are part of a "director society" which is busy every day subduing, controlling, "improving," developing and otherwise dominating the "directed" societies. We cannot see that "our" culture and in many places "our" religion continue to be imposed on the poor, and that since ours is not a culture they have participated in creating, both our culture and our religion become means of control. Because we are a part of the imposed culture we cannot understand why a flat renunciation of all imposed culture is an indispensable step in the Third World's developing independence. As representatives, albeit often unwilling ones, of the imposed culture, we are baffled by the way dominated peoples often use their religion to express their rage in the battle for cultural and political independence.

I have used words like "cannot understand" or "baffled" here as though we were observing something whose meaning we cannot quite grasp. The situation is even worse. The religious aspect of the Third World insurrection rarely even claims our attention. The result of this distracted inattention is that, unless our theology is fundamentally "deprovincialized," we may not even notice the most important religious revolution of our time: the "conversion" of the peoples of Africa, Asia and Latin America from enforced lethargy and self-deprecation to anger, pride and self-emancipation. On these formerly colonial continents millions of people are beginning now to refuse to be the mere receptacles of a reality created outside. Increasingly they are entering into the real vocation of man: the making and remaking of culture.

How then can our theology be deprovincialized? In the last few years I have tried to chip away at my own provincialism by immersing myself in the folk religion and Hispanic Catholicism of Latin America. It has been an exhilarating quest. I have haunted the village churches, saint's day fiestas and pilgrimages of the Mexican hills. I have swayed and sung at Chilean Pentecostal rallies. I have been blessed by a dark-skinned holy man in the blackness of a Rio *favella*'s lurid Umbanda ritual. I have read and listened and watched and sniffed from the Rio Grande to the far south of Argentina. I still know very little, but I am learning. Latin America is not unique. I might have learned from the proliferating independent churches of Africa, or some other Third World religious movement. But I have a hunch that what I'd find would be similar to what I've discovered in South America: not the death of God, but the birth of a New World. Therefore in the rest of this chapter, although I will be talking about the whole Third World, most of the examples I use will be drawn from Latin America.

America Latina is a continent swarming with the images of saints and revolutionaries—Simón Bolívar, Jesus Christ, Che Guevara, Pancho Villa, Eva Perón, San Martín de Porres. Today a new image is appearing. Out of the filthy *favellas* and hacienda shacks a new human reality is stubbornly asserting itself, and it is doing so by a process so fundamental that merely to call it "revolution" is to underestimate its significance, especially since in South America, as elsewhere, the rhetoric of "revolution" has often been debased into an ideology of repression.

I do not accept the widely circulated but mistaken notion that there is a radical *church* in Latin America, at least in the conventional meaning of the word "church." The organized church in Latin America, like all institutions everywhere, is trying most of all to *survive,* and it is placing its bets with an eye more to institutional safety than to social justice. Nevertheless an unprecedented mutation of Christian faith is emerging, though it is doing so often despite a divided and often opportunistic institutional church.

The new faith has nothing to do with the cynical pandering of popular religious slogans to con the poor into following demagogues of the left or the right, though this happens too. Rather the new consciousness expresses itself in a transformed recognition of the self's relation to the world, an awareness *both* of freedom and agency *and* of the systems of control that have heretofore perpetuated dependency and quiescence. Millions of poor people are beginning to see themselves for the first time as the active subjects of history rather than as its passive recipients. This new way of seeing the self and the world is an example of what we in theology call "metanoia" or conversion.

The Brazilian educator-philosopher Paulo Freire grasps this conversion process better than anyone else I know. He calls it "conscientization" and sees it as a crucial stage in what Teilhard de Chardin described as the "hominisation" of reality, the present step in cosmic evolution. For Teilhard hominisation meant the spread of Homo sapiens' web of meaning to the globe's farthest corners. He saw it as one stage in humankind's pilgrimage toward Spirit, toward the culmination of evolution. Freire has read Teilhard and makes use of his ideas. But Freire goes further than Teilhard and gives his thought a needed political twist. He argues that the present patterns of Western cultural dominance will prevent any hominisation from taking place unless captive peoples break the existing political structures of dominance and learn to "name the world," to join the never-ending process of creating and re-creating culture. Freire is a Brazilian, at this writing still a political refugee from the Brazilian military government. His ideas therefore represent in part a political enlargement of Teilhard's theology growing out of Freire's actual experience in the struggle of the Third World.

This emerging consciousness is the "new reality" I am referring to. It is making possible an "uomo nuovo," a new person. As it happens, the objects of history become its subjects; those named by others begin to name themselves; those who lived in worlds of values invented by others begin to create their own. The process is a planetary one. Eventually it will alter the total consciousness not only of the Third World but, because of global culture's interactive nature, of everyone. We do not yet have the theological idiom to understand this worldwide "metanoia" of the outcasts. But it sets the main agenda for any non-provincial theology today.

Like the "new humanity" of Christian eschatology, the new reality is hard to describe or even locate. Like the Kingdom of God, it will not win out tomorrow. It will be clubbed and exiled, bought off or betrayed, temporarily. But even when I find myself believing in very little else I still feel sure it will win in the end. Latin America is only one scene in the drama that is convulsing the whole Third World, including its outposts still incarcerated in the other two. The actors in the drama are the faceless ones who have always been the material of history but who now fiercely assert that they intend to become its makers. They will use every shred of their cultural life, including its rites and myths and songs and stories, in their titanic battle to *be somebody*. They presage a new era that is being born, sometimes almost completely unnoticed, right under our noses.

What does all of this mean for theology? It means that the basic metaphor of radical theology today can no longer be *death*, of God or anything else. It must be *birth*. Death for a while was a powerful religious image. But birth is an even more powerful one. Birth includes blood and screams, but it suggests a beginning rather than an end. It includes an organic continuity with the past, but in birth something undeniably unique appears. Our task in theology will now become impossible unless we shift root metaphors. Let the dead bury the dead while we attend to the New Thing that is happening in history. In fact, only when we turn our attention to the New Thing do we begin to grasp what the "death of God" really was. It was the gasping demise, after violent birth, amazing virility and then inevitable senility, of Western "bourgeois" culture. This means we must now read Nietzsche, who coined the phrase "God is dead," in the light of Fanon, Mao and Ho Chi Minh, the diagnosticians of the decline of Western dominance.

The death of God means the dissolution of the religious basis of the age of Western dominance. If so, it is not only a religious fact, as Tom Altizer has correctly told us, or a cultural fact, as Gabriel Vahanian knows. It is also a *political* fact. It should therefore have political consequences. If so, "radical theology" should be more concerned with the emerging new world culture (and I don't mean just the overpublicized American "counterculture") than it is with the expiration of the old culture in which our theology was so firmly ensconced. Any theology meriting the designation "radical" should be facilitating the emergence of that new era. Our nation now looms as one of the main *barriers* to the birth of the new world, and the religion of America still largely endorses our empire. That religion requires from us a relentless critique. Theologians have interpreted; the time has come to change.

Notebook Jottings

The hulking old cathedral of Cuernavaca, Mexico. Spanish colonial, peeling gray-pink stucco. Inside a noisy crowd has gathered for the Mass of the Feast of the Assumption of Our Lady. The celebrant, Bishop Don Sergio Mendes Arceo, is being vested in rich pastels in the middle of the central aisle, jostled by the gawking congregation (right "on stage," as Genet and other artificers of metatheater have urged). Babies howling, the trumpets and violins of the mustachioed musicians begin to wail. The procession picks its way toward the altar. The Mass begins: Alchemy, the magical transubstantiation of Latin American folk piety into a radical fiesta. Don Sergio, though in his sixties, is one of the mutants, a radical Mexican Catholic with a deep sense of irony. He is preaching on the Assumption, using the Magnificat as his text: "My soul doth magnify the Lord." He continues with a modern Spanish translation that in English would go something like Luke 1:49–53 in the New English Bible:

"His name is Holy . . . the deeds of his right arm disclose his might: the arrogant of heart and mind he has put to rout, he has torn imperial powers from their thrones, but the humble have been lifted high.

"The hungry he has satisfied with good things, the rich sent empty away."

The church is jammed. Everyone seems to be listening. Don Sergio speaks vigorously but simply: Mary is poor like the oppressed people of the Third World. The "Assumption" does not mean she "goes up" (he's read Tillich, Robinson, et al.) but that she is now united with Christ, who is "the liberator in our midst." Together at this very moment they are "tearing the imperial powers from their thrones" (our

older version says "casting down the mighty"), sending the
rich away empty, lifting up the downtrodden, supporting "us"
in our fight against dependency and imperialism. Therefore,
on with the battle. He crosses himself. The sermon is over.
Banks of incense swirl. Bells chime. Broken bread is distributed. Mass over.

   Courtyard outside the cathedral. Dogs romp. Children hawk
balloons and plastic birds on sticks. Women fry tamales.
Across the valley Popocatepetl, the venerable volcano of the
Toltecs, glistens serenely. The late summer sun browns the
hills of Morelos province, a land where two great mythic
figures suffuse the popular mind: Emiliano Zapata and Our
Lady of Guadalupe. On this Feast of the Assumption one
can almost imagine the two of them, either in a sacred
marriage atop Popo, or cleaning their rifles in the hills.
Message (?): The myth making of the poor is still producing,
and the content is more and more radical. If both Emiliano
and the Virgin be for us, who can be against us?

I made the above entries in my notebook in August 1971. I
include them here because the famous Mariachi Mass of Bishop
Mendes Arceo is one of the few examples of a successful blending
of "folk" and "popular" religion. Obviously it is not the kind of
Mass one would come upon in some remote village in Yucatán.
Notice its bold use of barroom music and vestments of contemporary design. But it is not just a campus pop liturgy either.
It faithfully adheres to the canonical elements of the Roman
Catholic Mass. Its success is demonstrated by the fact that both
illiterate *campesinos* from the nearby villages and wash-and-wear
tourists from a dozen different countries take part every Sunday.
It is an example of that emergent blending of the folk and popular types of people's religion.

   What interests me most about the Mariachi Mass is that it represents the dawning of Third World "conscientization." My sketch
of its significance will illustrate my understanding of radical theology in two ways. First, the analysis exemplifies what I think more

theologians should be about. Second, the Mass itself is a concrete instance of the radicalizing of false piety and the political energy of poor people's religion.

What would throw off most theologians at the outset about the Mass I witnessed is that it was a celebration of the Assumption of Mary, the passage to heaven, body and soul, of the virgin mother of God. What could possibly be "radical" in any sense about that?

It was George Santayana who once said, "There is no God, and Mary is His Mother." I know of no theologian who has yet quipped, "God is dead, and Mary is His Mother," but no Latin American Catholic would be terribly shocked by such a notion. "God," in Hispanic popular piety, is almost always pictured as dead: as Christ in a casket, being lowered from the cross, being placed in the tomb. Mary on the other hand is the radiant incarnation of life and flesh. Her two main manifestations tell it all. *Concepción* symbolizes the always mysterious *beginning* of life. *Asunción* personifies the anti-spiritualist (and very Spanish) insistence that eternal life without *flesh* would be terribly dull. Given a choice between the two standard Resurrection heresies, immortality of the spirit (Anglo-Saxon) and the "assumption" of the human flesh (Latin), I lean somewhat toward the latter. Our overly spiritualized sentiments about immortality reveal yet another way in which our curious blend of technology and Victorianism has removed us from our own bodies. If pressed to a choice between symbols, I vastly prefer the Assumption to Ethical Culture. If God is dead, Mary is alive and well, and she deserves our attention.

Mariological piety is only one example of thousands of kinds of poor people's religion. Like the rest, it has been exploited and abused by the rich time and again, and a clerically controlled Mary always changes from the advocate of the oppressed into the haughty dispenser of regal largesse. Still, there was something real there to corrupt, and Mariological devotion remains a vastly important subject for radical theology. One way to begin such a study would be to ask a simple but widely ignored question:

Why do we find women leaders and female imagery so much more frequently among the religions of the oppressed than we do among the religions of the privileged? Christian history brims with male guardians of orthodoxy burning and banishing people like Sojourner Truth, Joan of Arc and Anne Hutchinson. Prophetesses and female charismatics continually appear and are continually exterminated in the history of Christian heretical movements. The fact that these movements were often made up of poor people protesting against a ruling religious ideology has been noted occasionally by historians of doctrine, but consistently ignored by theologians. Many examples of women leading innovative religious movements are noted by Norman Cohn in his book on medieval heresies entitled *The Pursuit of the Millennium*. In discussing the fourteenth-century heretics called the Society of the Poor, who influenced Jan Hus and the later violent Bohemian revolution, Cohn says, "Their leader was a woman, named Jeanne Dabenton. She was burnt; and so were the body of her male assistant, who had died in prison, and the writings and costumes of her followers."

How I would love to see those writings, and those "costumes"! But they are lost to us forever, to our impoverishment. During the same period, Charlier de Gerson, the Chancellor of the University of Paris, was busy publishing a whole series of tomes to condemn a movement called the Spirit of Liberty, which was led by another woman Gerson describes as of "almost incredible subtlety" named Mary of Valenciennes. Gerson's books did not, however, quench the Spirit of Liberty movement. It was still lively enough in 1545 to elicit from no less a personage than John Calvin himself a treatise entitled *Contre la secte phantastique et furieuse des Libertins qui se nomment Spirituels* (Against the Fantastic and Furious Sect of Libertines Who Call Themselves Spirituals).

The fascinating thing about this "heretical" movement was that it not only relied on women for its leadership, and did encourage considerable sexual freedom, but that it used female mystical imagery in its piety. There are crucial connections, still largely unexplored, among heresy, mysticism, religions of the oppressed, women's leadership and female imagery. But repressive religions, which are usually patriarchal, have succeeded time and again in stamping out or co-opting such movements. "*Cherchez la femme!*" is the cry not only of police sleuths but of anxious theologians. Watch out for witches, goddesses and prophetesses! They can make life difficult for religiously sanctified establishments in any age.

How does official Mariological piety relate to the Spirit of Liberty? It represents the most magnificently successful attempt by any religious hierarchy in history to channel, defuse and control female religious symbolism. In Protestantism the female element is repressed, but reappears in the aquiline-nosed androgynous Jesus of Sunday school literature. In Catholicism, through prescribed Marian piety, the anger and aspiration of women is sapped and deflected. Give them a goddess! Thus, through denial and sublimation, or by means of carefully defined pious practices, the female component is shorn of its protest element and made almost completely an "opiate."

I said "almost completely." In medieval Europe there were convents to tame overly volatile young ladies who were headstrong or religiously opinionated, or both. But just as the fiery prophetesses of the late medieval and Reformation periods could not be channeled and accommodated by the convents, so Mariological piety has a way of breaking out of its orthodox definitions. The portrayal of Liberty as a woman did not die just because Gerson or Calvin condemned it. The "armed Liberty" of the French Revolution and New York Harbor's torch bearer both bear witness to its persistence.

Mariology as a feminine religious devotion is important for another reason. It provides us with a living link to two forms of religious expression that are both of crucial significance in the coming "conscientization" of the Third World, but from which Western Christianity's theologians have become almost totally alienated—the "preliterate" and the so-called "non-Christian" religions.

Today preliterate peoples are by definition oppressed and harassed peoples. We see them as pathetic holdouts in the progress of the world toward color TV, heart transplants and 747s. We test our H bombs on their atolls or burn their villages to save them. Still they possess a secret we may all soon need to know: how to live simply and in harmony with nature. Mariology helps us understand them because it embraces, more than either Yahweh or Jesus do, such timeless, repressed but essential ingredients of religious life as fertility, sexuality, the womb, the earth, the stars and moon.

This is a risky point to make today, because I fully agree with women's liberationists that for centuries men have identified these qualities exclusively with women and then used this identification to hold women in peonage. What we are taught to call "feminine qualities" are present, albeit repressed, in men too. But one way for defeminized and overly phallicized men to reappropriate the repressed feminine element is to recognize that the Great Mother symbolizes a part of all of us.

Popular Marian piety is a link to preliterate forms of faith. Our Lady of Guadalupe, for example, whose shrine stands just at the edge of Mexico City, is clearly a reappearance, in a quasi-Christianized setting, of Tonantin, the Toltec fertility goddess. Her basilica rises on the very site of that pre-Columbian goddess' holy place. Unlettered Indians, despite four centuries of Christianity and endless corrections by well-meaning priests, still say as they go to the basilica that they are "going to Tonantin." A radical theology of Mary supplies an important entrée. We all know we have much to learn from the preliterate (once called "primitive") religions, but how can we begin to understand them if we ignore or disparage a kindred religious reality that lives right down the street?

Mary as a woman also provides access to the non-Christian traditions. Some might argue that a female deity provides common ground in relation to, say, Hinduism but not to Islam or Judaism, the allegedly more "masculine" religions. Again this makes it important to recall the distinction between elite and people's religion, between textbook theology and popular piety. In "official" Islam, Allah is indeed thought of in exclusively masculine terms. But in Shiite piety, an important popular version of Islam, Fatima, the prophet's daughter, has often assumed a place similar to that of Mary in Christianity. One popular belief holds her to be a reincarnation of the Virgin. Likewise in that cabalistic tradition of Judaism, there is the Shekinah, the feminine aspect of God, through which the world is created. Examples could be multiplied. Nowhere does male dominance in religion, or the closeness of women to other dominated groups, show up better than in the frequent attempts by patriarchal cultures to either downgrade or control the feminine elements of the deity. But popular piety has a way of returning to bury its orthodox pallbearers.

Liberated women today are not always enthusiastic about efforts by male theologians to reinstate Mary. I know this very well from the articulate and angry women in my own classes. Still, I don't think we should overlook the fact that in some of her manifestations Mary is not just a woman but a powerful, maybe even a liberated woman. The very depictions of Mary that shock orthodox theologians turn out predictably to be the most important ones in this respect. As Queen of Heaven, Mary is depicted *without any child* in view. Although she started as a mere auxiliary to Jesus, she has soared in the (popular) Western religious consciousness to her present power. And she remains there despite the zealous demythologizing of post-Vatican II (male) theologians, trying, as it were, to keep her in her place. Maybe Jung was right after all when he said that the proclamation of the doctrine of the Assumption was the most important religious event since the Reformation.

Women theologians like Mary Daly and Rosemary Ruether are right when they insist that the overload of masculine symbolism in orthodox Christianity has contributed both to the oppression of women and the narrowing of men. And when they say that it will require primarily a change in the fabric of society to bring about the death of patriarchal religious symbols, they are correct. But I hope women theologians avoid being too monodirectional. Symbols are not *merely* the ethereal nimbus of social structure. They have a mind of their own, at least during some periods of history. They can *influence* society, even inspire changes, as well as *be influenced by* those institutions Marxists call the "infrastructure." The causal flow between symbol and society is seldom simply one-way. I think we are now at a stage of human collective consciousness *and* of changing social roles in which it is imperative to induce change both ways.

Mary as woman, mother, queen or comforter is a focal symbol for one of the largest subjugated minorities in the world, the women of Christendom. Especially for millions of very poor women, Mary is the central religious reality in their lives, the spiritual energy center that gets them through many tiring days and trying years. Admittedly, Mariology often functions, among poor men and poor women, in ways that are cruelly alienating and regressive: Mary as royal benefactress, a cosmic lady bountiful; Mary as virginal mother; Mary as sentimental pleader to Those Higher Up. But these are not the only meanings Mary has and need not be the predominating ones. Official Mariology is a form of seduction, a calculated misuse of the spirit. But we should be careful not to confuse genuine piety with its official abuse. Those who support justice for the poor cannot spit on their devotions. They must realize that the faith of the poor is not *just* opiate but also cry. It is the collective interiority of a people even when it is twisted and used against them. Therefore, to dismiss all Marian devotion as a priestly shill or to leave Mariology to the curial hacks is to cop out on one vital aspect of "radical" theology: listening to and learning from the religions of the losers.

One refreshing thing about Mariology is that learning from it takes us completely away from our obsession with true-or-false games. She puts us literally "beyond belief." Mary is so obviously an aggregate of human fantasy, myth making, projection and all the rest that it seems beside the point to worry about whether she really was conceived immaculately, is Theotokos, or went bodily to heaven. When we talk about God, Christ, even the "death of God," we are still often stuck at the level of what we can "believe" or "not believe." But Mary, as always, is easier on us. Just as she has always been softer on sinners—the one you approached when you were afraid to go to God or Christ directly—so she is easier on theologians too. She doesn't care about our doubts.

Mary is myth *par excellence*. She permits us, therefore, in a way that Jesus cannot, to find a radically different *modus* for approaching her. With Mary we may, indeed *must*, become mythic and symbolic if we are to approach her, whereas with Jesus Christ the belief-unbelief axis still tempts us. Appreciating Marian piety forces us to shift into another religious epistemology; Mary allows us to plumb again, in ourselves and in our cultural unconscious, that psychic sector which lies dormant but not dead beneath our overdeveloped cognitive intelligence.

Once we have found the appropriate religious sensibility for Mary, maybe we can then generalize it. We need to, because Mary is really not all that different. The radical relativizing of religious consciousness caused by pluralism has fundamentally altered our *total* consciousness. We don't ask now, or shouldn't, how *much* to believe, or *whether* to believe this or that. Rather we are looking for, and finding occasionally, a *way* to embrace it all. Not all, really, but all that can contribute to our inner and outer liberation. By starting with something so obviously "incredible" as the Assumption, we can learn to outgrow our credibility-incredibility hang-up and appropriate the *meaning* of this doctrine and devotion. To "appropriate" does not mean merely to analyze, as a lepidopterist might analyze a moth. To appropriate means to accept it as a religious reality personally significant to us.

But then comes the next step, and that is the perilous one. Having learned this all from Mary, we can then apply it elsewhere. Ironically, precisely because she *is* a myth, maybe only through Mary can we learn to pray again. And theology, as St. Thomas said, is a form of prayer. So as theologians we must learn, as ordinary people do, to pray, even though we may be "beyond belief." If we do, curiously enough, Mary *does* become the mediatrix of grace, and Pius XII was right, for all the wrong reasons, to promote her in 1950.

Ignoring poor people's piety is not the only source of weakness in the radical theology movement. It has also been shaken by internal divisions. One of the most severe tensions, and one that has plagued the movement since its inception, is the dispute between those theologians who emphasize the radical redefinition of faith and those interested in the radical restructuring of society. The argument became even more abrasive when in more recent years the concept of "play" began to occupy the attention of theologians. Some saw a total contradiction between theologies of play and theologies of revolution.

There is no such contradiction. My own realization of the essential agreement underlying the two theological approaches came from an odd source, an article I chanced upon in a psychiatric journal. In that piece, two psychiatrists, Bergen and Rosenberg, make the following important point about play:

> . . . in play the external environment is no longer perceived as dictating the actions of ego, the conscious center of life as purposive activity becomes the shaping and reshaping of the meaning of reality . . . projections, fantasies and myths are seen for what they are. *Players feel themselves to be real in a way they know the system is not.*

Play is not about fun: Play is what links instinct and imagination with politics and social reconstruction.

How does play inform our approach to religion? Play is doing freely something we know is symbolic, whose procedures we know are in some ways different from those of other worlds we inhabit. Play is something we do for the values and satisfactions inherent in the activity itself, not for some extrinsic purpose. Play, furthermore, is the best model we now have for how we can be joyfully religious in our self-consciously critical era. The claim the theologians of play make should be much more ambitious than the one made so far, for play must be understood as a heightened form of consciousness. I call it "ludic consciousness" from *ludus,* the Latin word for play. As such, play provides the link between our new theologies of religion and theologies of liberation. It connects rite and revolution. Play is not one activity among others. It is a *radical form* of consciousness and therefore a radical form of faith.

What is important about play is that although it projects meanings and myths, as Bergen and Rosenberg show, it does *not* "require the maintenance of historical continuity between the self and any given manifestation of projected meaning." In other words, players know they can change the rules, so the posture of the self toward what is labeled "reality" changes. In play we see the boundaries set by the political structure as something human beings create in their attempts to cope with reality. When I play I know I am more real than the rules. I can alter them, if the other players agree, make up new rules, make up a whole new game. Even if I'm prevented from doing so, I know it *could* be done, that the game is not eternal or immutable. But most of all, knowing all this does not prevent me from playing. As the writers say, "Moral proscriptions and notions of orderliness and continuity" are no longer used to prevent the self from pursuing its activities.

The incalculable political potential of play as a form of consciousness is that the external environment is no longer seen as dictating the self's projects. Man becomes the continuous shaper and reshaper of the meaning of reality. "The most salient feature of 'play' as a modality of interaction," Bergen and Rosenberg continue, "is that projections, fantasies, and myths are seen for what they are. *Players feel themselves to be real in a way that they know the system is not.*"

Note that a culture of liberated play would not be one that ascetically attempts to live *without* myths, fantasies and projections. It would not be an antiseptic *Walden Two* or a completely rationalized planet out of the old science fiction comics. A culture of liberated play would abound with myths, rites and symbols. It would be more like the worlds portrayed in *Dune* or in *Stranger in a Strange Land*. But such a culture would see myths for what they are and recognize both their worth and their mutability.

A playful society would not be a permanent pot party (which does tend to observe some fairly fixed forms), but an unending cultural revolution. People would continue to spawn fables and institutions, but they would also continually go beyond them. In the process the myths that stifle joy and justice would be transgressed or transfigured, or a little of each.

Obviously, to move toward a culture of liberated play will require political action. How does play become politics? I think play is the first step anyone must take from bondage to freedom. In the "little" man's present historical transition from object to subject of history, "play" provides an alternative to either cowed submission or empty nihilism. As a player, the tyrannized person no longer sees the colossal social structures around him (and internalized within him) as permanent fixtures. He realizes that his captivity is a cruel game whose rules someone else has set. He recognizes that institutions are not fixed orders of creation but human inventions that *can* be altered. The player who knows he is more real than the system is never the safe vassal of a despot again.

To make the changes he wants in the system the player-revolutionary may create new metaphors (socialist man, polymorphous perversity) and new institutions (the commune, the cadre), most of which are imaginative adaptations of older ones. But these new images must also in turn eventually be seen for what *they* are. They are no more eternal than the ones they displaced and must therefore be reshaped when their time comes. The revolution is never completed, and the most dangerous tyrants are usually those who have already had their revolution, or think so.

The reluctance of anyone to see his own myths melted down for resculpting also explains why the Old Left gets more terrified of the New Left than anyone else does, and why the New Left is unsettled by the yippies, the yippies by the religion freaks, and so on. A always wants to see B's game as a "mere game" but his own as "the way it really is." Play as radical consciousness means we see all our games as games; then we can play them, alter them, or play something else. The insight is as frightening as it is liberating. Does it leave us with no standards for judging bad games or no way of judging between games? Can you have a real revolution without "taking the myth seriously" (thus presumably *not* playfully) at least for a time? Revolutionaries, we are solemnly assured, usually by people very far from any revolution, *must* be serious. They can't just "play games."

We have never yet had, to my knowledge, a "playful" revolution. That helps explain why so many revolutions fall into reaction. But it does not mean we cannot have a revolution that is both playful and successful in the future. Such a "ludic revolution" is the only one I think we *can* have or *ought* to have in the future. Not only our religious but also our political fundamentalism has been broken. Revolutionaries of any stripe who seriously believe they are ushering in the last stage of history or who actually think that their ideology (myth) is the ultimate one are often temporarily effective. But in the long run they devour their own children. May turns to October. The fall of the Bastille leads to Napoleon and the fall of the Winter Palace to Stalin. The myth of revolution cannot be exempted from the caldron of criticism. It must be open to re-examination even *in medias res*. Can there be a form of revolution that is self-critical even while it is effecting a revolution?

I think there can be. That is why the Chinese Cultural Revolution is so important, though it appears to have questioned only one part of the myth in the name of another. Also important was Dubcek's heroic effort to construct a self-critical Czechoslovak form of socialism, an attempt which was crushed by one of the world's most conservative states in the name of "putting down a counterrevolution." But there is still a problem. Both Mao's cultural revolution and Dubcek's "human face of socialism" became possible only *after* a revolutionary party had achieved power. Are there examples of a self-critical "ludic" element in a revolutionary movement *before* this critical stage?

The most important example in recent times of a playful revolution that *almost* "succeeded" (though it is hard to say just what that would mean) was the Paris May of 1968. I personally believe this fascinating few weeks constituted one of the most portentous periods in modern cultural and political history. The participants in the May upheaval would just not take their own symbols with the teeth-clenching gravity usually required of barricade stormers. On one wall along the Boulevard St. Michel they chalked "*Je suis Marxiste, direction Groucho,*" and they announced their intention not to take over the societal pyramid but to dismantle it. They enraged old-line leftists as well as conservatives, yet they aroused the support of millions of young workers, came within a hair of unseating DeGaulle, and were defeated at last only by a desperate alliance of Gaullist and Communist party bureaucrats.

But the word "defeated" does not quite apply to the Paris May. The crowds in the streets and at the Odéon were not just trying to "seize power" in the usual sense of the term. They were engaged in a much more fundamental enterprise. Power over people rests not just on gun barrels but on the authoritative social symbols those in power utilize to rule over others. André Malraux, the great French writer and a supporter of DeGaulle, declared that the alliance of students and workers constituted a crisis of civilization. I think he was right. The Paris rebels were undercutting the operative myths and structures of a whole historical epoch. They were engaged in a "revolution" that redefined the meaning of that term. In a sense, of course, they "failed"; but can it really be said today that the Russian Revolution "succeeded"? In another sense the Paris May succeeded beyond anyone's wildest expectations. Its surrealist insurgents showed how precarious a card house the allegedly monolithic modern industrial state really is. They also lit up in one fireworks flash the vision of society without hierarchies and the feel of an erotically open culture.

In one way conservative critics of the French May like Raymond Aaron are also right in calling it "psychodrama." That is just the point. Paris 1968 broke down for a few dizzying moments the boundaries between theater and "reality," between play and politics. The May revolutionaries knew that any "revolution" which does not dismantle and decentralize state power is a mere palace coup, and that any "revolution" which does not liberate people's heads and bodies, psychodramatically or otherwise, leaves us with our massively internalized oppressors.

As it happens, I visited Paris a few months after the May uprising and talked with people who were part of it. Since then I have read many of the countless descriptions that have appeared. I do not believe anyone has yet grasped the profundity of its import or its originality. But I also do not think it can be understood apart from its place in the tumultuous history of Paris during the course of the successive French revolutions. Louis Greenberg's *Sisters of Liberty*, a study of the Paris Commune of 1870, for example, provides a fascinating comparison with May of 1968, especially on the question of dismantling state power. It documents the fact that the commune (and similar but less known movements in Marseilles and Lyons) must be seen as part of a nationwide struggle *against* the growing power of the centralized state and *for* regional and municipal liberties. The commune is a chapter in the history of decentralizing socialism, and the leading symbol is a working woman (not a fine lady) with a banner in one hand and a lance in the other.

"All religion," said Peguy, "begins in mysticism and ends in politics." When play becomes, as it now must, our defining stance toward "reality," both our mysticism and our politics become playful. Then our myths and our institutions are seen "for what they are." This is the next big step human consciousness must take. Any really "radical" theology must take it also.

The most important change needed in radical theology goes beyond its relating more imaginatively to the feminine element, the non-Western faiths and the mythical. It must also address the anger of the poor. Again, Mariology supplies a clue. Mary is the goddess of the poor. She represents an essential form of people's religion, the missing factor in our widely touted return to "human experience" as a crucial object of theological inquiry. Marian piety and similar devotions raise an unavoidable question: *Whose* experience? From a biblical perspective there is one clear answer to this question: God speaks to man through the poor. But *how* does God speak, and what is the message?

Karl Marx, child of the Enlightenment that he was, though right in many things, was wrong in his estimate of religion. He not only undercalculated its durability but he also overlooked its seldom tapped potential for catalyzing political and cultural transformation. And even Marx himself is often misunderstood on this point. In the classic passage he not only said that religion is the "opiate of the masses" but that it is "the sigh of the oppressed creature, the heart of a heartless world, just as it is the spirit of an unspiritual situation." In another place Marx also correctly reminded us that history is "written by the victors." What he forgot was that the history of religion is also written by the victors—and writers have tended to ignore the "losers," who, however, often "lost" not because they were less intelligent or less devout but because they were burned or beheaded by the victors. Radical theology needs to begin to pay more attention to the "losers" (read "heretics" or "schismatics"). The process is already beginning. My Harvard colleague Dieter Georgi has recently shown how the history of the battles over how to interpret ancient texts can be read as the history of class struggle. There have always been battles between stabilizing ("orthodox") and destabilizing ("heretical") interpretations of Scripture. This welcome rereading of Christian history is beginning to spread. We see it in the growing interest in Münzer and Karlstadt, Luther's more "radical" contemporaries, not just as midgets snapping at his ankles, but as competent theologians who "lost" more for political than for intellectual reasons.

We do not have to go back four hundred years for examples of poor people redefining faith in the midst of political struggle. A more recent example is the Golconda Movement in Colombia, inspired by the martyred rebel priest, Camilo Torres. The priests and laymen of Golconda had the good sense to reject the orthodox Communist dismissal of religion as always and only an opiate. Nor would they cynically "use" the poor people's faith in demagogic ways. Rather they believed that if they listened attentively to the people and actively took sides in their cause, then the revolutionary meaning of the religious symbols of the poor would begin to assert itself. It did, and the Golconda Movement has now been suppressed by church *and* state.

Our attitude toward poor people's religion in general, or Mariology in particular, should never be disingenuous. Men have been tortured and enslaved in the name of Mary. The perversion of Marian piety for anti-Communist purposes, for instance by the history of the Fatima devotion, and for other forms of repression is too well known and too notorious. But the same can be said for almost *any* pious practice.

The faith of poor people reveals not only where their pain is and what they yearn for but how their hopes have been confused and blurred by the very religion that gives them the images they use to cry out in protest. The religions of the poor show us, more graphically than anywhere else, both the glory and the curse of religion, including our own. But our first task as radical theologians vis à vis the religion of the poor is *not* to criticize it. We must first allow it to speak to us, to feel what it says, to detect that heartbeat in a heartless world. Exposure to the pain of the poor can help us feel the pain and outrage within us, the cry we stifle because we are a lot better off and a lot better controlled. Our criticism should be aimed not at the poor, to tell them how stupid and debilitating their religion is, but at the rich and powerful who cause the hurt and impose false pipe dreams on the hope.

Here is where all "demythologizing" and most so-called "radical theology," whatever its intention, turns out to be reactionary in operation. Detecting myth, it sets out as the very young Marx did to straighten out the thinking of the adherents of the myth. This is a classic instance of blaming the victim for the crime. A real radical program would follow another tack. Given the fact that myths are often misused against people, as *radical* theologians we should seek first to expose the structure of mystification. We should be dismantling the cultural, educational and politico-economic pyramids that keep us opiated and colonized. This, incidentally, is what Marx soon decided to do. He gave up writing atheistic tracts and began the serious work of making a revolution.

We expose ourselves to poor people's religion not to stamp it out but to be changed ourselves by its elemental power, to learn what the deepest feelings of the losers in our greedy world are. We expose ourselves to poor people's faith so that we can share something common to all of us and equip ourselves better for the battle against the powers who keep poor people poor.

The Mariachi Mass in Mexico and Don Sergio's sermon on the Assumption (and there are thousands of other examples) show the transformation of the religions of oppressed peoples from expression to protest, and from protest to action. But this raises one unavoidable question: How does it happen? We know it has happened in the past. We can see it going on around us today. But if theologians, as I believe, are called on not just to *observe* but to criticize and guide the life of faith, then this process of "radicalization" cannot be left to indeterminate or unrecognized forces. We should be helping it happen.

Don Sergio's interpretation of the Assumption may not find many supporters in the curia. But the fact is that Mariological piety is changing in Latin America. In by far the most cases it still serves to defuse anger and sacralize quiescence. But here and there it has fed righteous anger and even insurrection. If Our Lady talks to God about casting down the mighty from their imperial pinnacles of power (revolution), and sending the rich away empty (confiscation), then little Juan Diego can talk about it too. And, again if Paulo Friere is correct, when the thought becomes word, the word soon becomes deed.

It is important to study Latin American Mariology not only as poor people's religion (which can often be *only* tears and opiates) but because it is a form of piety *in process of political radicalization.* That is the real meaning of Don Sergio's sermon. Religion, again reverting to Marx's *locus classicus,* is also *protest.* At times it focuses, energizes and motivates the fight against the tyrant. It provides transcendent symbols of aspiration and lustrous images for exposing the slick control mechanisms of any society. It perforates the stifling enclosure of the one-dimensional world. It keeps hope alive when all the empirical evidence looks bad. It permits us to spit at mere "facts" and not become slaves to rationality. It allows us to be a little mad.

To discover *how* religion moves from hapless cry to effective protest, from opiate to stimulant, is a matter of great urgency. It is urgent because if theologians are to criticize and guide piety, then we must know how this kind of change in religion occurs. We must stop merely interpreting religion and try to help change it. When we move to that stage, we quickly see (as the Golconda priests did) that people's religion provides an unexpectedly rich source of sparks for political action.

But this should not have come as a surprise. In Latin America insurgency has often broken out under the banners of people's religion. In the backlands of Brazil mystical prophets have often led uprisings. Glauber Rocha's film *Black God, White Devil* depicts one such movement. In Mexico, Father Hidalgo organized his Independistas under the insignia of Our Lady of Guadalupe. A century later Emiliano Zapata led his machete-wielding rural guerrillas beneath the same sign. More recently the Chicano grape strikers marched from Delano to Sacramento under an identical image.

What this means for our urgently needed critical restudy of religious history is that we must ask more cogently where and how religion has been used as Mace (to blind and paralyze the protest) and where it has informed liberation. We must learn how to expose the first and nourish the second. More precisely, we must learn to distinguish between the ways a people's faith enables them to survive and the ways that same faith is used to seduce and misuse them.

But when one begins the search for materials and methods for this kind of radical theology, it immediately becomes clear how impoverished we are. We have been badly miseducated, rendered virtually incapable of dealing with poor people's religion. We are taught, for example, to rely very heavily on texts (whereas the poor have not usually been able to write, or their documents have been burned by the "winners"), on consensual documents and pronouncements (made *to* the people, not *by* them), and on what clerics preached or taught instead of what people believed and did.

Of my deceased and somewhat eccentric former colleague at Harvard Divinity School, Arthur Darby Nock, it has recently been written that he "saw that the essence of religion cannot be found in philosophy or theology alone; it resides also in piety and cult, in the practice and expression of the common man." He was able, the description continues, "to treat the actual manifestations of religion without condescension."

"To treat the *actual manifestations* of religion without condescension"!: an admirable and indeed indispensable methodological principle for theologians of all stripes. But for "radical" theologians, especially those like myself who are willing to carry the label "Christian," it is especially the actual manifestations of the religion of the poor, the hurt, the captives, the mad—the victims and the losers—that we should learn about, not only without condescension but with love and appreciation.

Finally, we cannot be satisfied only to study something admittedly a bit exotic, like Mexican Mariology or Vietnamese Buddhism or African neo-Christian nativism. In America there is a turbulent story to be heard in poor people's religion, black and white. Black theologians have begun to show us that any theology concerned with the liberation of America cannot ignore the black religious experience. The same could be said for the religion of Chicanos, "ethnics," and poor whites. For the most part white radical theologians have been alienated not only from the religious experience of the Third World abroad but also from the religion of the poor and forgotten here in our midst. And the only way we will ever be able to know the faith of these captive peoples is to share their struggle and listen to their pain.

What I am advocating here is not really a marked departure from the best of modern theology. History shows that critical theology first arose as an *emancipatory* activity. It was inspired by the desire to deliver men from political absolutism and the religious superstitions that undergirded it. To be true to its history, modern critical theology must once again become emancipatory in its objectives. This means, however, that theologians should recognize that people are held in bondage not just by archaic ideas but also by institutions that are sacralized by beliefs and values. Theology which does historical criticism but stops short of institutional-ideological criticism absconds from its historic mission.

Ultimately radical theology is not something which can be done *for* people *by* theologians. To try to do so would perpetuate a very *un*radical model of the relation of theologians to other people. Radical theology's very premises point to a democratization of the critical, emancipatory purpose of theologizing—the participation of the people themselves in the unmasking of the sacral myths by which they are controlled. Again there are precedents for this. Throughout Christian history there have been unlicensed preachers who have helped people expose the idols used to rule over them. And from Jan Hus, the angry iconoclast of Bohemia, to the inmates of Attica who burned the chapel as their first act of rebellion, captive peoples have entered enthusiastically into the idol toppling.

There is an even more far-reaching implication to the task of radical theology as I propose it here. In order to grasp the meaning of people's faith we cannot avoid sharing in the experience of those who produced it. Since in Christianity it is always the oppressed and afflicted with whom God is present, and among whom the New Reality is appearing, we cannot do our work without identifying their cause as ours. The text of the Bible can only be understood by someone who has, in some measure at least, identified with the stance and struggle of the "losers." This stance will in turn enable us to see, maybe for the first time, the winsome untruths by which the powerful always perpetuate their rule. Then comes the task of criticism, not of the faith of the poor but of the way it has been twisted and used against them by those who sit at the symbol-manipulating switchboards of society. The liberating contribution of theology will come from exposing the false myths of the powerful, not from trying to straighten out the thinking of the poor.

In the religion of the poor we hear the cry of the oppressed creature in its most poignant form. In it beats the heart of a world more heartless than most of us ever dreamed it could be. And if their faith is often an opiate, as it surely is, we know that TV, higher education, reading and making money can also drug us into their own forms of coma. We should also know by now that the way to treat addiction is not to tear the victim away from his pipe but to cure the cultural pathology that drives him to it.

"A specter is haunting Europe," Karl Marx once wrote. The specter he had in mind was Communism. Today another specter haunts us. It is the grin on the skeletal face of a god we have inherited, worshiped, misused and finally killed. But while the leering specter still besets us, a new eon is tearing its way from the womb of history. Should radical theologians be morticians or midwives? We have nothing to lose.

CHAPTER EIGHT

Naked Revival: Theology and the Human Potential Movement

Each he took by the hand, and when their eyes were shut by the magic of his touch, the circle formed. Krishna sang an air in praise of autumn. The Gopis responded, praising Krishna, and the dance began to the tinkle of their bracelets.

Occasionally dizzied by the round, one or another would throw her arms about her beloved's neck and the drops of his perspiration then were like fertilizing rain, which caused the down to stand forth on her temples. Krishna sang. The Gopis cried "Hare Krishna!" Where he led, they followed; when he turned, they met; and for each, every moment was a myriad of years.

Thus the Being Omnipotent assumed the character of a youth among the women of Vrindavan, pervading their natures and therewith, too, the natures of their lords; for, even as all creatures, the elements are comprehended of ether, air, fire, water, and earth, so also is the Lord everywhere, within all.

—*Vishnu Purana* 5 : 13

THE ESALEN INSTITUTE at Big Sur, California, is known as both the Bethlehem and the Mecca of the encounter-sensitivity-sensory awareness-Oriental meditation movement that hit America during the 1960s. Though I once thought the wave was receding a bit, I still see its ripples everywhere. "Bethlehem" and "Mecca" are religious metaphors, so they are unusually apt ones for Esalen. Biblical scholars tell us that the New Testament accounts placing Jesus' birth in Bethlehem may be mainly legends. The encounter movement was certainly not born at Esalen, but lots of people think it was. Besides, Esalen is where the star hovers overhead, where the wise men journey and where the angels sing, so why bother with the factual history? The aura suffuses Esalen. And as the frontier editor says in the film *The Man Who Shot Liberty Valance*, "When there's a conflict between the facts and the legend we print the legend."

As for Mecca, I am told that it often turns out to be a crushing let-down for those plucky Moslems who complete their arduous pilgrimages. But having waited so long and worked so hard to get there, they can never admit it to themselves. Besides, it is part of the religion. You've just *got* to go to Mecca before you die or you're not much better off than the infidels. Esalen too.

I didn't go to Esalen as a pilgrim, however, not even as a seeker. At least not the first time. Prosaically enough, I went there first to lead a weekend conference, together with the late Bishop James Pike. Maybe that is why Esalen hit me so hard. Since I was not a pilgrim I had no illusions to be shattered, so I was taken in my innocence and naïveté. Also, what Esalen felt like to me was neither a saviour's birthplace nor a pilgrimage center, but my mental picture of an old-fashioned American camp meeting.

I had heard a lot about Esalen before I arrived, and some of it had been pretty wild: people freaking out in all-night encounter marathons, tears, screams, moans, hoarse sobbing and hysterical hugging, sex in thirty-eight flavors and, of course, the nude baths. So as we crunched into the driveway that January Friday afternoon I was getting scared. But along with my fear I detected another more fugitive but still identifiable sentiment, a sort of determination: I didn't want to let this place defeat me. There were other things scheduled that weekend in addition to our conference. I wanted not only to lead our own little show but to sample, yea *master*, the whole scene. As I climbed out of the car and checked in I smiled a lot and talked volubly. I hoped no one would notice that I was trembling. They didn't seem to.

It was not until the next morning that the rain cleared and I actually saw where I was. It was almost overwhelming. Esalen couldn't be better situated to conjure its peculiar mystique of warm promise and craggy threat. Perched on the seaward face of Big Sur, its tiny grounds seem to hang precariously out over the Pacific breakers crashing into pieces of soapy foam on the rocks hundreds of feet below. Teetering there between sky, mountain and endless sea, the site seems to say to you, "If it doesn't happen here, it isn't going to happen at all. There's no place else to go."

So I decided to let it happen. I joined a group on the lawn and clumsily extended my arms and legs in the rhythmic movements of Tai Chi (Chinese body meditation). I touched, smelled, tasted and listened to grass blades, tree bark, wet stones and pine needles in sensory awareness exercises. I fell over backwards and was caught by my partner in a trust-development trial. I looked into people's eyes in an encounter group. I lay still in quiet ecstasy as a deft masseuse, her fingers sweet with berry-scented oil, skillfully kneaded my body in one of the Institute's famous long-stroke, deep-muscle massages. I hammered ferociously on a huge home-made drum, and I languished by candlelight in the hot mineral baths. I did not freak out.

It was all great. As it turned out, neither my fear nor my determinations triumphed. Instead, they both slid gradually out of my mind as I let myself be carried along by a kind of gentle assent I had rarely felt before. I did not "master" Esalen. Nor did it master me. We decided, together, I think, not to pursue that contest. We both just let it happen; and ever since then my relationship to Esalen has been one of trysts, fantasies and interludes. It's like an episodic love affair with a woman whose nutty ideas embarrass me but whose presence is warm and inviting, who knows I'm kidding a bit in the attention I pay her, but who doesn't really care, because she has lots of other lovers, and for some reason she likes me too.

After I'd been back several times to Esalen over a four-year period, the director, Mike Murphy, finally presented me with one of Esalen's rare "perpetual guest privilege certificates." It is a small yellow ticket-sized card on which it is stated that the bearer has the right to visit Esalen and use its facilities, as the card modestly reads, "forever." They call it the Forever Card.

Since I got the card I haven't been back to Esalen. I'm not sure why. Maybe it is like the inevitable freeze that sets in when a lover starts to talk about marriage. Maybe it's because I was just getting over my Esalen stage as this visa to immortality was bestowed upon me. But I liked the Forever Card anyway. It told me that it was okay that I knew the star overhead is really the reflection of a San Bernardino schoolteacher's flashlight on the Pacific fog as she picks her way down to the baths. And the angels singing are car radios blaring on the road from Monterey down to L.A. The card is a nice mixture of messianism and self-caricature ("Forever"!), so it is Esalen at its best. There are some fanatics, I know. But the people who are closest to Esalen are not. They know they have hit on something important, but they also know it is not the Final Answer. They know they can safely give you a Forever Card, because the Esalen Institute will not be there forever. And when you accept the card you know you won't last forever either. It's good for everybody's humility.

What I remember most about that first weekend at Esalen is not the view or the conference. Nor is it the baths or the Tai Chi. What I recall most clearly is the ad hoc discussion that occurred on Saturday night. It had not been planned that way at all, but on Saturday afternoon, after Bishop Pike and I had finished our talks and everyone was napping or getting massaged, Gary Snyder, the Zen poet (and author of *Earth House Hold*), and Allen Ginsberg arrived with some of their followers to meditate and cavort in the baths. Someone suggested it would be just splendid if the four of us—Bishop Pike, Allen, Gary and myself —would hold a sort of panel that evening on "The Future of Religion." We did, until the early dew dampened the paving stones around the darkened studio of the Esalen lodge, with sixty or seventy people lying on the floor around us, the whole scene lit by only a few aromatic candles, and the surf and the wind outside.

Ginsberg was a boyish bearded Siddhartha. He sat cross-legged in a robe, the candle flames glinting on his glasses, and told us the future of religion was now entwined with the future of LSD. He described how he used Hindu meditational techniques while tripping on acid or mescalin and confessed that the only thing Christian that made any sense to him was the rosary because of its repetitive, trance-inducing power. It also helped him on trips, he said, when he felt himself freaking out, to cling to those hard beads in his hands. It gave him something to hang on to and something to do. He also talked about masturbation and screwing as religious experiences, at points with a little more visible embarrassment than I would have expected. While he spoke, several of the young girls and fellows who had come to Esalen with him sat on the floor near his feet with their eyes half closed, nodding and smiling and occasionally snapping their fingers or groaning appreciatively.

When Gary Snyder spoke he told us about his rigorous training in a Zen monastery in Japan and then explained why for him some form of Buddhism rather than of Christianity was the only suitable religion of the future. I thought he took a little too long cataloguing the vices of Christianity, all of which I already knew, and not enough on why he himself had found the Way of the Buddha so satisfying. Still, I knew in listening to Snyder that he was not dealing in pop Buddhism or instant Zen. He had served his hard spiritual apprenticeship in that bare monastery at the foot of Mount Fuji. He knew what he was talking about, and I felt I wanted to know him better. After he had finished speaking he and Allen chanted a mantra. Then Bishop Pike began.

Poor Jim. Although I never knew him very well, I liked him despite, or maybe even because of, some of the qualities that turned other people away. It is true that he talked too much. Endlessly. And much of it was disjointed and ill prepared. He smoked king-sized L & M's one after another, dragging at them furiously, and seemed harassed by some terrible nemesis. But what won me about him was his driving desire to push back the boundaries of experience, to explore dimensions of religion that had been taboo for ages. He was a harried wanderer who was never at home for very long in any church or with any theology. I always felt a little freer after I had been with him. Though he died before his time, the manner of his death was entirely fitting. I confess I once thought it was a little staged, but then that would have been true to Jim's style too. There was a large dash of the thespian mixed with his priesthood. He died two years after our Esalen meeting while exploring some wilderness where, legend says, Christ met Satan and was tempted. Jim was there on what many people would consider an ill-advised fool's errand or a PR stunt. But for him I'm sure it was a momentous spiritual exploration. It is just right that his widow, Diane, who was with him on that Esalen weekend, has started a center in his memory which is designed to help people "in spiritual transition." Jim Pike never stopped being in transition.

But Jim Pike was in a tough spot that night. He had a compelling need to be at least as far out on the edge of religious evolution as anyone else, farther if possible. But there he sat, surrounded by cross-legged freaks, mantra chanters, plates of incense, and the sensuous aroma Esalen itself exudes. Pinioned there where crazy California meets the sea, he seemed, despite himself, to look very much the part of the Anglican parson. He had left or been fired, I've never been sure which, from being Episcopal Bishop of San Francisco because he was too radical. But he was still a Christian, an Episcopalian and a priest. He was still even a bishop. After Snyder and Ginsberg it was hard for him to upstage anyone. He expatiated at some length, mainly about communication with the dead, especially with his own dead son. People were moved, even those who were skeptical about his reports, including me.

I forget now what I said that night. But I know I have never felt straighter. I only wish that my colleagues at Harvard, who still twit me occasionally about being the resident radical, could have glimpsed me that evening. In comparison with the other three panelists I felt like Mr. Conventional Christian himself. But somehow at another level I didn't really mind. In fact I felt marvelous.

Since that evening I've thought about it a lot and I think now that I know why I felt so much at home. The whole weekend at Esalen was a turning point for me. It marked a return to trusting the element of *experience* in religion, my own experience in particular, as a legitimate source of direction in life, and also in theology. As I look back now I realize that I had been moving toward that return for some time. But it often takes a particular occasion to jell something for me. Still it was not something utterly new. It was a return; and one reason I felt good at Esalen was that it seemed so *familiar*, not strange or new at all.

My boyhood religion had been heavily experiential, and after years of studying theology I was ready again for religion. The encounter group there did not provide my first experience of public crying or deep emotion, and the sulphur baths did not supply the first purgative waters I had passed through. Years before, there had been prayer meeting and baptism. Also the darkness and candles of the Esalen lodge were familiar. Hadn't they also illumined the last night of Bible camp? And now here were Gary and Allen and Jim giving—what? Their testimonies! The Human Potential, Sensitivity, Encounter Movement is the cultural successor and heir of the pietistic Christianity of my own and many other people's childhoods, with all its strengths and weaknesses, its warmth and intimacy and its excessive sentimentality.

Esalen and its sister growth centers and human-potential encampments are no foreign import to the American religious scene. Despite their reappropriation of the Oriental spiritual idiom, their predecessors are really not so much Benares or the Tibetan plateaus but Asbury Park, Ocean Grove and a hundred arcadian revival sites across the Midwest. The emotional intensity and spiritually approved fascination with feeling of the great pietistic awakenings would not be strangers at Big Sur. There are differences in rhetoric and ritual and especially in mores, but the underlying melody still sounds like the one I first heard so many years ago at the little Methodist church in Malvern:

> Floods of joy o'er my soul
> Like the sea billows roll,
> Since Jesus came into my heart.

People who patronize the growth centers and imbibe the ideology of the encounter movement are frequently very critical of conventional Christianity. They often speak in disparaging terms of "puritanism" with its alleged anti-body bias and its suffocating uptightness. But most American religion is not puritanical, at least in this sense; it is pietistic. Pietism not only allows but revels in feeling. And anyone who remembers the last night of High School Bible Camp—the fever pitch of religious intoxication mixed with adolescent sex that is reached, the campfire dedications and the sweaty necking in the bushes—knows what I mean. At Esalen I remembered all that again, and I am glad I did, because it was slipping from my memory.

"Higher education" exacts a price. Most of the time I am grateful for my years at Penn, Yale and Harvard. But not always. Because I know full well that living in those centers of cerebral cultivation did lure me away from my earlier trust in my own experience. It costs a lot in repressed rage, postponed satisfaction, and just plain lost goofing-off time to acquire a Ph.D. Sometimes I think the cost is too high. In any case, by the time I visited Esalen I was beginning to suspect I was cerebrally overdeveloped and experientially atrophied. What I discovered about myself there was simple enough, and I probably would have learned it somewhere else if I hadn't learned it there. I saw that I didn't have to be Allen, Gary or Jim—an LSD guru or a Zen poet or a wandering bishop. That was their experience, not mine. All I had to do was to accept myself and maybe to hum a few bars, under my breath of course, of "Just As I Am Without One Plea."

So far I have not said much in this reminiscence of the Esalen camp meeting about the part most people want me to get to first, the mixed nude soaking in the hot sulphur baths. I've delayed because I haven't known how to avoid the Scylla and Charybdis of descriptions others have made. Some Esalen initiates make light of the whole thing by assuring you that it "isn't really sexy at all," and by referring condescendingly to the horny misfits who actually feel or fondle people in the purifying waters. They stress the spiritually uplifting quality of the immersion as though it were some fleshless exercise in transcendental meditation. Other people, most of whom have not passed through the thermal flood, are sure it's just a staging area for later hanky-panky back in the cabins, or an orgy for people who would die before they would attend one advertised in an underground newspaper, because they want their excesses to be sanctified by the authorities, in this case the encounter group gurus.

Well, for me the "bath experience" certainly *was* sexy, and anyone reared in our culture who says it is not either baffles me or arouses my deep suspicion. I did find it "spiritually" satisfying too, if I catch what those who describe it with that term mean. I am also sure there is a lot of fondling, patting, poking and pinching going on under the water (and over it) and that this probably culminates in roughly the same amount of sexual intercourse that takes place whenever groups of consenting adults find themselves away from home for a weekend at a ski lodge, sales training meeting or YMCA conference. So my description does not steer *between* Scylla and Charybdis, it encompasses both of them. For me the "bath experience" was *both* sexy and spiritual, both voluptuous and innocent. It was all the contradictory things people had told me about it and more; and for that reason it was different from anything I had anticipated. But maybe the best way to explain it is first to describe what happened.

"Does everyone *know* about the . . . bath experience?" ventured the husky social worker from San Jose, looking around the group thoughtfully. "Do you think we're . . . ah . . . ready, or do you think we should . . . talk about it before we . . . uh . . . go down?" He had been to Esalen before and he thought it was "time to raise the question." It was. My watch told me we had now reached eleven o'clock on opening Friday night of our weekend conference. The sixteen people in my conference group were sitting or lying around on the rug, feeling a little tired and a lot relieved that the inevitable opening session anxiety was behind them. But their coziness was being cut short. They were now confronted by something they must have expected when they came but which, however mildly it was being proposed, would have seemed unspeakably audacious anywhere else. He was asking, "Are we ready?" What he meant was would sixteen total strangers (except for one husband and wife and one former student of mine who had driven down from San Francisco for the conference) now pick up large fluffy towels, walk the two hundred yards down the narrow ledge to the open-sided bathhouses, take off all our clothes and climb together into a pool-like tub where the sixteen of us would be closely packed—skin, inevitably, to skin—there to continue our getting acquainted in a different mode?

Were we *ready?*

My thought was that no sixteen strangers anywhere in America were ready, but that we were all, or most of us, going to do it anyway. Ready or not. And furthermore there was probably nothing we could "talk about" now that could conceivably get us any readier. All talk would do, I felt sure, was to build up tension, anxiety or anticipation, and I had already reached my limit of all three.

Up until that evening my experience with nudity had been about par for an average American middle-class male. In short, when it came to groups, my nude experiences were not mixed and my mixed ones were not nude. From fourth grade on I had shared many damp smelly locker rooms and swum *au naturel* in the eye-scorching chlorine of YMCA pools. Later I parboiled myself occasionally in college gym steam rooms and was periodically herded through various group medical exams by colleges, camps and the Selective Service System. But all these activities were restricted to members of my own gender: nude but not mixed. My high school buddies and I had occasionally sneaked into burlesque shows, and I had pulled off some Peeping Tom tricks as a small kid, but on each of these occasions *I* was fully clothed. All my unclothed experiences with unclothed *women* had been strictly *à deux*, not groups at all. I don't believe I am unusual in the poverty of my exposure. So this was new.

When we got to the baths the moon was overcast, but someone had thoughtfully placed dozens of candles around the edges of the small pools. Their yellow glow softened the epidermal colors of those already there. In fact their skin seemed almost to glow. So much so that we clothed ones felt a little like furry Visigoths encroaching on the inner sanctums of cultivated Romans. We gawked and blinked for just a second or two, but with clothes on in this setting it was we, not they, who seemed out of place. A few people in our group had stayed behind, telling us this was just not their scene. We had all murmured our approval of their decision to abstain. But now the rest of us, the venturesome ones, were here. The moment of truth had arrived. We unzipped and unbuttoned fast, just like in the Y locker rooms, hung our clothes on little wooden pegs, glancing but not staring as we did, then climbed into the warm mineral-rich water and settled ourselves on the pool's grainy bottom.

The water is just deep enough to reach to the armpits of a seated person of normal height. The sensation was delicious. At first we all looked at one another in a kind of ecstatic relief. We were *there*. We had transgressed the outside world's arbitrary borderline, demarcated by briefs and bikinis that mask but do not hide the essentials. We had broken taboo and we were not dead. That alone gave us all a little lift. Furthermore we were floating together in a kind of free zone where progressing from nakedness to intercourse was not required, was indeed hardly possible. We could loll around and laze with one another in the brine without the performance anxiety that in our culture infects even, or perhaps especially, the act of coital intercourse.

What an ironic twist. The same act our deranged culture has decreed as the quintessential gesture of personal freedom, even of rebellion against conventional authority, has also been transformed into a performance to be accomplished according to well-circulated standards. But in the sweet vapors of Big Sur it was different, and in an age so preoccupied with the freedom *for* sexual expression, being freed *from* the standard seduction scenario soothed us like a salt breeze of grace. I think everyone there felt the same way. Almost every other backdrop our world provides for men and women to disrobe also requires them to follow the standard script. The exceptions are saunas and doctors' offices. But obligatory intercourse is a *contradictio in adjecto,* and so the gentle waters of the Esalen baths provided a paradoxically liberating environment. No one seemed to expect anyone to do anything except just *be* there; and in an age clutched by *doing,* that alone is a foretaste of heaven.

The water itself was nice too. Because of its calefactive qualities and its high sulphur content it seems to prickle and soothe the skin at the same time. If you inhale, it exudes a fragrant steamy bouquet, and if you lean back it buoys you up more than ordinary water does. Then when you climb out and stand damply exposed to the balmy Pacific air, it evaporates, leaving a strange tingly residue. No wonder the Esalen Indians who roamed these cliffs long ago liked it so much and believed it was the source of a holy power.

Ordinarily each pool-tub, of which there are eight at Esalen, holds about a dozen people, but packed a little more snugly, each can accommodate fifteen or more. Consequently, if the pools are full, isolated meditation is difficult. So after the first splashdown and the subsequent quiet languor another mood usually sets in. It begins with chanting or with quiet conversation, then often escalates into group massaging or boisterous horseplay. The massaging is a complex affair, with one person rubbing another's back while he/she kneads someone else's toes and simultaneously has his/her neck tenderized by the fingers of a third or fourth person. In the semi-darkness it is hard to know whose limb is whose.

Though the group massage sounds vaguely promiscuous, it is not. In fact after I'd enjoyed the sheer sensation of it for a while,

I even began to have a vision. The candles seemed to expand and I caught a glimpse of Teilhard de Chardin's Omega Point, a suprapersonal future in which individuals become joyous corpuscles in a more inclusive organism. Was I a muscle cell, a brain nerve, a bit of stomach lining? It didn't seem to matter. That dream danced in my brain for a long time, then it dimmed and I felt myself slipping back into childhood and infancy, into what Norman Brown calls "polymorphous perversity," that generalized form of sensual enjoyment children seem capable of but adults have lost. "Except ye become as little children" blended with "We are members one of another" in a shifting collage of faces, hands, candles, mandalas, omegas, and unending future vistas.

Time, I have no idea how much, passed. Now all the candles were one flame and all the fingers were on one great hand. The combination of water, chanting, body dissociation and massage was moving me beyond a pleasantly sensuous swoon into something closer to what I could only imagine was either a fanciful reverie or a mystical trance. I could feel the hydrogen and oxygen molecules of the water seeping into the amino acids and carbohydrates and bone cells and nerve endings of my body. The hands touching me became mine, and my own hands slid off my wrists to fuse with the dampness in and around me. Again the vision faded. Now I felt something I had read about many times before but never understood, the underlying unity of Brahman and Atman, the oneness of self, other and All. With an infinitesimal corner of critical consciousness still looking on, like that part of you that knows a dream is a dream, I thought about the fact that the modern Western convention which draws the border of "me" at my epidermis, and posits "you" and "me" as two entirely separate entities, is after all only one way of looking at things. We are all in some ways one with the water, the sky, the air, each other, and in the sulphur baths the reality of a collective self seems a little less bizarre than it does in the everyday world.

I doubt that those who shared the limpid pools of Esalen with me that night, or any of the other times I was there, ever thought they were adding to my theological wisdom. It is not the sort of environment where one *thinks* of anything at all in the usual sense. And even though I tend to be an almost compulsively thought-obsessed person, most of my cerebration about the "significance" of the baths occurred *after* I had clambered out of them. Still, they did enrich my theology. I had heard for years about the classical Eastern religious idea that the "self" is an arbitrary concept and that the I and the Them can be subsumed under an impersonal or suprapersonal It. But I doubt now that any amount of reading of Buddhist or Hindu philosophy would ever have helped me visualize the meaning of this doctrine as much as one evening in the baths. Some people may have learned the same thing I did through meditation, intuitive insight or through an LSD experience. Some may even have learned it while reading. I am simply recounting my peculiar way of glimpsing the internal significance of something that others may have discovered in their way but I learned in mine.

After I had returned home from Esalen I began to have some doubts. Isn't a nude mineral bath with candlelit massage an odd place, maybe even a questionable place, to hit upon a mystical insight? But my doubts soon faded. In the Hindu Gitas, Lord Krishna frolics with the nubile goat girls, charming them with his melodious flute. In Hinduism, "eros" and "agape" are not divorced, and though it began as a secret cult, the ancient Tantric tradition with its emphasis on erotic rites has made an important contribution to all forms of Indian religion and to Mahayana Buddhism as well. The same element is richly present in the biblical traditions as any reader of the Song of Songs knows.

Admittedly the pool itself is no place to theologize. There is a time and place for everything. In the pool, on that evening and during subsequent visits, I just floated, psychologically and physically, on a crowded cluster of unusually delightful feelings—watching men and women, old and young, shuck off the outer garments of the workaday world and splash at first hesitantly, then eagerly into one of the brimming tubs of people; seeing the play of candlelight and shadow on thigh and breast and hip and shoulder; sensing in everyone the fear and anxiety that quickly mellowed into trust, exhilaration and even frolic; seeing skinny men, tiny children, people with warts, burn scars, ungainly legs, pot bellies, thin chests and overly ample behinds enjoying one another in the same condition in which they had entered the world.

I never saw a white flash.

I was not converted. I did not return home preaching the illusory nature of the self or the superiority of the Tantric tradition. I did not come away rejecting Christianity and convinced that Hinduism is right in its emphasis on reunion with the universal soul. But I was able to grasp much more fully what such a doctrine, previously opaque to me, was about. I even discovered that I might be able to catch something of its import from the inside without discarding my "Western" Christian identity.

My passing through the Esalen waters makes me wonder even more now about the way we teach religion. It gives me grounds for hope that we may not have to explore the great world religious traditions only from the outside, as curious observers. Nor will we have to view them as a series of painful options or forced choices. Perhaps rather we can experience them as variant modes of consciousness, different ways of symbolizing self and world. Further, we may be able to experience for ourselves more than one such mode of consciousness.

When I emerged from the waters of Big Sur I joked a good deal about it with people. I minimized the elements of ecstasy and vision, because I had not expected very much to happen. But like that earlier baptism in the First Baptist Church of Malvern, more had happened than I anticipated, and finally I had to admit it. For all its vulnerability to excess, sentimentalizing and other abuses, pietism—new and old—has an undeniable potency. As much as we can and must reflect critically on the feelings when they have fled, we can never doubt they were real when we felt them.

As people left the baths, drying and pulling on their jeans and T-shirts, I sensed some of the spell was ebbing but that it would never disappear completely. The mandalas and omegas were gone as I trudged back up the hill to the lodge, but I would remember them. Also, I thought a lot about clothes and what they mean.

In our society clothes do make the man, and the woman. Despite their current rebellion against fashion fads, young people flash cues by the way they dress. So do we all. Our pants (straight or bell-bottom), scarfs, ties, blouses (plunging or coverup, tight or loose), shoes, hats and jewelry all send out constant messages. My wife Nancy is a student of costume history and has managed in the past few years to persuade me that what Columbus or Elizabeth I or Napoleon *wore* on a certain occasion may have been just as important as what they *said*. It is true of us too, and only in a no-clothes situation do we realize how much of our relating to one another is regulated by wraps. There is nothing wrong with that. Clothes at their best help us tell our stories, to say who we are, how we feel, what we hope others will think of us. I can see this especially in the recent second coming of those used sashes, fancy capes, epaulettes, long frocks, boas, cloaks, spats and assorted junk-store finery adolescents and others display today on the city streets of America. This flamboyant parading of body décor changes some of the meaning we had heretofore attached to apparel. Wardrobery, formerly one of the surest signs of rank and station, is now being democratized. One's dress now tells little or nothing about social status but much about individual tastes and moods. Every day is a masquerade ball. The clothing behavior of young people is becoming less a panicky mimicking of what the media dictate, though that persists to some extent. It is increasingly a caricature of the pretentious use of dress.

Doing without clothes temporarily makes one think about what one's own story is and how to project it without any veils, props, masks or visors. But a temporary tryout of living without them does not make clothes less important. On the contrary, just as words become even more significant after you've had to keep silence for a few days, or food tastes more succulent after a fast, clothes assume a subtler meaning after you have gone without them.

We could apply much more of what we have found out about the meaning of clothes to liturgy and celebration. What does it tell us about worship that some people often feel they want to "dress up" for church? My parents spoke of "Sunday-go-to-meeting clothes." Why do some other people rebel so stridently against the custom? Maybe they suspect that if we are expected to come to God "just as I am," putting on ties and shirts and gloves seems hypocritical. But on the other side, why did the Bostonians of all ages who flocked to Byzantine Easter dress themselves and one another so expressively? And why do our children and younger siblings love to rummage through attic trunks for old evening gowns and cutaways? What do we really want to say to ourselves and one another with the copes, cassocks, chasubles and cowls of ecclesiastical vestment? There is a universal human desire to use clothing for more than mere warmth and protection. Clothes are not just our furs, they are also our plumage. They are not just coverings but bits of communication stamped with meanings and innuendos. We use them to say things words will not express. But like all other media of communication, clothes can be used to intimidate as well as to liberate. Policemen's uniforms, judges' robes, bishops' mantles and admirals' gold braid are intended to inform us at a glance about the authority they hold. Costume certifies position in a hierarchy of power.

Some equalitarian movements in religion and in politics strive to abolish rank by requiring everyone to wear the same thing. Quaker worship is devoid of all the surplices and soutanes to remind people that all are equal before God. To tell one another and the world that class privilege is on the way out in China nearly eight hundred million people wear the same plain brown or gray pants and jacket. Where oppression has been symbolized by apparel in the past, stark and uniform simplicity is an understandable counterstrategy. But I prefer the strategy of caricature and hyperbole to that of uniformity and colorlessness. The adolescent boy who strides down the street wearing the field jacket of a four-star general strikes a blow against rank without losing out on the fun of strutting in style.

If we want to laicize and equalize liturgy, which I think we should, the same principle applies. Instead of burning the popish trappings, we need only make sure everyone has a key to the vestry. This would abolish clerical privilege and priestly domination without draining any color from worship. If ordained clergy were convinced of the necessity both of democratizing liturgy and of redistributing the *symbols* of religious power, they could demonstrate to a hierarchy-ridden secular society that jobs and callings do not carry with them the right of lording it over anyone else. They could show that the professional does not need to hoard the badges of office in order to render a service.

Whenever I lead a religious celebration I try to practice something I learned from attending Bishop Mendes Arceo's Mariachi Mass in Mexico. I wear liturgical vestments, but I put them on over regular clothes in the presence of the congregation. This tells everyone I am not a person set apart permanently, only for this occasion. Next time it could be someone else. At the end of the liturgy I remove the liturgical garments, again in everyone's presence. Every congregation should have a closet full of celebrative attire. Human beings have always donned such paraphernalia to approach the gods, and they always will. But the fun, and responsibility, of wearing it should not be reserved for a clerical elite. If, as Luther said, we are all priests to one another, then let us dress the part.

A visit to the Esalen camp meeting sends one away thinking not just about clothes and unclothes but also about touching and its nearly complete absence from contemporary Christian worship. Friends laugh, nervously I think, when I only half-facetiously suggest that the next step in liturgical reform, after the Kiss of Peace, might be the introduction into church congregations of some form of massage. It would have to be completely noncoercive, of course, unlike Esalen, where there was a strong social pressure to participate. And it would have to discourage casual curiosity seekers. But if these conditions were met, what theological arguments could be arrayed against it? On every side we hear that the body has been for too long overlooked, denigrated and disparaged in Christianity. I think this is true. I also think that our sexual feelings have been so overly pinpointed on coital intercourse alone that we do not know what else it might mean to love and care for one another's bodies as well as one another's souls.

In our confusion we have so narrowed the range of allowable physical contact that most adults live with a constant, if only dimly conscious, need to be touched, cuddled and embraced. But since there are so few occasions where friendly touching is encouraged, it is easy to confuse the need for mere gestures of affection with the need for coital intercourse. Because of the rarity of times when touching is culturally okay, and the continuous use of sex to sell products, it is understandable that many people experience any touching at all as the first step toward the bed. A potent mixture of fear, attraction, repulsion and fascination sets in and attaches itself to the slightest bodily expression of warmth and care between adults. The result is the crazy blend of repression and promiscuity that besets us now.

Making massage an integral part of religious life would help change the situation markedly. I don't mean professional massage parlors or the back-thumping workovers administered by track trainers. I mean friends taking time out from the pursuit of money to learn to communicate by subtle gestures and caress as well as by word, overcoming their fear and fascination of the flesh, enjoying and serving one another without exploiting or manipulating, exploring a type of sensuality that is not narrowly sexual, and finding out after generations of anesthesia what it feels like to inhabit one's own shoulders and fingers and elbows.

Not all segments of the Christian church have derogated or ignored the body. A few years ago when I was visiting Brazil I attended a long session one night of a fast-growing Afro-Brazilian religious movement called Umbanda. Sometimes known also as

Macumba or Condomblé, it is an intricate synthesis of African gestures, beliefs, rites and deities brought by the slaves plus the Roman Catholic faith they were baptized into in Brazil. The worship takes place three or four nights every week from ten P.M. until the early morning hours. During the night drums beat, devotees dance and brightly costumed priests and priestesses invoke the spirits of various animals, and natural forces—lion, stars, serpent, sea, bird—who also bear the names of popular Catholic saints. When the spirits descend, those who receive them pass on the healing powers to others. Everything about this throbbing poor people's liturgy underlines the potency of touch. The dancing is ecstatic and exhausting. There is much greeting, hugging and embracing. When the suppliants kneel before the seated persons who have experienced the presence of the saints, the spirit-filled ones transmit the vivifying current by rubbing, stroking and patting the suppliants. There is healing in that touch which even an uninitiated bystander cannot deny.

Standing in the Umbanda meeting hall that hot night in Rio, I remembered that touch was once central to Christianity as well but has shrunken in recent years to a mere residue. Jesus himself regularly touched the people he healed and forgave, and the crowds tried to touch him. In one significant incident he even felt the tapping of his strength by someone who had touched him without being seen. Both Jesus and the outcasts who flocked around him knew that touch sometimes says even more than speech. Later on the disciples passed on the energy they had felt in Jesus by "laying on hands." The earliest Christians believed one's conversion to the faith was not completed with merely hearing and responding to the word; it required the placement of hands on heads and bodies to open the channels of grace fully. Traces of this old practice remain today in confirmation rituals, ordinations and the "Kiss of Peace."

During the last days of his life Jesus set two examples of how his followers were to signify their new-found unity. Both actions rely heavily on bodily metaphor. But the churches since then have practiced one and ignored the other. In one precedent, Jesus shared the eating of bread and the drinking of wine with his friends, equating it with sharing his flesh and blood. He said as he did so that his companions were to continue this sharing of loaf and cup until his new era appeared on earth. The churches have indeed continued some form of communion ever since.

But even before the Last Supper, Jesus had demonstrated another sacrament of love and unity. He had washed the feet of James, Peter, John, Matthew and all the others. When he had finished, Jesus clearly instructed his followers, in words just as unequivocal as those used to institute communion, that they should continue this practice. "Do you know what I have done?" he asked them, then continued,

> If I then, your Lord and Master, have washed your feet; ye also ought to wash one another's feet.
> For I have given you an example, that ye should do as I have done to you. . . .
> If ye know these things, happy are ye if ye do them.
> —St. John 13 : 14–17

This is a very explicit "ordinance," more explicit than the words Jesus used to institute communion. But his unequivocal instruction has been ignored. With the exception of my distant theological cousins, the "foot-washing Baptists," and the pope, who once a year touches someone's toe with a damp cloth in a ritualized nod to the command of Christ, the church has abandoned foot washing. We have kept the eating and drinking rite and discarded the touching one.

Why *feet?* It could be argued that foot washing was common in the Palestine of Jesus' day and so his choice had no special significance. I disagree. Jesus' choice of the most "distant" members of the human body was not an accident. Eating and drinking bread and wine were also commonplace then, but we do not dismiss their spiritual potency for that reason. Jesus chose foot washing because our feet provide a test case of whether we really inhabit our own fleshly frames and whether we recoil from or reach out to the flesh of another. Feet are generally viewed, in our culture at least, as funny, awkward or misshapen addenda to the human corpus. We joke about flat feet, splayed feet, big feet, "sticking our foot in our mouth" and stubbing our toes. Lovers gush over almost every square inch of a beloved's body from flowing tresses to shapely ankles. But I have never seen an ode to anyone's toes. I am told that in Japan feet have sometimes become the fetishes of passion, but in the West kissing someone's foot is a sign not of affection but of slavish subservience. In choosing feet as the bodily members on which his followers were to begin in their caring for one another, Jesus wisely foresaw that once we fully accept one another's most ungainly parts, and accept our own most removed members, our painful separation from ourselves and from one another would already be in the process of healing.

Perhaps the first step toward the reintroduction of our lost sense of touch in Christianity would be to start following Jesus' command and example about foot washing. It would unite people in service, touching and cleansing, and it is a practice religious groups could legitimate in our culture as an antidote to our present combined aversion to and compulsion about the human body. Maybe some form of massage would soon follow. In some places this practice or something like it is already beginning. There will always be people who will anticipate shameless abuses of massage or even foot washing. But the church has sensibly kept the swallowing of an alcoholic beverage as a sacrament for many centuries even though no one denies the dangers of excessive drinking.

Whatever form it eventually takes, a renewed appreciation for the sacramental power and human importance of touch is sure to emerge from the present spiritual ferment, part of which, though only a part, underlies the encounter-sensitivity movement. The ethical and political consequences of such a renewed appreciation of the beauty and fragility of human flesh could be considerable. Dan Berrigan once, when we were talking about a slightly different subject, expressed the theological meaning of flesh with characteristic Berriganian succinctness. "It all comes down to this," he said. "Whose flesh are you touching, and why? Whose flesh are you recoiling from, and why? Whose flesh are you burning, and why?"

Like every other religious revival in history the sensitivity-encounter movement does have a theology even though its rhetoric is anti-theological. It is beginning to have a church even though it is anti-institutional. It is beginning to face the problems all previous religious revivals have had to grapple with. The encounter theology sometimes locates the fall with Cotton Mather or with Queen Victoria—depending on whether sin is viewed as "puritanism" or "Victorianism"—or sometimes with the beginnings of Western society, or sometimes as far back as man's differentiation from matter. Wherever sin entered, in the encounter theology, our own complicity in the curse of the race is that we continue to deny our feelings. Salvation comes, as it did for the early Methodists, in small, intense and avidly honest groups, usually gathered in sylvan retreats. But salvation, also as with the early Methodists, is never fully assured merely by a conversion. One can easily backslide (into phoniness or uptightness) and one must constantly strive to "go on to perfection," as the old Methodist theology has it, this time a perfection of unending growth. This usually requires periodic perk-up visits to sensitivity groups, encounter sessions or human potential centers.

There are circuit preachers too, the traveling revivalists and wandering specialists in psychodynamics, primal scream, basic encounter, "rolphing," body awareness, bio-energetics and techniques for inducing joy, openness, enhanced feeling and inner peace. They travel by jet instead of on horseback today. Posters and handbills hail their coming, and at every meeting site they are welcomed by the once-saved and the would-be-saved. Sects have developed, doctrinal squabbles have broken out, and some of the preachers, now as before, do not seem averse to peddling a little snake potion along with the true and living word. Also, like the two Great Awakenings of yesteryear, one in the eighteenth century associated with Jonathan Edwards and one in the nineteenth century associated with people like Charles Grandison Finney, the encounter movement presents a disquieting challenge to the established religious institutions. For all these reasons and more, the encounter wave has already called forth a host of theological critics.

Some of the critics believe the dangers in the new surge of group-grope pietism far outweigh any constructive contribution it could possibly make. When they look at Bethel or Esalen, what they see is a pusillanimous retreat from politics, a weary abdication from the strenuous struggle our species must carry on if we intend to survive: in short a cop-out. They are afraid that the recent hard-won re-emergence of a politically aware stance in American religious groups, their commitment, such as it is, to peace and racial justice, could easily disappear in a maze of touchy-feely gimmicks, self-induced trances, chanting and navel gazing.

I think there are good reasons to be concerned. Without a doubt the new pietism like the old is susceptible to abuse, exploitation and even a kind of fanaticism. Not every guru or group leader is a dependable guide to the mysteries of community. Not every psychic discipline delivers the inner depth the pamphlets promise. Still, the current surge of interest in groups, encounter, sensitivity and the literature and practice of spiritual discipline is understandable. Though subject to fraudulent misuse, the impulse itself represents a stubborn survival instinct in millions of people who, often without fully realizing it, have begun to kick back at a society that tries to pack them into its routines like bearings around an axle. Therefore the critics of the new religiosity should be careful to distinguish between the real human hunger which motivates it and the pandering to hunger that occurs in every age.

For me there are two equally serious dangers stalking us today as we look for a viable faith for our time. The first is indeed the peril of a new quietism, a unilateral retreat from the kneel-in to the lotus position, from the picket line to the self-awareness group. There is a danger in the zealous cultivation of that spurious form of "spiritual" life that recklessly turns the "outer" world over to greed and power. This pseudo spirituality would eventually defeat itself by producing a world where no inwardness of any type could long survive.

Another disaster, however, would be to reject any expression of faith in which we cannot see any immediate political relevance or any help in addressing the accumulated social grievances that so plainly need addressing now. Long-term "relevance" is not always easy to spot. Any religious movement, Christianity included, brings to a social crisis some genuinely relevant dimension only because its concerns are longer and larger than any one issue. Paradoxically, faith is politically relevant only because it comes to any given moment with a perspective that seems a little out of phase, even odd, to those with no such perspective. This out-of-phase quality gives faith its leverage, its critical perspective and its capacity for moral suasion. Praying on the courthouse steps and singing hymns at the draft board are politically powerful, and we should do them without embarrassment. I've done both. I once sat in a jail cell for a couple of days for carrying a cross at the head of a civil rights procession (we were "parading without a permit"), and more recently I was apprehended for handing out a peace prayer of St. Francis of Assisi on the grounds of the U.S. Air Force Academy in Colorado. But everyone should realize that the power of these gestures derives from the fact that they are not *just* political ploys. Their political efficacy comes from their appeal to something that goes beyond politics. It is that "something" that I think the new spiritual quest, with all its perversions and susceptibility to escapism, is seeking to uncover. I think the quest is a valid one and should be honored. A religious relevance bought at the price of interiority or transcendence soon loses both its religiosity and its relevance. It disintegrates into an impotent ideology. It is neither prayer nor politics but a transparent flimflam, and those against whom it is used know it.

The sickness of our time is not the movement toward interiority but the disappearance of it. The problem for me is not *whether* we should recover our waning sense of subjectivity and centeredness but *how?* I do not think the sensitivity movement, in the long run, can provide it. I agree with Dan Berrigan that we need a "new breed of gurus," a mutation of monk and militant; for most of the swamis we have, Eastern or Western, can only take us so far. This includes not only the encounter group prophets but people like Meher Baba, and the Maharishi Mahesh Yoga who introduced the idea of transcendental meditation to the West. It also includes Alan Watts, the most eloquent of the contemporary Western mystical writers. These spiritual masters are men of acute insight. They correctly see us as a people so locked into the jangle of outer signals that we cannot hear our inner voices. They know we feel inept in coping with the spiritual stirrings within us. The skills they teach us are indispensable. With their help we are learning both from the discoveries of psychology and from the storehouse of mystical wisdom how to hear our own pulse and breath, how to reclaim our impulses, and how to feel ourselves once more from within.

But at one point most of the new pietism fails us. Like its predecessors it underestimates the *extent* of the threat to the inner person and it fails to recognize its political sources and consequences. Take for example the new gurus' emphasis on wordless meditation. Their love for silence (or in the case of Alan Watts, for nonsense syllables) powerfully challenges the reign of chitchat, but they fail to notice the millions of people who are held in silence against their wills. They rarely comment on the fact that people with power can talk as much as they want while other people are forced to listen and obey. Some gurus even say that all words are illusory. What they don't see is that speech can be a means of self-defense. To break out of imposed silence and talk back to an oppressor, as even a bullied kid knows, is the first step toward dignity and resistance. Put in religious terms, those who distrust the word so much they want us to discard it seem never to have understood the significance of what I call "testimony." They have never learned that testimony is not just talk. It is the painful reclaiming of words from their bondage to selling and ruling and avoiding. It is the liberation of speech for its primal purpose: the creation of a human universe, one where persons can know others, be known by them, and know themselves.

Most of the group-process facilitators would agree with this critique of silent solitude. The whole group movement teaches that personal interiority cannot become actual without some supportive web of relationships. What some do not see, however, is that a world where greed reigns and people are set against one another by racial, sexual and hierarchical roles cannot provide such a web. Such a world twists this fragile net into distorting nooses. When the group adjourns, life is still choked instead of linked with the big world outside. Subjectivity can only emerge in a community of subjects, but we now inhabit deformed communities that produce deformed persons. We need a new web.

Saving souls inevitably entails politics. Interiority arises within us only as community emerges amidst us, and vice versa. Daniel Berrigan's choice of the title *The Dark Night of Resistance* to describe the spiritual basis of his non-violent struggle against war is remarkably apt. In one phrase it joins the two currents that now must flow together if we are to save our souls or preserve the planet. The "dark night" is the "religious" tradition of inwardness, spirituality and mystical discipline represented by St. John of the Cross in his *Dark Night of the Soul*. "Resistance" represents the "political" tradition of prophecy, dissent, opposition and just plain fighting back that human beings have turned to wherever tyranny reigns or rulers lose sight of the value of human life. There was a time when I believed that any politically "relevant" theology must eschew mysticism, turn from interiority, and base itself on something more ethically explicit. But the

Berrigans and many, many others have proved me wrong. The inwardness of mystical vision need not result in torpor; it can lead to struggle.

Periodic awakenings, religious resurgences and spiritual revivals seem endemic to American history. We traverse cycles of charismatic bubbling and institutional hardening, emotional intensity and phlegmatic tepidity, theologically motivated activism and peace-of-mind tranquillity. All the signs indicate that we are now entering into a new phase of religious awareness and searching. The encounter-sensitivity movement is but one wavelet in a large cultural tide. It is part of a movement in which the Jesus people constitute the orthodox wing, the mescalin trippers form another contingent, and the neo-Sufis, transcendental meditators and primal screamers fall somewhere in between. Where will it all lead?

In the past, periods of awakening in American religion have led to both dire and beneficial outcomes. The Second Great Awakening, for example, produced a plethora of reforming societies and fed the growing anti-slavery sentiment, at least in the North. However it also encouraged the early stirrings of American imperial fervor and whipped up enthusiasm for such questionable causes as prohibition. The politics of revivalism is not fully inherent in the revivalism itself, so the social expression of pietism can move in many different directions. The present Third Great Awakening is no exception. It could result in a massive defection from politics by millions of people who prefer the more manageable dimensions of the small group to the frustrating uncertainties of macrosystem issues. It could produce a totally internalized ethic which, like the worst of the old pietism, allows people to profit blissfully from institutionalized injustice as long as they are warm and open with the individuals they meet personally. Or it could generate a powerful social vision that will render thousands of people discontent with present constrictive, competitive institutions and spark large-scale change.

No one now knows which way the Third Great Awakening will develop. Part of the answer will depend on what happens in the larger social milieu in which it is placed. Part will come from the dynamics of the movement itself. Much more will depend on those who lead it and give it direction and definition. It is too early for either sweeping indictments or for sanguine celebration. But it is also important not to underestimate the import of the new religiosity, for weal or for woe, in the long run.

CHAPTER NINE

The Search for a New Church

Religious beliefs are always common to a determined group. . . .
They are not merely received individually by all the members of
this group; they are something belonging to the group, and they
make its unity. . . . A society whose members are united by the
fact that they think the same way in regard to the sacred world
and in relations with the profane world, and by the fact that
they translate these common ideas into common practices, is
what is called a Church. In all history we do not find a single
religion without a church.
—Emile Durkheim, *The Elementary Forms of Religious Life*

By the time you are grown up, the form of the Church will have
changed beyond recognition.
—Dietrich Bonhoeffer, *Letters and Papers from Prison*

THE RELIGIOUS revival which is under way all around us is already
searching for new corporate forms. The new faith is looking for
a new church. It has always been so. Man is an irreducibly social
animal. His religion, whatever its content, invariably inspires him
to look for other like-minded or like-spirited beings with whom
to celebrate his hopes and enact his rituals. Sensitivity-encounter
groups, experimental liturgies, communes, the rebirth of people's
religion—all these have one thread in common: They demonstrate the quest for new forms of collective interiority, the search
for a new church.

As this quest proceeds there are two blind alleys some of the
searchers have already stumbled into. The first is the widely
touted return to ethnicity. The second is the effort made by some

well-intentioned people to use the family as a substitute for what the church once provided. I hope these detours into ethnicity and familialism will not last long or eat up much more energy. Ultimately neither the family nor the ethnic group can possibly answer man's need for new forms of collective interiority.

The family will not do as a new church, mainly because we already load it with too many emotional expectations and because in its present form it perpetuates an obsolete form of male-over-female dominance. This makes it all the more unfortunate that conventional Christian churches today put such a continuous emphasis on the allegedly sacred quality of family life. Once a year at least, every local Protestant minister finds his mailbox brimming with multihued pamphlets from his denominational headquarters urging him to get moving with plans for Christian Family Week, culminating in Christian Family Sunday. I am sure Catholic priests and Jewish rabbis are deluged with similar kits and leaflets, for if there is one common creedal thread running through the popular piety of America it has to do with the "sacredness of the family." It is something most religious people either believe in or feel they should believe in, often despite all the evidence of experience and observation. So most churches go through the motions of celebrating and sanctifying family life annually, repressing for the moment all the doubts and suspicions, guilt and uneasiness they feel about it. Consequently Christian Family Sunday becomes for most people a festival of nostalgia and hypocrisy.

The charade becomes even more puzzling when we notice that what is being celebrated as "family" has almost nothing to do with the families pictured in the Bible. What we see on the covers of the church bulletins that week is almost always a contemporary "nuclear" family—a mother and father with their own children, usually two or three in number if it is a Protestant picture, five or six if it is Catholic. The old days when the "Catholic family of the year" had to line up a minimum of twelve offspring now seem to be passing. In any case, what is pictured is neither the "extended" family of three generations back, consisting of grandparents, aunts, uncles and cousins living in close proximity; nor is it the postnuclear family now emerging everywhere around us, those groups of individuals or couples who live together sharing home life and child rearing on a wider basis.

No wonder we feel queasy on Christian Family Sunday. We should. What we are really being asked to sacralize is not the "Christian family" at all, but one limited and very recent form of family, the late-industrial nuclear (or one might even say "residual") family of the mobile-technological society. And it is not a very successful form of family life at that. It is time we stopped talking about it as in any way "sacred," especially since it is always hard to criticize or change "sacred things." Like any other human institution the nuclear family is neither sacred nor eternal. It is one way, among many others, of organizing human life. Furthermore, it seems now to be one which has outlived most of the usefulness it ever had and is in need of remolding. Of course we should celebrate periodically the joy and pain of family life—just as we should celebrate friendship, collegiality and neighborhood as forms of human association. But let us not be misled into expecting the family to take the place the church once had. And let us not sacralize one form of family at the expense of other forms which, in our time, could be even more viable. What then *is* this "Christian Family" we toast?

Those who turn to sacred writ for help on this question are in for a surprise, especially if they are looking for some legitimation for the nuclear family. Not surprisingly, the Hebrew Scriptures know of nothing like a modern nuclear family. Nor are their stories of husband-and-wife or parent-child relations particularly exemplary, at least in terms of conventional "family" ethics. Abraham the ancient patriarch, father of many nations, is not above selling his own wife, Sarah, to the Pharaoh's harem. Isaac and Jacob are unabashed polygamists. The less said about King David the better. With a thousand wives, Solomon was hardly a paragon of monogamous intimacy. Though it could be argued that the stories of Bathsheba and of Solomon's harem are included in the Bible more to warn than to inspire, there is not much else there to support the present attempt to sacralize the family either. When the Hebrew Scriptures do discuss what we would call "family," they use a term better translated as "household." It includes wives (*nota bene* the plural), concubines, slaves, off-springs of all the preceding, relatives, and various dinner guests who just stayed on. Not the kind of family generally pictured on the cover of a monthly church magazine.

But if all this describes the actual state of affairs, sorry or otherwise, in the olden days of the patriarchs and prophets, surely, it will be argued, they were all engaged in human deviations, understandable but regrettable, from a clear standard? Wrong again. The Ten Commandments not only carry no brief whatever for the monogamous ideal, they also provide little comfort for those who want to find in them any support for women's liberation. There are actually two versions of the Ten Commandments in the Bible. The oldest, in Exodus, forbids the coveting of a neighbor's house, or wife or manservant or maidservant or ox or ass or anything else, *in that order*. By the time of the "deuteronomic" version of the Decalogue several centuries later, the wives had somehow made it to the top of the list of chattels, followed by houses, fields, servants and so forth. All along, incidentally, the Hebrew men seem to have had the right to divorce their wives for almost any reason. They were only required to prepare a bill of divorcement, which most women were probably unable to read anyway. Women had no right to a divorce, but if caught in adultery could be stoned. Most scholars feel this rarely happened in fact, but only in the more recent history of Judaism did the Talmud supply any grounds whatever for a woman's divorcing her husband, and then it was only one ground—if he contracted a loathsome disease.

I am not here criticizing what Christians somewhat condescendingly call "the Old Testament" for not providing a model of family life, women's rights and sexual morality for the late twentieth century. The New Testament does not provide much of an ideal of family life either. If anything it is "anti-familial." Despite conjectural Sunday school paintings of the lad Jesus helping his father amid planes and saws, we actually know very little about the family life of Mary and Joseph except that it began under what Joseph considered to be highly suspicious circumstances. Jesus himself never married, and furthermore every time he actually says anything about his family it sounds curt or negative. His parents, for example, in the single incident the Bible does record about his boyhood, did not understand why he stayed behind in Jerusalem at twelve to converse with the elders in the temple. When they came to retrieve him Jesus spoke to them testily and with a severity even few modern parents would accept from a preteenager. St. Mark in his Gospel reports later that Jesus' family thought he was crazy. Well they might have. In a society which did attach a certain sacral significance to kinship, Jesus was audacious enough to say that only those who would leave behind "father and mother and son and daughter" could follow him. When someone asked him about his own brothers and sisters, he brushed the question aside with the insistence that his brothers and sisters were those who did the will of God. He assigned no special place to kith and kin.

But Jesus was no sworn enemy of the family either. His statements about it, though they sound negative, were not intended to abolish it. Rather, Jesus wanted people to see that a new form of human community was appearing in history and that it went far beyond the ties of blood and kinship. With Jesus, family bonds were relativized. Water became thicker than blood. People could become "members one of another" in communities that were not defined by organic ties. The one time the word "family" appears in the New Testament in a positive sense is in the Epistle to the Ephesians, written fifty years after Jesus' death. In that passage, "family" does not refer to a nuclear family or even to an extended family but to "the whole family of heaven and earth."

It is callous and insensitive, as well as theologically wrong, for the churches to use the notion of the "Christian family" as a sanctification of the nuclear family. Churches do include married couples with children, but they also include the non-married, formerly married, twice married, not yet married, and those with no intention of getting married. They include people living together, living apart, living alone, and people living in couples, communes, collectives, cooperatives and clusters. The churches encompass people whose children are gone, or yet to come, as well as those whose progeny are still very much present. They include bachelors and divorcees and those women for whom our male-dominated culture has no positive equivalent of the word "bachelor," but whom I refuse to call "spinsters," "old maids," "maiden ladies" or "unclaimed treasures." The church also includes children without parents, parents without children, parents without partners, and partners without children.

Amidst this heterogeneous diversity of living styles, to elevate one particular form of family life as "*The* Christian Family" is narrow and idolatrous. Even worse, it allows Christianity to be misused by the still powerful forces of male superiority which defend the nuclear-bourgeois family because it keeps women in their place, and suspect any questioning of "the family" as a women's liberationist plot.

The Bible does not provide a model for family life. Nor does it supply many images of truly emancipated women, though there are a few. Rather, the importance of biblical faith for the freeing of women from the cultural and religious images by which they have been held for so long in bondage lies elsewhere. It lies in the inclusive vision of biblical religion which sees God's ultimate purpose as the liberation and maturation of all human beings, and of all creation, to their full potential in a cosmic feast of love and joy. Thus the current thrusts toward liberation—of colonialized peoples, blacks, children, women and even of nature from its thralldom to man's greed—can be interpreted as the groanings and reachings out of this universal process. Men and women of faith sing out for these movements, struggle within them, and discern in their anger and aspiration the luminous signs of a coming new era.

No society can be a human one, or even encourage the maturation of the untapped universes of human potential, so long as institutions remain in which one person or group dominates,

manipulates or subordinates another. Sadly, no socialist revolution has succeeded in abolishing the cultural domination of
women by men. Nor has any capitalist society. My hope is nailed
to a transformation which goes beyond either, which frees people
not only from the debilitating quest for property and power but
also unleashes them from their need to possess and control other
people. Therefore, finding some economic system other than
capitalism—with its built-in emphasis on competition and consumption—is a necessary but not sufficient condition for human
liberation.

Man's domination of women is the oldest and most persistent
and may be the most basic form of seignioralty. It suffuses all
societies with the bacillus of over-under hegemony and therefore
fuels both racial tyrannies and the corporate caliphates that
despoil the peoples of the Third World. Furthermore, this spurious hegemony has for ages been sanctified by Christianity in
theology, liturgy and polity. God and Jesus Christ are both
depicted as men; even the Holy Spirit is referred to as "He."
Many churches, and most particularly the Episcopal and Roman
Catholic churches, still exclude women from the full exercise of
priesthood and ministry. Churches have been the accomplices of
other powers in holding women down. It does not surprise me
that the insignia under which oppressed Indians and *campesinos*
have gathered time and again in the revolutionary history of
Mexico has been that of a woman, Our Lady of Guadalupe.

As in every liberation movement since the dawn of history, the
freeing of women must and will be principally the work of
women. No oppressor ever willingly hands over his power (or
what he *thinks* is power) to his restive vassal. What role then can
men play in female liberation? We can first of all be honest about
how much it scares us. This is the first step in taking it seriously.
Only then can we allow ourselves to fantasize on how marvelous
it would be for all of us if not only were women liberated but if
the female potential within *men* were allowed to flower instead
of being rooted out at age two and a half. Then we can at least
not retard female liberation, not minimize it, not try to co-opt it,

not divide it (by secretly enjoying the way some women criticize it or the disputes between gays and straights). And we can avoid ridiculing it. Sometimes I think man's major weapon in keeping the cultural chastity belt on women has been ridicule. But it is not funny any more. For women it never was.

We are in the midst of a women's liberation movement now partly because the idea of human freedom is one whose hour has come. The idea has been around for a long time. Although culpable in practice, Christianity did make a crucial contribution to the ideology of liberation. This is important, and those who think Christianity is solely to blame for male chauvinism should take a quick look at the status of women in Islam, Hinduism and even in Judaism. Christianity's guilt seems more striking, and may in fact be, precisely because of the absurd contradiction between theology and practice. In women's liberation a not-so-new idea has now come to that irrepressible moment when it will no longer remain merely an idea. The contradictions between idea and practice are so palpable that no one can seriously pretend otherwise. Of course there will be opposition, stronger and more tenacious, I believe, than most women foresee, mainly because the monstrous masculine regiment has not yet really taken female liberation seriously. When it does, the opposition will surely stiffen.

The idea that a woman should be a "full-time wife and mother" is a very recent one. It may be a product of the reduced labor supply needed by late capitalism's high technology and the consequent need to curtail the size of the labor force. Women now supply reserve labor. So the TV housewife, depicted by the media barons as idiotically agog over whiter whites and crisper pie crust, can be transmuted into Rosie the Riveter with a flick of the corporate wrist. Later she can be shipped back to the ironing board and won't even appear in the unemployment statistics. This is the way it worked, until recently. Now the flesh-splitting contradictions of this replaceable coolie's role no longer escape the wrath of women. Many of them feel that the job of full-time diaper changer and pot scraper is a shill, and will no longer be pushed on and off the work force like colored beads on a play-pen. The most pathetic outcome of all this would be the sight of blacks, Chicanos, women and poor whites clawing one another for the limited number of job slots in the Big Machine we call the economy. The crisis energized by the anger of these groups cannot be accommodated within our present economic myth of accelerated acquisitiveness, instant obsolescence and resource squandering—all in the interest of making profits. A women's liberation movement that can be brought off *within* the limits of acquisitive society will be a defeated movement, even if it doesn't realize it. Whose heart really beats faster at the idea of living in a world of female four-star generals and bank presidents?

The nuclear family supplies today the key link in the transmission of the blight of male superiority from generation to generation. Like the "full-time wife and mother," this mangled torso of what the word "family" used to signify is also a newcomer on the scene. Four generations ago it was a rarity. Today mobility has ripped us away from our extended families, economics has reduced the size of our broods, and home architecture has incarcerated us in separate cells. Of course, male chauvinism was present long before the nuclear family developed. Women have also been repressed by men in seraglios, harems and polygamous households. Male domination might well reappear in another guise after the present nuclear family disappears. Consequently the mere transformation of our present reduced form of family life into something more flexible and equalitarian will not by itself free women or anyone else. It is another necessary but not sufficient step in human liberation.

We need something beyond the nuclear family, but until such alternatives begin to emerge I think it would be wasteful and reckless to try to destroy what we have. The nuclear family, for all its weaknesses, remains one of the few institutions people rely on to cushion them from the slings and arrows of the big outside world. They will leave it behind only when some alternative form of family life becomes available. Therefore, we should be. inventing these alternatives. Merely uprooting the nuclear family could even cause the atomization of the culture to increase. We need new familial forms as much as we need new cities and new patterns of relationships between people and land. Exploding the nuclear family will not by itself emancipate women. Making it into a new church is asking for disaster. But to try to free ourselves from sexism inside the nuclear family is to transform a needed revolution in psychic relationships into one more set of New Year's resolutions. And you know what happens to them.

What replaces the nuclear family is not necessarily the commune. That may be the answer for some people. But for many others an intermediate structure is needed, one that preserves some of the values we have found in monogamous marriage and even in nuclear families, with some of the liberation that can only come from a different domiciliary style. Margaret Mead has shrewdly suggested that for many of us the "cluster family" is the next reasonable step. A cluster is a group of families who live close enough together spatially to allow for unplanned and spontaneous meetings, and who begin sharing such elementary things as food buying, child care, cooking, and equipment ownership. What single family requires the full possession of a power saw or a lawn mower or a slide projector? The participants would then edge slowly toward the enlargement of the areas in which they share, at a pace that allows for everyone to move without panic from one life style to another. A setting like this would go a long way to freeing men to share domestic tasks and women to assume a more active role in penetrating and altering society. Such an arrangement would also benefit those of us for whom monogamy, however modified, seems to meet our needs best. We could eat our cake and have a little of it too. (More theologically expressed, we could taste the fruits of the new era of the Kingdom while still struggling "here below" in the old.)

I do not mean this to suggest that everyone must stick with monogamy forever. We are now learning from African Christians that monogamy is not an absolute requirement in Christian life. The Africans remind us that neither the Bible nor Christian history can be read to endow monogamy with exclusive or eter-

nal validity. In the history of biblical religion we have had patri-
archy, concubinage, celibacy, group marriage, and serial
monogamy. We should not invest monogamy with the sacred
significance of being the only legitimate Christian or human form
of familial structure. Even St. Paul, not an avid proponent of
marriage in any case, prescribed monogamy only for certain
officers within the church, not for everyone. The place of
monogamy is a question that will come up more frequently now
that women's liberation is upon us. I think I could defend it as
preferable to other forms, even theologically. But I would never
try to pretend it is the *only* acceptable style of Christian marriage.

Men can expect, eventually, to be "liberated" in some important ways by "women's" liberation. It could unlock the repressed
and throttled "female" potential in all of us. That will happen
when we no longer associate hammers with men and needles with
women, when I can be just as "emotional" as I want to be and
women can be just as "rational." I disagree with the argument
advanced by some women that there are *no* biological differences
between men and women, that *all* differences are cultural accre-
tions. I think personally that women would be wrong to base
their struggle for liberation on a denial of differences. But that
decision is not mine, and I must sadly agree that men have twisted
healthy differences between the sexes into the shackles of bondage. Example: Maybe men *are* more instrumental and less intuitive. I don't know. But to create a society in which instrumental-
ism is rewarded and intuition is punished, and then to deprive
women of equal participation on that basis is an obvious fraud.
Let us not try to eradicate whatever *other* differences there turn
out to be between male and female human beings. That would
amount to what the Nazis called *Gleichschaltung*. Rather let us
envision a new city where our differences delight us and in their
depths we find our common humanity.

If the family is not the answer to our quest for a new form of
collective interiority, a return to *ethnicity* is not the answer
either. Like the family, ethnicity served, and still serves, a valid
human purpose. Ethnic groups, as we have them in America, are

based on shared language and customs, a common ancestral home-land and an experience of migration or displacement. If the homeland happened to have a predominating national religion, as do Italy and Ireland, then religion becomes a key element in ethnicity. But the religious ingredient does not play much of a role in those ethnic groups whose homelands had a mixed reli-gious cast. For this reason neither Germans nor Czechs nor Lebanese, for example, make much of the religious dimension in their ethnicity.

In American history ethnic grouping was an inspired and inventive response on the part of immigrant peoples not just to the dominant Anglo-Saxon mores of the new land but also to the bewildering plethora of other immigrant groups. It enabled the embattled Ellis Island arrivals to cherish the beliefs and practices they had brought with them from the old country while they were getting a foothold in the new one. It cushioned the cruel transition.

But as urban historians are quick to point out, ethnic enclaves were never merely transplanted Italian or Irish villages. New York's Little Italy was not a Sicilian piazza. For one thing, as Richard Sennett has shown in his books on American cities, individuals from one ethnic group had to interact constantly with those from other groups. Despite a certain degree of ghettoizing, the newcomers all shared the cheapest housing and the poorest streets. They sold things to one another, negotiated about the politics of their block, and argued with one another in unions and workers' circles. The lives they lived were never bounded by their own group. Little Italy was not Italy, mainly because it was crawling with Jewish merchants, Irish policemen and Slavic immigrants bidding for the jobs and rooms the Italians were vacating. It was a potpourri where the *paisanos* relied on their kinsmen for essential support but lived cheek by jowl with jumbled multitudes whose dress, language and religion were dramatically different from anything they had met back in Tuscany or Umbria.

The experience of America was, for the immigrants, an encounter both with Yankee predominance and with intense national diversity. In that encounter, always a dangerous one for anyone, the ethnic groups pulled together with those sharing roots in the old land, which enabled them to survive both physically and psychologically. But the question we are faced with today is a different one. Instead of running the danger of being torn to pieces by a chaotic immigrant city or pressed into an Anglo-Saxon mold, the person in today's America faces the relentless leveling down by a society seemingly bent on erasing all traces of diversity, whether it be regional, ethnic, sexual, religious or just idiosyncratic. Instead of physical survival and adaptation to a new environment, the need is for authentic group and personal identity. Our society is in quest of satisfying contemporary forms of interiority and for the politics and institutions that will make them possible. Can ethnic belonging provide it?

I doubt it, at least for most people. Ethnic groups drew not only on a fund of national memories and linguistic subtleties but also on commonly shared recollections of a harrowing trek. They served their purpose well, and will continue to do so for the generations immediately subsequent to the passing over. But what we now need are analogous forms of collective interiority that can do for us, in the troubled transitions we must make, what ethnicity did for some of our forebears. Being Italian or Polish today in Newark or Gary is surely not what it was in Naples or Lodz or what it was on the Lower East Side in 1890. Especially if your mother was Scottish and you're married to a WASP. Although ethnicity does seem to persist longer than one might expect in some groups, we cannot assume that the reason it survives is that great numbers of people find in ethnic groups a satisfying identity and a sense of collective interiority. People may also remain ethnic because they have nothing else to turn to. I doubt that all traces of ethnicity will disappear from America for many years to come. I hope not, for ethnicity adds diversity and gusto at a time when both are in decline. But as a basis for genuine collective interiority, I seriously doubt if it will work except for a minority of people. That leaves the rest of us.

My scenario for the future of America, tilted admittedly by my hopes, envisions a pluralistic commonwealth of communities that will include ethnic groups and other groups as well. Musicians, disciples of the Hare Krishna movement, divorcees, elderly citizens, athletes, sky divers, homosexuals, and people organizing grocery-buying co-ops come together now across ethnic lines. They often find in these groups a sense of human solidarity that is deeper than ethnicity. So it should be. Christianity itself began as a movement in which Jews, Greeks, barbarians and Scythians enjoyed equality and fraternity.

Cultural diversity today is not just a cosmetic need. We are becoming aware that in order to survive as a species humankind must avoid a single locked-in and highly interdependent world economy. It would be just too risky ecologically. The same survival insurance holds for culture. We need cultural heterogeneity not just for its own sake but to equip us to face unforeseen crises in the future. Yet at every level today we see massive leveling, bleaching and homogenizing influences at work. So we do need ethnic diversity; but it is only one expression of particularity and must not be allowed to overshadow other lively forms of small-scale human community.

We are hearing today in America a lot about the persistence of ethnicity and even about a rebirth of ethnic self-consciousness. If this is happening, it is surely a welcome change from all the "melting pot" propaganda we were fed not too long ago. I think the significance of this ethnic revival has often been overstated, both by its defenders and by its critics. The new ethnicity cannot fulfill its apologists' hope to restore a wavering identity to confused people. But I also doubt that it will loose the monsters of xenophobic racism and narrow clannishness its detractors fear. All the talk about the "ethnic votes" Edmund Muskie would draw seems to have been vastly exaggerated. He was even defeated in Polish districts of Milwaukee by candidates with Anglo-

Saxon names. This would have been unthinkable in the old days of "ethnic politics" when voters automatically checked only those candidates whose surnames clearly indicated they were "one of ours." But no matter what happens between various political candidates, the "new ethnicity" will neither provide the identity nor relapse into the purblind loyalties of the old.

The difference is that if ethnic self-consciousness does come back, it will be to a culture which is not only already thoroughly pluralistic but to a society where that pluralism is part of the identity of most individuals. The great difference between today's ethnicity and that of the generations who invented it is this: It is no longer the case that my original identity comes from my ethnic group, and *then* I interact with all those others. The reverse is true. My identity *emerges* in a pluralistic world, albeit one threatened by new forms of uniformity. Dissatisfied with the insipidity of the superculture's signals or bewildered about who I am, I look elsewhere, perhaps to an ethnic group. People turn to ethnicity now as *one* form of community *among others* that can give them a sense of history and tradition. For fewer and fewer people does ethnicity confer a primary, unreflective identity. That in itself is a massive and, for me, welcome change. It means that a person can now choose, within limits, which community will provide him with his primary point of reference. If I choose to know myself and to be known as Polish, Jewish, German or something else, I can. With blacks, of course, the element of choice is reduced, though not eliminated. In one way you cannot choose *not* to be black, but you can decide how "black" to be. One hesitates, for example, here in Massachusetts, to refer to Senator Edward Brooke as "black." I doubt if the black community is his primary one.

There is another difference. In addition to my choosing *whether* to be ethnic today, I also decide what *relative importance* that loyalty has to other loyalties. This dilution of ethnic identity can be seen in what some people still call "mixed marriages." They occur all the time, across religious, ethnic, class and racial lines. There is no evidence that they are diminishing in frequency. In fact, between Catholic and Protestant ethnic groups the most recent census shows them to be increasing. There are probably even more such couplings than the statistics indicate, since someone who leaves a church to marry is usually not counted. I hope more men and women marry across such boundaries. Such weddings are our clearest evidence that more and more people now make important decisions on a personal basis rather than following a script composed by custom. Ethnicity today can never be more than one loyalty among others.

I have no doubt that my skepticism about ethnicity comes in good measure from my own life history. Although half my forebears were Welsh, and therefore I am technically not an Anglo-Saxon, most writers on ethnicity would still probably classify me as a "WASP." And since even the most avid ethnophiles do not like *that* ethnic group, I tend to be on my guard immediately. But, like everyone else, I do have an "ethnic" quality, and a pretty interesting one at that. My earliest ancestors on my father's side were Quakers who came to Pennsylvania from Wales in the early 1700s to escape religious persecution. Remembering the consonant-clotted village names in the old country, they called the settlements they found Narberth, Bryn Mawr, Bryn Athyn, Duffryn Mawr and Llanerch. My own home town, Malvern, is named for a chain of hills near the border of Wales. The high school I attended was called Tredyffrin-Easttown. On my mother's side my ancestors were Scottish and English immigrant peasants who intermarried with German pietist refugees from military conscription. I feel a profound continuity with this "ethnic" tradition, so I sometimes smile about the alleged "uptightness" and incapacity for emotional feeling among Anglo-Saxons, especially when I hear the singing of Janis Joplin, James Taylor, the Beatles or Elvis Presley. And I wonder what people can mean by our notorious northern European sexual frigidity and distrust of the flesh when I compare the freewheeling sexual mores of Sweden and Denmark with those of Spain and Italy. My own ethnic tradition includes a lot of things other people are now starting to appreciate, like a deep suspicion of the military, bagpipes screaming "Amazing Grace," a fierce belief in simplicity and lack of pretense in religion and elsewhere, a respect for genuine personal centeredness, and much more. But all those family jewels are not enough to live on today. My "ethnic" heritage has helped make me what I am. But I view it as investment capital, not as gold bullion or heirlooms. I see it as an important resource in helping to create new forms of interiority. Besides, my ethnic heritage is already mixed. It includes, besides all that I have listed, my own experience of being American and, even more, of being an "earthman." To choose among ingredients now would constitute an impoverishment.

This is a crucial point for me. I will not write off Zen or the Taj Mahal or druidic worship or the Koran as "theirs." They are mine too. My ancestors have been mostly Protestants, but that does not have to delimit me. I will not let the Catholics keep St. Theresa or the Unitarians have Michael Servetus or the Jews have Martin Buber or the Hindus have Lord Krishna all for themselves. I live and work in a miscellaneous pandemonium of Marinis, Kennedys, Stefanskys, Bronsteins, Eichfelds, Arujos, Fosters, and Chos. Everything I enjoy in life depends on pluralism, variety and crossbreeding. Within a span of weeks I have sensed the presence of the holy at an Apollo temple in Delphi, a Toltec pyramid in Xochicalco, and a Moslem mosque on the island of Rhodes. What would an anthropologist from Mars make of our family's rituals and the cultic objects in our house? We celebrate a Seder at Passover. We often attend Catholic Masses, never missing on Christmas Eve. A straw Mexican Indian crucifix blesses our living room, and a Jewish *mazuzah* enclosing a text from the Torah stands watch at our doorway. A serene Buddha gazes down from just over the inside windowsill of our front room. Nearby stands Ganesha, the elephant god, who is the Hindu patron of sagacity and worldly wisdom.

I doubt very much that some newly refurbished ethnic group —for me I suppose it would be Anglo-Saxon Protestant—could furnish the community of collective interiority I need. I am neither an agnostic nor a "true believer," but one whose parish is the world, not just the present world but many past ones as well. Sometimes I suspect I may have the theologian's equivalent of the "medical student's disease" (suffering the symptoms of every sickness in the book). There is a part of me that says yes to some elements of every religion I learn about. But I see this as a sign of health, not of sickness. Likewise I have no interest in retreating from the admittedly incomplete and imperfect ethnic and racial heterogeneity of urban America to some new ethnic regrouping. Ethnicity may be the answer for some people but not for many, and not for me.

We live during a historical period in which a new religious sensibility is struggling to be born. It is far too easy to criticize this barely emergent new expression of the spirit, because at this stage it seems diffuse, vague or eclectic. My house and my life are marked by the symbols of so many different historic faiths because whatever is coming, in the world and in me, must in some way include what has gone before. Those who ridicule "eclecticism" as superficial or stupid express their own bias. The most "successful" religions in history have all been syncretistic. The difference is that previously the fusing of old traditions occurred at a civilizational level. Today we can do it on a much smaller scale.

As men and women of faith in the present century, marked as it is by planet-wide communications and the uncovering of previously unknown civilizations of the past, we have available to our spirits rich veins of religious wealth hardly imagined before. The symbolic treasures of the full sweep of human history are available to us—everything from the oldest cave drawing to the newest image of utopian hope. They are available, furthermore, not just to be catalogued and observed but to be shared and used. But how do we go about it? For myself, I need a company of confreres that is much smaller than humankind with whom to quarry and refine the deposits. But no merely ethnic or sexual or racial group will do. I need a community that has not yet quite emerged, a church that has not been founded, a collective interiority still in the making. But what does all this mean for the churches we already have today?

A couple years ago I was asked by *Commonweal*, a Catholic weekly magazine, to answer the question "If you could make one single change in the Church today, what would it be?" It is an intriguing thought to play with, and the magazine had asked several contributors to respond to it. Most mentioned changes in liturgy, social action, the ordination of women, and the need for theological renewal. I found myself dreaming about a church that would be in constant touch with the poor because it would have no wealth of its own, and a church that would open itself to the songs and rites of many ages and cultures, a church that would encourage cultural and theological diversity by a dramatic gesture of decentralization. To make my point more tellingly I wrote my answer in the form of a fictional news release about a new encyclical. Here it is:

> *Rome and Geneva, Oct. 5, 1975, UPI.* In a historic joint encyclical issued today by both the Vatican and the World Council of Churches, both religious bodies announced that they were beginning "forthwith" to divest themselves of all earthly possessions. The unprecedented pastoral letter, the first ever issued by both groups at once, was known in Rome as *Lucrum Salax*, after the first two words in its Latin text, "dirty money." In Geneva the encyclical, recently adopted by a special session of the Central Committee of the World Council of Churches, appeared in French, German, English, Russian and Swahili. The document is signed, shattering another precedent, not only by Pope Paul VI and several other members of the WCC's Central Committee, it also bears the signatures of hundreds of laymen from various parts of the world, including Juan Gonzales, a parishioner of San Martín de Porres, a small Catholic church in Bolivia, and by Franklin P. Jones, a sharecropper and a deacon in the Mount Pisgah A.M.E. Zion Church of Meridian, Mississippi. The statement was released today, it was explained, because October fifth

is the Feast of St. Francis of Assisi who, it was pointed out by Vatican and WCC theologians, actually did obey the command of Jesus to sell all his wordly goods and follow him.

Lucrum Salax states unequivocally that all branches of the Church now in communion with Rome, and all member churches of the WCC, must now begin to sell or give away their property, buildings, investments and jewelry or risk excommunication. When queried by reporters if this was an infallible pronouncement, Paul VI raised his shoulders and palms in his characteristic gesture of puzzlement and said, "We don't really know ourselves what it means for us to be infallible, but if we ever were, this is it." The six presidents of the WCC said in their statement that this "new program emphasis" represented a consensus of the member churches, arrived at in debate at synods, diocesan conferences, and presbyteries over the past two years. When pressed, however, the WCC spokesman was hard put to explain how this movement had spread in the churches and, smiling with some obvious embarrassment, said that it "might just be something inspired by the Holy Spirit." A theologian from Notre Dame explained to reporters that the "Holy Spirit" is the seldom-mentioned Third Person of the traditional Christian Trinity, the one that "bloweth where it listeth."

A short explanatory text accompanied *Lucrum Salax*. It states that beginning within the next few weeks all church-owned chapels, convents, retreat centers, bingo halls, basilicas, cathedrals, shrines, rectories and schools would be turned over to local community corporations. Where such local community corporations do not exist, it was thought that the possibility of receiving church properties might stimulate their creation. It was strongly emphasized both in Rome and Geneva that no church properties would be given to state, federal or municipal authorities. The property will be given in every possible case to local indigenous organizations in an effort, interpreters explained, to strengthen the position of powerless and voiceless groups in the world. All stock portfolios will be dissolved. Retirement funds will be returned to church employees to give away if they desire or to reinvest in annuity plans of their own choosing. The monies accumulated by the investment of these funds will be given to groups representing poor, minority and other oppressed people. St. Peter's Cathedral in Rome will become a "palace of celebration," with an agreement *in perpetuo* that it will always be available for Masses, papal coronations, funerals and ecumenical councils. Monasteries will become retreat and conference centers. Vatican City will retain its independence but will become a sanctuary for political refugees, military deserters and other expellees. Some of the Vatican's buildings will be used for a Free University of the World.

It was clear that the ecclesiastical divestment program, or "the St. Francis bit" as it was being dubbed, would have enormous implications for the churches. Most clergy would now work, at least part time, in secular pursuits. Bishops and vestries would have no real estate problems to discuss. Church buildings would be used for community purposes throughout the week. Parochial schools would become community schools, under the control of neighborhood boards, an alternative to the so-called "public school" system. Smiling delightedly as he raised his fist in a salute, a black priest from Harlem said the whole thing looked to him like "All religion to the people!"

In the Rome stock market, speculation was rife as investors waited for thousands of shares of Alitalia and other Vatican holdings to hit the counter. The Reverend Carl McIntyre, longtime opponent of the World Council, denounced the statement as a "satanic and modernist plot to undermine property," and suggested that Communist-influenced persons in the WCC and Vatican had engineered the scheme. Meanwhile in Los Angeles James (Cardinal) McIntyre came out of retirement, entered the archdiocesan chancery office and personally attached a lock to the safe where the deeds and stocks of the archdiocese are stored. He then left to celebrate a Mass at St. Basil's in honor of St. Francis.

It is not probable that this release or anything like it will appear in 1975 or in any other year. In the meantime we are left with the question of what kinds of religious communities we need and whether there is any chance that the churches we now have could ever provide them.

After pondering this question for many years I have come to the conclusion that it is just not a very helpful way to think about the issue. No matter what our present churches do or do not do, the present quest for new forms of collective interiority will inevitably produce new kinds of religious and political communities. As these new forms emerge, they will replace or transmute our existing ones just as any new form of life both uses and discards elements of what was there before. Therefore it is simply a waste of time to ask whether or how our existing religious (or political) forms can be altered or reformed, or whether they can provide the wineskins for the new wine. Instead, we should be trying to discern the lineaments of emerging new communities and discovering what shapes our new consciousness will require. After that we can ask what, if anything, our existing forms of polity can contribute to the emergence of the new. What will the new communities be like?

We can start by saying what they will *not* be like. They will not, I think, be communities composed of people of the same racial, sexual or "ethnic" coloration, although these groupings do give many people a sense of community today. Nor will they be national sovereign states or organized religious denominations, two of the main forms of polity that people "belong to" now. Positively, the new communities will probably be ones in which the distinction between "civil" polity and "religious" polity begins to fade. This blending of the two realms was always the case in premodern societies and is reappearing again in intentional communities and communes. It can be very dangerous, as it is when a whole nation sees itself as a religious entity with a mission to inflict on others. But if the communities are small enough and diverse enough, the civilization they produce could be an enormously rich one.

When I say that neither national states and denominations on the one hand nor racial or sexual minorities on the other will provide the communities/churches of the future, I do not deny that the former were once valuable forms and that the latter still are today. I am talking about the next stage. Religious groupings, for example, did once help people from different nations to dejingoize their national self-consciousness because they were members of a larger community of faith: "Let's put aside our national differences, we're all Christians here." Likewise national states once helped people from different religious communities to defanaticize themselves, to find an identity that united them on a different basis: "Let's put aside our religious differences, after all we're all Americans." So denominations and nations helped relativize each other. In that way they once served an invaluable purpose.

The process continues. Today we sometimes hear that people should put aside national and religious differences and unite around the fact that they are black or young or female. There are many who are very critical of this new sorting process and see grave dangers in it. Erik Erikson calls all such groups "pseudo-species" and deplores them as a plague. But part of this new group consciousness springs from the undeniable fact of oppression—against women or blacks or other groups—and for this reason a sense of corporate identification is a survival strategy. The struggle that ensues will undoubtedly produce for those who engage in it some of the collective interiority everyone needs. But it can provide their "church" only in the short run. In the long run we cannot count on it any more than we can on ethnicity or the family. The people who expected to win some sense of selfhood from their struggle in groups have already run into snags. Even before they achieve justice, the strugglers begin to see that the longed-for collective interiority still somehow eludes them. They find that, however crucial it is to be consciously black or young or female or all three, they still have other loyalties than those tying them to these groups. Though for some this is a conflict and a vexing personal trauma, my point is that such a realization can also be a liberation. Through it one learns that "no one owns my soul." The self-conscious black woman in America today is in a particularly advantageous position to see this. Her bond with other women who are white sometimes complicates her ties to black men, and vice versa. At first she may experience this as a conflict, but then she begins to see that neither of these communities of sex or color can lay a *total* claim on her. She achieves a measure of personal distance from both without losing her involvement in either. It is at this moment of awareness that the deeper question appears: Where does any person look for collective interiority today?

There is no answer to this question which is not fraught with loneliness and peril, with the fear of freedom and the possibility of liberation. But what makes the black woman's question significant for all of us is that in one degree or another this same awareness is now emerging for the first time in the whole human species: No one owns my soul, but I want to belong somewhere. Paradoxically, as more groups emerge to claim my loyalty— groups based on color, sex, language, age, religion, or anything else—the less power any one of them has actually to give me a full identity or claim my total loyalty. This is the irony of the age of racial caucuses and the new ethnicity. The more of them we have, the less inclusive any one of them can be.

The form human community takes in the future will *not* be defined by age, sex, color or ethnicity. Those are transitional forms of community springing from situations of oppression. They are forms the struggle for liberation takes, not the form of the liberated community itself. This does not mean, however, that in whatever comes next all these differences will be "transcended." Nor does it suggest that communities will be mere conglomerates of colorless ciphers. On the contrary they will be constituted by people who feel even more deeply than we do today the distinction of having brown skin or speaking Italian or being female (or male). But they will be made up of people whose probes of particularity have led them to hunger for communities where, through ritual, play and dramatic enactment, they can learn actually to *become* one another, to learn one another's histories, to feel one another's wounds from within, to taste one another's joys. They will look for communities in which particularity will be saved not by hoarding it but by sharing it. They will search for places where celebration and suffering are not sundered, where ancient and modern symbols quicken each other, where sinners, saints and skeptics co-inhabit and absorb one another's legends and heroes, sniff one another's cuisines, worship one another's gods—all without losing the poignancy of the peculiar.

This may sound utopian, but I suspect it already goes on in some religious ceremonies I have witnessed. Among black Afro-Brazilians the Umbanda and Condomblé rituals give people a chance to become infused by the personalities of a wide variety of spirits, to feel different roles from inside, to try out new identities, to walk and grimace and talk, temporarily, like other people. Also utopianism is sometimes the only valid realism. Humankind has been surprised before by the realization in fact of what was daydream only very recently. Our technological fantasies become facts overnight. Why not our spiritual fantasies? Can we really live another people's history? I think we can. Those who have been touched by great rituals know it. One purpose of myth and ritual is to enable one to *experience*, not just to *hear about*, the history of someone else. The purpose of Passover, to take one obvious example, is to make every Jew feel as though he or she were actually present on that terrible night when the unleavened bread was baked, the angel of death passed over the bloodied lintels, and the slaves escaped the Pharaoh's chariots.

> And thou shalt declare unto thy son on that day, saying, This is done because of that, which the Lord did for us when we came forth from Egypt. It was *not our ancestors only* that the Most Holy, blessed be He, redeemed from Egypt, but *us also* did He redeem with them, as it is said. And He brought *us* from thence, that He might bring *us* to the land which He swore to give unto our fathers.

The logical question is, if a ten-year-old kid from Nyack can make this ancient history his or hers, why can't anyone? If the answer is that only one people's history can possibly be mine, I ask why? Admittedly few seventeenth-century Christians could make both Luther *and* Loyola part of their own history, but many do today. Why should this capacity for enlarging what constitutes *my* history or the history of *our* people become inflexibly fixed now?

Even the sex barriers are not all that immutable. Carl Jung tells us we are all both male and female deep down. We know we each have the residual organs and the repressed feelings of the other sex. If we look closely at the rituals of so-called "primitive" peoples we can discover the various ways they played out different sex roles at stated times—reversing costumes, men cutting miniature vaginas into their bodies, fathers ritually giving birth to children. And we still do it. Everyone knows that on stunt night at camp it is the most "masculine" men and boys who most love to dance onto the stage with the biggest grapefruits under their T-shirts and the shortest skirts revealing their hairy legs. Religious ritual at its best does not simply seal us into past categories, it enables us to breathe into our lives the histories of others and to weave new forms of habitation.

It is still too early to make out very clearly what shape the emerging forms of human polity will assume. I have already suggested that the future has no place for two of the major ways we have organized religions and political communities in previous years—sovereign states and religious denominations. Both will certainly continue to hang on for a while through accumulated power and the inertia of history. But both are the institutional residues of a previous stage of human consciousness in which exclusive citizenship or membership in a single collective made sense. They are now misleading and even destructive forms of polity for two reasons. First, they stress *exclusive* loyalties by teaching that you can't be an American *and* a Russian at the same time, or a Catholic *and* a Hindu. Second, they focus loyalty at the wrong *level*. What we need now are communities of shared symbol and decisional power that are *non-exclusive* in character and *global-local* in focus. By "global-local" I mean we need a universal church that will correspond to our growing awareness that the only adequately inclusive religious community is humankind itself. But this universal church must at the same time nurture the growing re-emergence of human community at the *local* level, the one where we exist daily in neighborhood and polis. If such a non-exclusive global-local "church" emerges, and if it combines "civil" with "religious" qualities, this obviously means that sovereign states and exclusive denominations are fated for extinction. But is there any evidence that they are even beginning to decline?

I think so. Air pollution, nuclear fallout, music fads, satellites, multinational corporations and guerrilla movements all ignore national boundaries. Why should anyone think the nation-state is eternal? It arose quite recently in human history, and if the low level of loyalty it summons among youth today is any indication of how most people will feel in fifty years, the withering process has already set in. National states retain a real grip on the loyalties of young people only in Third World countries where they focus anti-colonialist anger. But when the war of independence is finally won we can confidently expect to witness a decline in the national fervor of young Africans and Latin Americans. Though national states will undoubtedly continue to exist for some years, they are marked for dissolution. They will never again provide the focus for group energy they did from Napoleon to General Patton.

The same "withering away" is even more obvious in the vast name-brand religious organizations of the world. The current rebirth of religion is *not* producing church members, not even among the Jesus people. If this quickly diminishing level of exclusive *denominational* loyalty means anything for the future, in fifty years our national and worldwide denominational organizations will either have changed their function completely or they will have expired along with national states.

What I foresee is not planetary anarchy or a "non-institutional" church. As a preference, I have nothing against institutions as such, and as a prediction, I doubt if human beings can ever do without them completely. But the political and religious institutions we now have are anarchic in the worst sense, i.e., they undercut a proper sense of ordered community. No one wants institutions that end up throttling the purposes they were originally created to serve. What I am predicting, or maybe hoping for, is a form of political and religious life that is both local and universal, with reasonable stages in between but with our sense of belonging refocused to the two ends of the spectrum. I foresee a new religio-political form that gives maximum freedom to those who interact at the most continuous level of life (local) and that really does include all people (universal).

This vision of a human polity that is both religious and political, both universal and local, probably roots back deep into my childhood. I grew up in a house nestled between the Baptist and the Catholic churches. On a windows-open summer Sunday the music from the two temples would actually form a kind of cacophonous ecumenical harmony in our back yard. So my utopian church has an earthy ancestry. Baptists have always taught that the essence of the whole church is somehow mysteriously present even in the smallest local congregation. The congregation is seen as a miniworld, a kind of religious microcosm. Catholics have believed that any truly Christian church must be truly universal. It must somehow, like Noah's sagging ark, find room for all the aardvarks, gnus and three-toed sloths. I am combining the chanted Mass with the gospel hymn, the planetary scope of St. Peter with the congregational freedom of Roger Williams. The religious community we need now must be both intensely local and inclusively universal. I think I see it coming. It will celebrate the hope and the history of people who share a turf and have time for one another. But it will not be provincial. It will include in its roster of saints and range of rites much more scope than any Catholic church does today. But how will it influence political community?

In order to blossom fully, local and global community will require politically viable forms of local and global polity. But anyone can see that it is at just these levels—local and global—that civic polities are weakest today. And it is equally obvious that our bizarre system of sovereign national states prevents the emergence of just the polities we so much need. National states, as I said before, may help colonialized peoples focus their anger and gain their freedom. But the irony is that in making the national state the vehicle for such liberation, the rebels inadvertently swallow one of the oppressor's worst poisons: the myth of national sovereignty. Eventually that poison, however necessary it may now be as an antidote, will take its toll. Sooner or later the national state must be seen for what it is: an enemy of our emerging forms of consciousness and community. It is common knowledge that it stands in the way of a *world* polity by chopping up the planet into a crazy congeries of plots, each grazing a herd bearing its sovereign brand mark. But it is not as widely recognized that sovereign national states also stifle *local* civic polity. They voraciously suck up energy, money, loyalty and leadership away from local areas, where life is really lived in city, town and region, and drain them into an improbable mythical entity called the "sovereign state." That would not be bad, perhaps, if sovereign states had a proper scale. But most sovereign states are just too large to be anybody's real *patria*. There are exceptions. We snicker at Lilliputian states like San Marino, Andorra and Liechtenstein. But maybe they are right after all. They cannot escape working things out with their neighbors. Their claims to "sovereignty" may seem absurd but hardly more so than those of the self-designated "great powers." The very existence of ministates helps us see how much like a comic opera the whole notion of national sovereignty is. In the meantime, none of these three funny little countries has dropped Napalm on a village or liquidated an internal minority, and they may just have a feeling for appropriate political scale we could all learn from.

The giant national state fixes its citizens' sense of belonging at precisely the wrong level and then pumps into their heads a steady stream of spurious collective interiority. Only Christmas gets more worldwide attention than the various national fetes. The myths and flags and heroes of national states have, until quite recently, held a nearly exclusive grip on the group consciousness of millions of people. But that grip is weakening, and the politics of emerging collective interiority, local and global, presages its eventual disappearance. What we need is a global village of miniworlds, infinitely deeper in particularity and broader in universality than anything we now have.

A world where people's loyalties fasten first on humankind and second on the actual polity in which they live every day will have little loyalty left to invest in sovereign states. I will be a citizen of the world, a cosmo-politan *and* a citizen of the city-region-town or even neighborhood where my own sense of daily reality resides. I will recognize only those communities that have any justifiable claim on my loyalty or participation. Then, the very idea of my being taxed, spied on, drafted, policed or in any other way controlled by a fictional entity called a sovereign state will seem as absurd to everyone as it does to a few visionaries now.

Does this sound like a 1940s Federal World Government debate argument or a return to frontier isolationism? That is not my intention. I oppose conventional world federalism because, given the present grotesquely inflated power of sovereign states, it would be dangerous to move now toward world government. Any world government that is formed before we dismantle and decentralize state power into more viable human units could be just as oppressive as what we have. My vision is not Daniel Boone–style isolationism, because I realize that localities must be linked to one another in regional groupings, cooperating on those issues that cannot be handled locally. What I am saying is the politics of our emerging human consciousness requires that the illegiti-mate power of states should be redistributed in two directions, up *and* down.

Do nations and countries then have no claim whatever to our loyalty? Perhaps they do. Maybe after we have thoroughly re-established the communities of place and planet, then the inter-mediate communities of nation and region can be given a place on our ladder of loyalties. But that can wait. Our task now is to build the real communities that will eventually supplant the ones we now endure.

A new form of politics is already emerging, like the Kingdom of God, in our midst. But we have a hard time discerning either one because our eyes are so accustomed to what we have called "politics" for so long. Revolutionary politics always locates new sources of power. Consequently it at first appears absurd to those who are accustomed to wielding what any given age calls "power." Who would have seen in fishwives or serfs or peasants a source of power? The real "new politics" today does not strive merely to usurp and wield power "over." Rather it shares weakness and risks vulnerability. In so doing it releases a form of power more potent than the power wielders ever imagined.

No one builds community without politics, and politics is about power. But politics is also about the purpose of power, its sources, its quality and its appropriate uses. The palace conspirator wants to grab existing power. The pseudo revolutionary wants to seize it and use it for what he feels are better purposes. The genuine revolutionary, who is also the authentic saint, wants to transmute power, distribute it, redefine and humanize it. His ultimate objective is to dismantle the obstacles and to make room for the newly inclusive community that is always coming to be in our midst.

Whether or not it will eventually be satisfied by a new form of church or by something else, I do not think our hunger for community today is mere escapism. People need a place to continue to tell their stories, especially in light of the avalanche of signals. They need a place to try out different ways of being, a place to learn how *all* life might be lived differently by living some of it differently on a smaller scale. All these are essential. Those who do not actually *experience* a different way of life on a smaller scale soon despair of its ever being possible on a larger one; and those who do not first *survive*, physically or spiritually, do not contribute anything to the larger picture. Faith has as much to do with survival as with hope for change.

When they are working right, the religious communities of oppressed peoples provide just this indispensable locus of survival and of alternative experience. This is why I think it is so important that poor people guard the integrity of their religion against incursions by developers, improvers, programmers and other seducers. For those of us who can no longer be fully at home in the religious communities of our forebears something else will be necessary. Without such a community we are all lost. Outside the church, *some* church, there is no salvation.

I raise my glass of tequila to that mural in Santa Fe, to the Mexican people whose gods and heroes it depicts, to the story of faith and struggle it tells. I know that in one sense it is "their" story, not mine. I will have to find or forge my own community. I cannot piggyback on theirs. I even realize with sadness that those against whom Zapata and Torres fought were in some sense "my" people. But still I lift my glass to their story and I know the toast is right, because at a deeper level, one we all can glimpse on occasion, "their" story is my story too.

PART THREE

THE ELECTRONIC ICON

CHAPTER TEN

The Image and the Icon

The image always precedes the idea in the development of
human consciousness.
—Herbert Read, *Icon and Idea*

THE THOUGHT habits of a lifetime can sometimes be sent reeling
by one disconcerting sentence, like a finger tap on a card castle. It
happened to me when my eye fell on the above idea expressed by
Sir Herbert Read. Image precedes idea. Always? What if it is
only "mostly"? It is still an upsetting thought for people like me,
who spend their lives probing and dissecting old ideas, or even
inventing and playing with what we think are new ones. If old
Sir Herbert is only half right, then even our most original theological productions are at best derivative. Theology has dealt
mainly with the ideational residue of the original image-reality.
Except for poring over black letters printed on white (or yellow-
ing) pages, it has not exercised its pupils and retinas very much.
But, jogged by Read and others, theology is changing. This part
of the book recounts my own groping efforts over the past few
years to learn how to see, to use my corneal tissue, to look up at
the theological import of the *visual* world. Formerly I had been
wandering through the landscape reading the signs. Now I've
begun to enjoy the sights.

But that doesn't make Sir Herbert's sentence any less disturbing. In fact he himself does not spare us the rather far-reaching
consequences of his argument, if it is true. It will not only require us, he says, "to rewrite the history of culture" and to

261

"reexamine the postulates of all our philosophies," it will also force us to ask, "What is the right basis of education?" We must also, I would add, take up a rather new way of pursuing the enterprise of theology. "Iconology" is the study of the meaning of visual images. It is not a very well tended field in theology today, even when it applies to *sacred* images. Secular iconology is virtually nonexistent. Most theologians lay aside their critical faculties while looking at films, TV commercials, apartment house layouts and magazine ads. If we really want to understand our culture theologically, we won't be able to do that now. These are the icons of our cultural faith. That accounts for the "icon" (*eikon* = visual image) part of my title for this section.

The word "electronic" in the title represents an interest which came to me a little less dramatically. Ever since my college days I have been impressed with the frazzling impact of technology on the modern sensibility. I even wrote my doctoral dissertation at Harvard (finished in 1963) on the subject of religion and technology. It was a wordy tour of the historical, religious and ethical significance of technology from the Tower of Babel to the Boeing 707. The thesis now lies quietly embalmed in Widener Library. It is impressively footnoted in three languages.

For several years after typing the final period on that dissertation I remained faithful to a solemn vow I had made to myself late one night while writing it: an oath never to think about technology again, ever. For some time I kept that pledge with zeal. In more recent years, however, my resolution has weakened. My mind has wandered back to technology, albeit in a different way. I'm now intrigued with the myth and the metaphor of technology more than I am with its moral and political implications. I am awed and disturbed by the fact, as Henry Adams saw many decades ago, that the dynamo has replaced the Virgin in our cultural pantheon. Hence my title. Cross the mythic power of the technological with the cultural priority of the visual and the offspring is an electronic icon. This, I think, is why we need a new theology of culture.

It was the late Paul Tillich who introduced most of us to the term. As early as 1919 he had written in one of his first published works, an essay on "The Idea of a Theology of Culture" (*"Über die Idee einer Theologie der Kultur"*). To my knowledge that article has never appeared in English. But in 1959, after Tillich had lived in America for a quarter of a century and had published two volumes of systematic theology, he revived his youthful, and to my mind more original, interest. "It is a source of great satisfaction to me," he wrote in the Foreword to his *Theology of Culture*, "that after the passing of forty years I can take the title for this volume from my first important public speech." Tillich had returned to his first love, to theology of culture, which is, in his words, "the attempt to show the religious dimension in many special spheres of man's cultural activity." Theology of culture à la Tillich has no denominational axe to sharpen. It seeks rather to uncover the often obscure or hidden spiritual import of man's many-splendored cultural creations. Its object of inquiry is the worlds of meaning that are assembled and polished by the inventive human spirit. Anthropologists define "culture" as the symbols and stories that pattern human behavior, as well as the artifacts, rites and gestures that bring the values of a society to expression. "Culture" does *not* mean merely the so-called "fine arts" or the classics. Thus no person is "uncultured," for all societies have their primal meanings and root metaphors. For the theologian of culture it is true, *par excellence*, that "nothing human is foreign to me." The whole world of crystallized human sensibilities is his domain.

But as a *theologian* of culture he is not only an explorer, nor can he be content with mere analysis. He also makes judgments. As with "people's religion" he tests the spirits "to see if they be of God." Without rancor or arrogance he nonetheless tries to sort out the healing from the hurting currents, the liberating images from the oppressive ones, the gracious from the demonic. However provisionally, he says yes or no, usually a little of each, to the spiritual powers he discovers in human handiwork. He must not be afraid to wrestle with angels, nor should he fear the fangs of devils. He will encounter some of each.

Like many other theologians of my generation, I was once a student of Tillich's, virtually a disciple. I still recall with mild nostalgia Tillich's "home seminars" held amidst Budweiser cans and cigarette smoke at his second-floor apartment on Chauncy Street in Cambridge, a few blocks from where I now live. At every gathering, after we had pulled off our galoshes and exchanged small talk, Tillich would have someone in the group take exactly thirty minutes to lay out the main ideas of his doctoral project. The half hour was measured by an alarm clock placed on a centrally located table. After precisely thirty minutes the others would chime in with questions and comments. Tillich always listened quietly, fingering the famous giant paper clip he called his fetish object. Then, finally, he would speak to the subject himself, gathering up all the dangling strands of the conversation, locating the heart of the issue and telling us what he thought about it. Those home seminars on Chauncy Street were among the most formative intellectual experiences of my life. I still think of them frequently when I walk by Tillich's old residence. Since Tillich's death in 1965, I have occasionally written critical things about his theology. But these criticisms should never obscure the fact that most of what I learned from Paul Tillich I still believe, and probably always will. Above all I inherited from him a continuing passion for theology of culture.

There is little point here in describing in detail Tillich's influential approach to theology of culture. In any case this job has already been masterfully accomplished in the best book ever published on Tillich, James Luther Adams' *Paul Tillich's Philosophy of Culture, Science and Religion.* Adams was my doctoral supervisor at Harvard, and so much of his method and of Tillich's has rubbed itself into my own, it would be difficult to extricate the separate elements. So at the risk of appearing negative, I will mention only those points at which my approach to theology of culture, especially in this book, differs somewhat from Tillich's.

The first departure takes us back to the quotation from Sir Herbert Read's Charles Eliot Norton lectures, *Icon and Idea,* about the image preceding the idea. Certainly, more than any other Protestant theologian I can think of, Tillich recognized the religious significance of the *visual*. He once wrote an important article on Rembrandt and an introduction to the catalogue of an exhibit at the Museum of Modern Art. His students remember his lifelong fascination for architecture and painting and his pre-occupation with Picasso's "Guernica" (a print of which hung over his mantelpiece) as the greatest piece of "religious" art of our era. Yet Tillich, although he would certainly have accepted the notion that *symbols* are primary in human existence, might have been less receptive to Read's insistence that *visual images* are prior to words and concepts in the formation of human consciousness. For Tillich, the old Lutheran emphasis on the Word still reverberated.

My own hunch is that Read is right, that the visual precedes the verbal in human culture. In Freud's *The Ego and the Id* the founder of psychoanalysis (an extremely *wordy* form of therapy) reminds us that "optical memory residues" and "visual thinking" are fundamental to man. Though "thinking in pictures remains a very incomplete form of becoming conscious," says Freud, it does "approximate more closely to unconscious processes than does thinking in words, and is unquestionably older than the latter both ontogenetically and phylogenetically." Man's consciousness evolves from image to idea, but the primal vision lingers on, coloring and framing the words that seek to express it.

Symbol is the central component of culture, and the visual symbol is more basic than the verbal. Therefore my interest in theology of culture centers more on images, films, artifacts, patterns and visible designs than Tillich's did. I think this is important. It used to be that when a writer wanted to clinch the case for the cultural unity of an era he would talk about Thomas Aquinas' *Summa Theologica* and the Gothic cathedrals. Who has not heard Notre Dame Cathedral referred to as the "*Summa* in stone"? Yet, as Read cryptically reminds us, Notre Dame had already been gathering moss for many years when Aquinas moved to Paris as a student. Maybe we should refer to the *Summa Theologica* as a "Notre Dame in words."

My point here is the one Susanne Langer makes in *Problems of Art* when she says that "rationality arises as an elaboration of feeling." Symbol is a highly compressed fusion of feeling and meaning. And among symbols, mime precedes myth, vision precedes story, the layout of the village space precedes the spinning out of the people's beliefs in epic and saga. We understand theology best when we grasp it as the elaboration of a primal vision.

My second point of departure from Tillich's theology of culture is that I give more attention to *popular* culture. If we accept the distinction between "high-" "middle-" and "low-brow" culture, Tillich devoted most of his attention to the first two. He wrote very little about cinema, nothing (to my knowledge) about photography, comics, commercial art, packaging, technical design. He preferred Dürer, Kafka, Tolstoi and Rembrandt. His tastes were refined, even aristocratic (despite his socialistic political leanings). He despised television.

A good case can be made for this focusing of theology of culture solely on creations which exhibit at least some chance of eventually becoming classics. I have no doubt that Sartre's *No Exit* or Kafka's *The Trial*, both favorites of Tillich, will last longer than Alfred Hitchcock's *Frenzy*, which is already slipping from my memory. Still, the flotsam and jetsam of mass culture tell us something just as important about a culture's elemental sensibilities as its elite creations do. We ignore Mickey Mouse and Frankenstein's monster only to our own detriment.

In his own aphoristic way, Marshall McLuhan has called our attention to the centrality of visual symbols in popular culture, especially those found in ads. Commercial artists, he says, "have tended to develop the ad into an icon, and icons are not specialized fragments or aspects but unified and compressed images of a complex kind. They focus a large region of experience in tiny compass." The products of the prodigally supported "ad teams" who create an advertisement, he says, "are magnificent accumulations of material about the shared experience and feelings of the entire community." What we need is an iconography of popular culture.

My third departure from Tillich stems from the fact that he showed less interest than one might have expected in the dynamics of cultural change or in what we refer to today as "cultural revolution." On those pages where he does examine cultural change he is sometimes carried away by the awesome clash of symbols with one another, of the divine and the demonic. He makes only skimpy reference to the social forces that mold weapons out of symbols and use them to perpetuate their own power. As he grew older Tillich wrote less and less on the politics of culture. Perhaps his bitterly disappointing attempt to forge new political symbols during the time of the "religious socialist" movement in Germany, together with the ghastly outcome of the man-made Nazi myth, discouraged him from delving further into the complex interaction of cultural, political and social change. It is one of the sad aspects of Tillich's life work that he wrote less about this subject as he matured. His best essays on the politics of art and the theology of social symbol were written before his emigration to America to escape Hitler.

Today, however, the politics of cultural images cannot be ignored. PR men probe our fragile psyches and use our hopes and terrors to sell us things. Candidates are packaged and delivered. Badges, hairdos, posters, bumper stickers, finger signs, and different cuts of costumes clash with one another in the struggle for symbolic hegemony. We have learned in recent times that when Carlyle said there is nothing more powerful than "an idea whose hour has come" he was not entirely correct. There is one thing more powerful, an image whose day has dawned.

There are good reasons why theologians of culture, and to some extent even Tillich, have neglected the visual dimensions of their field. One is the long-standing Protestant and Jewish suspicion of all idols and images. The Second Commandment is, after all, quite explicit: "Thou shalt not make unto thee any graven image, or any likeness of any thing that is in heaven above, or that is in the earth beneath, or that is in the water under the earth." That covers just about everything. Also there is an age-old tradition of iconoclasm in Christianity, and it flames out most forcibly during critical reform movements. The Hussites and Savonarola, the Radical Franciscans and Thomas Münzer, how-ever they differed on most things, agreed in a spirited hatred for icons. Calvinism harbors a severe suspicion of pictoral depictions of the holy. Cromwell painted over the murals in English churches. Protestantism has produced great preachers, brilliant poets and unsurpassed music. Its visual creations, however, are not its forte. The Protestant spirit lives in Bach and Milton. It took the Catholic spirit to produce Chartres and the Sistine Chapel. Why should people reared in white clapboard or plain brown meetinghouses be expected to display an acute sensitivity to the visual aspects of religion and culture?

Nor should we brush easily aside the religious suspicion of making images of holy things. In a way it shows how accurately the power of the iconic has been gauged. The Puritans, for example, were hardly cultural philistines. They knew something about visuality that worried them, perhaps rightly. In religion too the media can become the message. W. R. Robinson has seen that in his contrast of movies with literature.

> For at stake ultimately in the difference between literature and the movies are the prerogatives of two moral universes, two cultures, and two ideas of creation. Both art forms, just by existing, pay tribute to their source, the power which makes them possible—literature to the Word, the movies to the Light. But beyond that, by implication when not directly, literature celebrates a God transcendent, the movies a god immanent; one affirms creation by fiat, the other creation by emanation.

Robinson may overestimate the opposition of Word and Light. In Christianity, both figure prominently. If in recent years we have emphasized the Word at the expense of the Light, it may be time to redress the balance a little.

There are vast untapped resources we can now begin to draw

on for a theology of visual culture. One, among others, is the elusive and subtle Eastern Orthodox theology of the icon. Fully aware of the pitfalls of idolatry, yet equally aware of the enormous significance of the visual for man, Orthodox writers have elaborated a theory of iconic meaning that can sharpen our consciousness today. To read them, and then to look again at their icons—and ours—is an experience in theological re-education. Such an investigation reveals immediately why it is important to consider *technē* and *eikon* in the same section, why we should reflect on the visual dimension of culture and the challenge of technology together. Consider, for example, the difference between sight and sound. Sound, especially the sound of speech, seems to address us quite directly, usually requiring a response of some kind. Although speech comes from somewhere, it seems to envelop us. We can close it out only by exerting the unusual effort required to stop up our ears. A sight, on the other hand, allows us to remain more passive and unhurried. Unlike words, sights are rarely addressed to anyone in particular. Physiologically we can close out sights by merely shutting our eyes. Nature relates us to sound somewhat differently than to sight.

In religious practice the same contrast appears between icon and pulpit. Both convey the holy message. But whereas the sermon speaks to us, requiring rapt attention, constant moral focus, and at least an element of cognitive reasoning, the icon does none of these. It is always there. Its expression is changeless. It permits us to move at our own pace, to come as close or to remain as distant as we choose. It does not pursue us. We must move toward it. It speaks more to feeling than to thought.

If the icon has been an aid to a contemplative rather than an instrumental attitude, technology in its Western setting has been just the opposite. It has been instrumental, not contemplative. We have used it to control and master nature, not to meditate on it or to enjoy it. "Machine" has meant manipulation. "Icon" has meant contemplation. The contrast is particularly evident in our attitude toward nature. Through our technologies we respond to what we think is a hostile challenge from nature, a *word* of defiance that requires a duel to the death. Thus our technologies usually place us in a pistols-at-daybreak confrontation with nature, or at least in a wrestling match or an argument. We thrust with pesticides and contraceptive pills; nature parries with resistant strains of insects and cancer. We launch rockets; nature counters with asteroids and lethal radioactivity. The metaphors are of "struggle," "conquest" and "battle." We find it hard merely to gaze at nature or to fondle her any more. We feel we must *do* something. Nature challenges us ("because it's there"), so we climb, explore, master, subdue. Even our own bodies become objects of technical mastery. The telephone bell tears us from our dreams at night. The wristwatch keeps us in step and on time all day. We control our moods with pills and our smells with deodorants. But suppose the depth of nature expressed itself to us as *icon* rather than as *word?* Would our attitude be different? Could we gaze upon it more, commune with it unhurriedly, let it *be* more than we do?

This contrast between iconic contemplation and technological mastery obtained by and large until quite recently. Now, however, the contrast is no longer valid. In fact sometimes the reverse is true: icons jostle and intrude and technologies help us contemplate. Our modern icons—film, ad, TV—are not changeless and unobtrusive. They are just the opposite. Also technology, ironically, can help us contemplate, as Lewis Mumford points out in a memorable chapter in *Technics and Civilization* on the camera. Although some writers have indicted photography for luring us into abstracted alienation, Mumford disagrees.

> The mission of the photograph is to clarify the object. . . . To see as they are, as if for the first time, a boatload of immigrants, a tree in Madison Square Park, a woman's breast, a cloud lowering over a black mountain—that requires patience and understanding. Ordinarily we skip over and schematize these objects, relate them to some practical need, or subordinate them to some immediate wish: photography gives us the ability to recognize them in the independent form created by light and shade and shadow. Good photography, then, is one of the best educations toward a rounded

sense of reality. Restoring to the eye, otherwise so preoccupied with the abstractions of print, the stimulus of things roundly seen as things, shapes, colors, textures, demanding for its enjoyment a previous experience of light and shade, this machine process in itself counteracts some of the worst defects of our mechanical environment.

How strange that Mumford, our most articulate opponent of mechanistic technology (see his two volumes of *The Myth of the Machine*), should appreciate the contemplative possibilities of one particular machine, a little black box with shutter and lens. It seems we can no longer assume the old contradiction between the *vita meditativa* and the *vita activa*. Nor can we symbolize their contrasting moods with the icon for meditation and the machine for activity. The relationship has grown much more complex, and we must now dig deeper if we are to discover what the icon and the machine actually mean in the lives of people.

As I delve further into the religious meaning of machines and of visual phenomena, another facet of my approach will become obvious; my way of doing it steers between the exclusively appreciative and the exclusively condemnatory stances. I try to avoid merely reveling in the things I examine (though that is tempting) and I try not to leap into exposing, demasking and demythologizing too quickly. I avoid the demasking strategy first because I enjoy masks and myths, but also because masks and myths are not just Potemkin façades. Captain Ahab, the demon-driven skipper in Melville's *Moby Dick*, saw the world as an assembly of masks hiding the true face of reality. He wanted to strike behind them. What Ahab may not have realized, however, is that what lurks beyond the masks not only hides itself *behind* them, it also expresses itself *through* them. As Bertolt Brecht once said, "Give a man a mask, and he'll tell you the truth." Man's "masks" today are his movies and his clothes styles, his advertising art and his jet plane fuselages. Admittedly he deceives himself with them, hides and distorts and mystifies. But in his very masking of himself he reveals more about his gods and himself than he ever suspects.

Ideally I suppose I should have a special interest in the mass media because they are so powerful, so mythogenic and so pervasive, and as a theologian it would be a dereliction of duty not to give them attention. My actual motivation, however, is not nearly so virtuous. The truth is I enjoy most of the mass media thoroughly. I have never outgrown my adolescent crush on movies, and although I prefer good ones, I even relish bad ones. Ever since I played the saxophone in a dance band called the Tophatters during my high school years (our theme song was "Harbor Lights," rendered with muted trumpets carrying the melody), I have retained an affection for popular ballads, dance music and show tunes. My still-sharp memories of the radio serials I listened to by the hour in the 1930s, like *The Shadow* and *I Love a Mystery*, make me a somewhat better than average contestant in trivia games and an easy mark for people selling nostalgia records and books. Although I am over forty, I still belong to what is probably the first generation of media kids.

I have also met the media from the other side of the mikes and cameras. After my first book, *The Secular City*, appeared and became a best seller, I began receiving invitations to show off on various radio shows, to appear on TV specials and on interview programs, and to write things for the media. I know the "other side" of the media in more than one way. I have frequently sat within their glassed temples, watched their whirring prayer wheels, blinked before their powerful lights, been anointed by their make-up crews, felt the expectant hush as the big sweep second hand glided toward the appointed hour. I have been praised, featured, berated, trivialized, rejected and ignored by the media. My books and other ventures have not brought me into the orbit of the media even a fraction as much as those people who spend their lives as "celebrities," but I have been burned enough times to respect their enormous power to tempt and torment, to inform and conceal, to interpret and corrupt. My feelings about media are ridden with conflict. But I think my ambivalence about them goes deeper than just a photo album of mixed memories. I see their enormous *promise*, and perhaps for that very reason I am more incensed at the distortion evident in the way they actually work.

In thinking theologically about the mass media I have come to dissociate myself from two groups, both of whom also have strong views on the subject. I disagree on the one hand with the anti-media defenders of "high culture," many of them fellow inhabitants of the academic world; but I also disagree with the media pros and buffs, the celebrants of popular culture and especially of TV, some of whom contend that the electronic media have already caused a transformation of consciousness more profound than anything since the invention of movable type. I suspect that the dismissal of electronic media by the first group—the one that includes so many writers, intellectuals and academics—reflects their desire to maintain a firm controlling grip on the "cultural heritage" which pre-electronic book culture and the scholarly tradition have placed in their hands. They sense, as we all do, that the electronic media *could* democratize culture. But they do not welcome the prospect, because they know it would break their own near monopoly control over "culture." My difference with them is that they want to avoid this change, I want to hasten it. They see that the electronic media pose a severe threat to the way cultural knowledge is presently produced, stored and distributed, and they are right. But they are secretly gratified that TV (especially most "educational TV") remains boring and vacuous; so much the better, it seems less of a threat that way. I both hate and love TV because I see what it *could* do to break the academic headlock on culture, and I am saddened that it is not doing it.

Our present anxious culture keepers are not the first to worry. There have always been mandarins who have gone pale at the thought of what the masses might do if they ever gained access to the means of cultural production and distribution. In our time this horror again haunts the advocates of "high culture." But it need not. I share the high culture's regard for Aeschylus, Bach and Dante, but not its disgust for popular culture or its dislike for the new media. I do not believe there needs to be a chasm between high culture and popular culture. Many societies in the past have avoided a cultural caste system. Shakespeare's and Sophocles' audiences included the ordinary people of their day. At its best, culture is a continuum. Its various levels feed and inspire one another. What happens to people in the everyday world becomes the raw material for great cultural achievements in the arts and music, and the artistic milestones become pivots for the consciousness of the whole civilization.

But this is not the way our presently fragmented subcultures relate to one another. It is frequently pointed out, often by scholarly critics, that industrial society has transformed culture into one more product to be packaged, distributed and consumed but that culture by its very nature is not a mere consumption item. When it is reduced to such a state, it becomes a method of psychological control and mesmerization. All this is true enough. But what distresses me is that academic institutions have allowed themselves to become one of the packagers and distributors of culture. This is even true for "religion" when it is thought of as an academic department. The result of the ivory tower control of high culture is that instead of providing the symbolic pivot points in the lives of ordinary people, cultural resources are hoarded and meted out by college departments in prescribed doses precluding feedback, countercreation, embellishment and the other ways culture is renewed. Aeschylus and Dante are distributed in credit-hour units. "Literature" is a catalogue entry. The academic packaging process not only withholds from ordinary people something that belongs to them just as much as natural resources do, it also has a damaging effect on the hapless students who "learn" it this way. The structure of the distributive system teaches them something frightfully wrong about culture: namely that it is a means to another end, in this case graduation, certification, graduate school, a career. I always inwardly shudder when I have to take part in faculty discussions about this or that student which fasten on how many "credits" she has "accumulated" or where his grade-point average appears on a graph. The banking and business idiom has so deeply infected the academic institutions of industrial societies that we rarely notice it, especially when our language itself is corrupted.

Western society now stands in desperate need of something like a cultural rebirth or renaissance. But for anything like such a spiritual renewal to have even a chance of occurring we must release the vast cultural capital now controlled by the ruling institutions of industrial states. This liberating of the cultural bastille must happen both politically and technically if the hoarded heritage is to be made available to the "masses" in such a way that they can both draw on it and contribute to it. I believe the electronic media contain within themselves one of the ingredients of a cultural revolution, the technical one. To ignore or dismiss them is to turn one's back on the most salient cultural fact of our era. No theologian with a serious interest in how the study of religion might be delivered from academic bondage to help spark the renewal of culture can afford such a back turning.

But if I do not accept the high culture's contempt for the new media, neither do I share the sanguine enthusiasm of the media buffs. They claim the media are already creating a "new man," a cultural revolution more pervasive and profound than any revolution previously imagined. At first glance these enthusiasts seem to have a point. My mind boggles when I remember that 723 million people in 47 countries watched Neil Armstrong step onto the moon on July 19, 1969, or that American children now spend more time watching TV than attending school. Also, TV did bring the Vietnam war into the American living room; and it is consistent for the racist South African regime to try to bar TV from their country. My students today do think in a less "linear" fashion, and this probably stems from childhoods spent in front of the tube. Still, it could be argued that more awareness of the Vietnam war did not make it any shorter or less bloody, it just made the powerlessness of ordinary citizens to do anything about it more evident. Also, for South Africans to learn via satellite how racist their national policies are will not help them to alter those policies. In short, until the pattern of power in the society itself changes, the control of the media will remain in the hands of those who will not permit their use for political or cultural renewal. Conceding the hours of exposure and the changing modes of consciousness to the media buffs does not prove their case. Media may broaden our purview and supply us with more data. But under present conditions of control and technology, if they do alter our consciousness, it is to make us feel more helpless and overwhelmed.

Still there is enormous promise in television, film and other new media. *In principle* they are more universal, equalitarian and accessible than previous modes of communication ever could be. Unlike books, for example, TV and film do not require the long expenditure of time required to learn to read or the even longer period required to learn how to write effectively. There are no *technical* reasons to prevent every TV or radio receiver from being a transmitter also, and this is just not true of books. Film is also *in principle* a radically equalizing medium. It has already been proven that illiterate Andes Indians and ten-year-old children can be taught to make films in a few weeks. This makes me ask whether there is something indispensable about writing, and whether print is necessarily a way human beings will always communicate with one another, store memories and information, or tell stories. This raises the even more basic question of whether everyone everywhere has to learn to read. As awful as it may sound to book readers (and even more to book writers), the new media may eventually help move us beyond a culture dominated by print with its inherently elitist characteristics. Eventually books may become a marginal mode of communication, while oral and visual modes, made universally accessible by new social forms and electronic technology, once again become dominant.

I say "once again" because, though we often forget it, book-and-print culture appeared only very recently in the sweep of human history. Everyone learns to talk but only a minority (though now a growing one) learns to read and write. For only a small minority of the world's people are books, newspapers and magazines the most important source of information. A best seller in America does not reach nearly as many people as watch a network TV show, and most people in the poor world still get most of their ideas and values from their neighbors and families. If it is argued that the "influential" people of the world, the "decision makers," get their ideas from print or from people who read print, this is just the problem. The willingness to cater to those who are presently decision makers is itself an expression of the elitist premises of print.

The electronic media *could*, given the needed changes in control and technology, facilitate a more democratic and more participatory society than we now have. Print cannot. I love books, but as one who has read and written many of them, I know how awkward and cumbersome they are as modes of communication. They take too long to write, cost too much to publish, encourage a certain snobbish reliance on a pretty style and vocabulary, and clutter up houses and libraries to a degree that is already becoming nearly impossible to handle. Also it takes a long time to reply to printed matter and it is not easily altered when you change your mind. Print does not reproduce the full range of human communicative sonorities and gestures the way tapes and especially films do. The readers of the world would do well to agree that we can save writing for *something* only if we stop trying to make it do *everything*. Writing will have an important place in the pluralistic communications culture of the future; alone, however, it cannot produce the cultural transformation we need. Films and TV, despite their present authoritarian structure, are inherently more capable of facilitating that revolution than writing could ever be.

This coming cultural revolution, from print to images, will have a shattering impact on the "religions of the book," those faiths that were spawned during that relatively brief period of human history during which writing assumed such prominence. It will also completely alter the authority structure of those faiths. Experts on Holy Writ will no longer hold such sway. Meanwhile, as a teacher of religion I am often made uncomfortably aware of the distortions introduced into our learning about religion by virtue of the fact that those who teach and study it not only came into consciousness within religions and cultures dominated by writing, but also presently live and work on tiny rafts of written pages adrift in an ocean of images. The inevitable bias this creates reveals itself in our study of religious history, where we rely mainly on texts—with a little welcome help from the pottery shards and temple lintels shoveled out by archeologists. It also distorts our study of "non-Western" religions, where we concentrate too much on merely reading the Vedas or the Gita when we could also be learning from these faiths by chanting, fasting, praying or meditating. Our book-print mentality also lures us into spending too much time reading what other theologians write and not enough examining what the vast majority of simple people, who never write about their faith, actually do.

We should prepare ourselves for the changes it will entail in our whole way of life when the coming culture transformation sets in. But it will not, given present prospects, be utopia; and I do not think we should liquidate our paperback collections too quickly. Sadly, the electronic media, like the "high culture" establishment from which they are so separated, are also in a state of captivity. Before they can facilitate any cultural change they have to be liberated themselves. But the prospect of *both* "high culture" *and* the new media being freed and then finding each other is a dizzying one. Such a combination might make possible the emergence of a worldwide spiritual community, one in which billions of persons and millions of groups could tell one another their stories, listen, respond and refashion in a thousand unimagined permutations. Only then would we truly have a "global village," something which, despite all the talk, we do *not* have today. A village is a place of instantaneous buzzing mutual communication among all villagers. We do not have that. Instead of a global village we have a global cluster of pyramids, a complex of vertical skyscrapers where signals come down from the tower tops but there is no way to answer back from the bottom. As long as this high rise stands, the electronic icon's spell will stupefy us. Its hypnotic power will tear us ever further from our inner selves and from the communities that keep us alive. But neither electrons nor icons are essentially evil, and we must never stop imagining a world where all pyramids are dismantled and we can use new technologies to see and hear one another on a scale never before possible.

CHAPTER ELEVEN

The Virgin and the Dynamo Revisited: The Symbolism of Technology

The great mythological themes continue to repeat themselves in the obscure depths of the psyche . . . It seems that a myth itself, as well as the symbols it brings into play, never quite disappears from the present world of the psyche; it only changes its aspect and disguises its operation.
—Mircea Eliade, *Myths, Dreams and Mysteries*

WE NEED you again, Henry Adams. Are you too long dead to hear? Who can ever forget his first wide-eyed tour through Mont St. Michael and Chartres with you as his slightly eccentric guide? Thank you for all that. But now we need you again. Remember another visit you made? Your visit in 1900 to the Great Exposition, with its famous forty-foot dynamo? What a colossus it was, and what an unwilling gasp it pulled out of you, what an imprint it etched on your fragile psyche! You became fascinated, in fact almost obsessed with the giant dynamo, Henry. Of course, at another level of your consciousness you were already mulling over your book on Mont St. Michel and Chartres. It appeared a few years later, brimming with antiphons to the spiritual power of the Virgin, the power, you said, that had built Chartres. With all that seething in your subconscious, your meeting with the sleek soaring dynamo became a kind of apparition. Why, you wondered, was the Virgin gone? Where was her softness and warmth, where the only partially sublimated erotic magnetism she exuded? "To Adams," you wrote, referring to yourself as always in the third person, "the dynamo became a symbol of infinity . . . he began to feel the forty-foot dynamo as a moral force, much as the early Christians felt the Cross . . . Before the end, one began to pray to it."

We need the sensibility of a Henry Adams today to understand ourselves. If he was that prescient about the dynamo, what could he have told us about those throngs of hushed pilgrims gathered around the blistered American space capsule at Expo 67, about our feelings toward our automobiles (family escutcheons?), the hydrogen bomb (apocalypse?), the computer (Delphian oracle?)? To understand ourselves and our technologies today we need an Adamsian fusion of Yankee shrewdness and Gothic fantasy.

Adams believed that about the year 1600, the year of the burning of Giordano Bruno, Western civilization went through a sea change from what Adams called the "religious" to what he called the "mechanical" age. He described this transition in terms of "energy," a popular word in his day. In our terms he was talking about how a culture orders and symbolizes its meanings, sanctifies its values and celebrates its hopes. Adams saw what so many commentators on technology since then have missed. He saw that the dynamo (read jet plane, computer, automobile, nuclear accelerator) was not only a forty-foot tool man could use to help him on his way, it was also a forty-foot-high symbol of where he wanted to go.

What is the dynamo? It was the symbol *par excellence* of technology. By "technology" I mean the tools and procedures men utilize to observe, cope with and modify their environment. By "symbol" I mean a highly dense and compact cluster of meaning. A symbol can be anything (a word, object, person, gesture) that focuses such significance and helps order or make sense out of raw experience.

By the "symbolism of technology" I have in mind those meanings technologies have above and beyond their merely technical function. Technological artifacts become symbols when they are "iconized," when they release emotions incommensurate with their mere utility, when they arouse hopes and fears only indirectly related to their use, when they begin to provide foci for the mapping of cognitive experience. The dynamo becomes a symbol when it begins to incorporate the self-understanding of a people or of an epoch, when it is placed on view at an exposition, when, as Adams said, one begins "to pray to it."

If Henry Adams' insight was correct it means that in the past two centuries or more certain technologies have begun to acquire an aura that is not only symbolic but religious. The dynamos and their assorted metallic kinsmen have stolen fire from the saints and virgins. In a classic passage in *The Elementary Forms of the Religious Life* Emile Durkheim describes what he calls "the ambiguity of the notion of sacredness." He argues that religious phenomena are of two contradictory sorts. Some are beneficent dispersers of life and health; others are evil and impure, the sources of disorder, disease and death. The good ones elicit feelings of love and gratitude, the evil call forth attitudes of fear and horror. The two sentiments, although both are "sacred," are very far apart, and are often separated from each other by rigid ritual rules. "Thus the whole religious life gravitates about two contrary poles," Durkheim declares, "between which there is the same opposition as between the pure and the impure, the saint and the sacrilegious, the divine and the diabolic."

But then Durkheim goes on to make a masterful observation. He shows that while these two contrasting attitudes at first seem contradictory, in practice there is a close kinship between them. Both positive and the negative are *sacred* as opposed to profane. In our terms, both have a highly charged symbolic character rather than a merely instrumental one. As Durkheim says, "There is a horror in religious respect, especially when it is very intense, while the fear inspired by malign powers is generally not without a certain reverential character." For Durkheim the tones by which these two attitudes are differentiated are so slight that sometimes it is not possible to distinguish one from the other. In fact an impure thing or evil power often becomes, through a simple modification of circumstances, a source of healthful power and goodness. "So the pure and the impure," concludes Durkheim, "are not two separate classes, but two varieties of the same class." This "class" includes *all* sacred things.

Durkheim's thesis about the ambiguity of the sacred is confirmed by other scholars. Malinowski, for example, in his famous studies of the Trobriand Islanders, shows that a dead man is viewed with horror and fear, but that ingesting part of his flesh is also the source of incomparably potent energy. In Hindu iconography important sacred figures are often depicted with more than one head so that the malevolent and the beneficent aspects can be shown as belonging to the same divinity. The Christian cross is not only the "emblem of suffering and shame"; it is also the assurance of God's love for man and life's victory over death. Wherever symbols reach a degree of intensity that could be called "religious" (and the borderline is always fuzzy) the devil turns out to be a fallen angel.

Symbols of the sacred, then, are characterized by a *high degree* of *power* and of *ambiguity*. They arouse dread and gratitude, terror and rapture. The more central and powerful a symbol is for a culture the more vivid the ambiguity becomes. A symbol becomes "sacred" when it reaches such a degree of priority that it begins to sanctify other values and symbols. This is an important point: A "religious symbol" is defined not by its *content* but by its *relative degree of cultural power*. Clearly there is nothing to prevent technologies of any kind from becoming sacred symbols in Durkheim's sense. Our question now is whether this is in fact happening. I think it is.

There are two identifiable classes of religious symbol: ritual and myth. A *ritual* is a dynamic symbol. It is enacted—sung, danced, mimed—and it is usually thought of as doing something for people, moving or changing them in some way. Baptism, confirmation and extreme unction are examples of ritual symbols. Each helps move the person from one state or stage to another. Rituals differ only in the matter of *from* where and *to* where they help people move. Paul Ricoeur in *Symbolism of Evil* suggests two main symbolic axes for ritual. He calls them the "bondage-extrication" axis and the "defilement-purification" axis. I think technologies are beginning to function as rituals in both senses.

The second main class of religious symbol is the *myth*. Rather than "moving" people, a myth "places" them in a history and in a universe of value and meaning. The two main types of myth are those of *origin*, which tell people who they are and where they came from; and myths of *destiny*. I think Adams was right about the dynamo. Technologies are becoming religious symbols in all these senses. Let us look at each in order.

Technologies are beginning to function as sacred rituals both in purification and in extrication. In the case of defilement-purification rites, there seems to be little argument. Who could deny our obsessive interest in sterilization, flushing and cleansing today? We have developed almost laughably refined technologies—sanitary, medical, prophylactic—to aid us in our self-purification. Our fascination with detergents alone is amply demonstrated by any evening's fare of television advertising. We also know, however, that compulsive cleanliness reveals a deeper-stated anxiety ("Out, damned spot") and that our technologies have also become symbols of defilement. The billowing smokestack, the auto graveyard, the oil slick—all have turned into icons of pollution. But the irony is delicious. The very detergents we churn out to cleanse us end up defiling our lakes. Vishnu is also Shiva.

The case for technology as a purification rite needs no further proof, but since technology as a rite of extrication from bondage is a little less obvious, I will concentrate here on it. Evidence is accumulating that in industrial-bureaucratic societies, despite the rhetoric of freedom, many people still experience themselves as trapped, powerless and immobilized. Ordinary speech abounds with phrases like "stuck," "hung up," "rat race" and "dead end" to describe work, marriage, and everyday life. The theme also appears in artistic creations. In a play ironically entitled *Happy*

Days, by the Nobel prize-winning playwright Samuel Beckett, both characters sit mired uncomfortably in piles of sand up to their waists. As the play proceeds, each act finds them more deeply buried in the sand until in the final act only their heads remain visible. The same writer ends his play *Waiting for Godot* by having Estragon say to Vladimir, "Let's go," and Vladimir answering, "Okay. Let's go." The stage directions then read, "They do not move. Curtain." In the same playwright's *Endgame* the characters peer out of garbage cans.

Themes of immobility and miredness are not new in contemporary cultural expression. Jean Paul Sartre's play *No Exit* is a classic statement. Luis Buñuel's film *The Exterminating Angel* depicts a group of people who for some eerie reason seem unable to get out of the salon where they are having a party. The American sociologist Ernest Becker discusses the striking frequency of such images in his book of essays *Angel in Armor* and attributes it to the perception felt by large numbers of people that they are totally incapable of influencing the vast and baffling social institutions they live in.

Whatever the historical circumstances that produce a consciousness of bondage, symbols of bondage recur constantly in the history of religion. One can be a prisoner in his own body, as Socrates described himself in *The Apology,* or a slave of the great Wheel of Fate, or chained to a rock in the Caucasus, or a captive in hell, or possessed by demons, or in slavery, or entombed. Whatever the symbolism, powerlessness means the inability either to get out or to exert significant influence over one's own destiny.

In view of this feeling of miredness, it is no wonder that one symbolic meaning of technology today, especially in the U.S.A., is that of *extrication.* Techno-power becomes the *deus ex machina* that lifts us out of our immobilized condition and delivers us from bondage. Two examples, one rather commonplace, one somewhat bizarre, illustrate this technological ritual of extrication. The first is the way jet tourist travel is increasingly sold with images of "escape" (extrication). The second is the infant (pseudo?) technology of "cryonics," the quick-freezing of human beings for possible resuscitation later, when cures for the diseases they have died of will presumably have been discovered.

Peruse the secular iconography of the travel pages of any large newspaper. It features a juxtaposition of bikini-clad women and jet airplanes. This is not surprising. Marshall McLuhan told us years ago that our culture's most commanding symbol is a "mechanical bride." When virgins wrestle with dynamos, curious hybrids can be expected to appear. The majority of the night dreams of people in industrial societies center on themes of sex and violence, or so clinicians tell us. The sex dreams reflect, they say, our hunger for belonging, the violent ones our desire for power. The admixture of woman and jet plane conjures both feeling clusters at once. The scantily clad girl smiling invitingly at poolside tells us we are loved, welcomed, nurtured—delivered from isolation and frustration. The soaring jet plane tells us it is all within our grasp. Technology extricates us, as the Air France ad proclaims, "from the ordinary." The airlines' omnipotent wings bear us aloft to an Elysium where, in contrast to our daily experience, the ad assures us, we can either be "deeply involved" or "left alone."

The theme of deliverance from the woes of this ordinary world to an extraordinary world, albeit even temporarily, through the powerful intervention of a benevolent saviour is an old one. In an interesting section on Shamanism in his *Primitive Mythology* Joseph Campbell says,

> Nor is he the victim of his trance: he commands it, as a bird the air in its flight. The magic of his drum carries him away on the wings of its rhythm, the wings of spiritual transport. The drum and dance simultaneously elevate his spirit and conjure to him his familiars—the beasts and birds, invisible to others, that have supplied him with his power and assist him in his flight. And it is while in his trance he is flying as a bird to the upper world, or descending as a reindeer,

bull or bear to the world beneath. . . . The early Russian missionaries and voyagers in Siberia in the first part of the eighteenth century noted that the shamans spoke to their spirits in a strange, squeaky voice. They also found among the tribes numerous images of geese with extended wings, sometimes of brass . . . in a highly interesting paleolithic hunting station known as Mal'ta, in the Lake Baikal area, a number of flying geese or ducks were found, carved in mammoth ivory. Such flying birds, in fact, have been found in many paleolithic stations. . . . Furthermore, in the great paleolithic cavern of Lascaux, in southern France, there is the picture of a shaman dressed in bird costume, lying prostrate in a trance and with the figure of a bird perched on his shaman staff beside him. The shamans of Siberia wear bird costumes to this day, and many are believed to have been conceived by their mothers from the descent of a bird. In India, a term of honor addressed to the master yogi is Paramahamsa: paramount or supreme (*parama*) wild gander (*hamsa*). In China the so-called "mountain men" or "immortals" (*hsien*) are pictured .as feathered, like birds, or as floating through the air on soaring beasts. . . . But the bird of the shaman is one of particular character and power, endowing him with an ability to fly in trance beyond the bounds of life, and yet return.

Of course the woes from which one is delivered by the bird vary from culture to culture. Philip Slater in *The Pursuit of Loneliness* shows how Americans today feel frustrated by conflicting quests for both privacy and community. We design technologies to insulate us from human contact (cars taking the place of trains, self-service devices). Insulated, we then begin to miss human relations. But when other persons do touch our lives, the experience seems intrusive, competitive or irksome. It is a vicious circle. We are on a pilgrimage in quest of both deeper involvement *and* more privacy. No wonder then that one travel ad assures us that on the sun-drenched enchanted island to which the huge bird will carry us one can have "all the involvement you want" or "none at all." The text of a recent Air France advertisement in the Sunday New York *Times* (February 8, 1970) includes the following:

Escape Your World, Embrace Ours.
Abandon the Ordinary. Fly with us to our exciting
European resort-villages. Where Internationals play. And
total involvement is up to you.
Join Escape Unlimited. Let yourself go. Embrace the uninhibited. Escape to any of three private and privileged resort
villages in the azure Mediterranean. . . . Now a limited
number of Americans may join Escape Unlimited and savor
the freedom of our continental Escape-Aways. . . .
Total Involvement Is Up to You. Escape Unlimited involves you in everything . . . or nothing.

The ad goes on to promise companionship with "fellow bons
amis" who are "lovers of the free and uninhibited life" and
"young in spirit" (if not always, I suppose, in chronology). The
key words are "involvement," "escape," "experience," "freedom," "excitement." The picture shows a generously endowed
woman frisking in the surf with a less clearly seen man. Both
appear young in years as well as in spirit. The sexual overtones of
the word "involvement" are underlined by the pictures, the
insulation from intrusion is guaranteed by the island's isolation.
Whereas in *this* vale of tears we lurch between deep loneliness
and bothersome interruptions, *there* we will experience both
perfect community and perfect privacy. No revivalist hymn ever
promised more. Sweet Beulah Land!

The link between our search for authentic community and the
hopes we pin on technology deserves further exploration. The
big bird is still swooping to save us in our need. But beware!
When we concentrate hopes so heavily, if the cure fails, the
disappointment, anger, and scapegoating of the false saviour sour
into righteous rage. The automobile, which promised to give us
privacy and mobility, freedom and community (or so we
hoped), turned on us. So now it becomes the object of that
peculiar kind of hatred felt by a lover abandoned or a devotee
betrayed. A group of college students, enacting a rite Henry
Adams would have savored, recently dug a grave and buried an
automobile. But they were really missing the point. Even a universal auto da fé of all our cars and jets would not really get at

the heart of our malady. The sickness is within. It is our inability, derived from our compulsive acquisitiveness and consequent fear of others, to fashion a more human form of community. No big bird can save us from that.

"The last enemy," St. Paul says, "is death." Although the fear of death and punishment after death does not haunt twentieth-century man as it did his medieval forebears, it still lingers in the recesses of the modern imagination. We fear death today not because dying entails physical pain—thanks to medical technology that can be dulled. Nor do we fear hell fire. Rather we fear death because it removes us from the human community. When we say that perpetual solitary confinement would be "worse than death" what we mean is that in both conditions we are deprived of human relationships, but that in death we are at least unaware of the deprivation.

All this is what makes the alleged science of "cryonics" so provocative, if admittedly in a somewhat ghoulish way. If death is the last enemy, then cryonics is surely the ultimate "technological fix." The theory is simple enough. Immediately after death, the body is frozen in a chemical solution to await the future discovery of cures for whatever caused the patient's demise. "Cryonics" comes from the Greek word for frost, *kryos*. Cryonics societies meet in New York and in California. The small journal of the movement, begun in 1966 as *Cryonics Reports*, was rechristened in 1970 and is now called simply *Immortality*. Several individuals are already stored in cryonic suspension awaiting the secularized last trumpet of a white-coated Gabriel in whose porcelain tureens, presumably, the first antidote to angina pectoris has just sprouted.

Alas, it is far too easy to hold up the cryonics crowd to ridicule, as I am even now tempted to do. Their argument is sensible enough. Organismal death (unconsciousness due to heart and lung stoppage) often precedes psychic death (destruction of cerebral cortex cells through lack of oxygen). Animals have been suspended after organismal death and returned to normal. Nor are the questions of cost of maintenance and the eventual ratio of caretakers to cryonically suspended souls in their liquid helium purgatory the really significant ones. Not even the seemingly overwhelming problem of finding space for all the bodies should detain us. One Robert Schimel, identified in *Cryonics Report* for December 1969 as "an experimental designer . . . employed as an instructor at Kent State University," has drawn up plans for a storage facility on the moon that would accommodate 1,437,969 patients. He calls it a "cryosanctorum."

It would be hard to imagine a more striking example of the contemporary reappearance of ancient symbols than the plan to store the frozen dead on the moon until they can be brought back to life. Since time immemorial people have seen the moon both as the land of the dead and as the sign that death is only a temporary state. Moon gods are frequently "chthonian" (funereal) deities as well. In the Hindu tradition recounted in one of the Upanishads the dead travel to the moon to await reincarnation, but since reincarnation is not ultimately desirable, the highest and most virtuous souls fly beyond the moon, where there is no more becoming. A slightly different version of this belief appears among the ancient Greeks, some of whom held that righteous souls are reabsorbed into the moon, from whence they originally came, but unrighteous ones must return to the earth. Moons and half moons appear on coffins, tombs and sarcophagi of the Babylonians, Hittites, Assyrians and Phoenicians. Residues of these old beliefs remain today in our popular superstitions and folklore relating witches and bats to the moon at Halloween, the day before All Saints' Day, and in the association of vampires, the living dead, with the full moon. There are also striking primitive religious parallels to Mr. Schimel's scheme, the belief that the spirits of the dead go to some nearby relatively inaccessible place and return when appropriate conditions are ripe—I think especially of Malinowski's work on the "baloma." But Mr. Schimel's point is not to resuscitate a myth. He is saying that once death is defined as a "problem" for which there is a technological "solution," then there is always at least a *theoretical* answer to every bug in the system.

Dispatching frozen corpses to the moon may seem funny, but the cryonics people cannot be dismissed with a laugh. Laughter can be a way of avoiding threatening issues, just as raising technical queries about cryonics is often a way to escape the philosophical questions it raises. Cryonics is interesting because it provides the clearest example of the refocusing of a perennial human hope (the conquest of death) from one symbolic object to another, from God to a machine. In one of the most familiar Greek Orthodox icons, Christ is seen striking open the caskets of the dead and consigning the newly awakened corpses either to bliss or to oblivion. In medieval theology the place where the resurrected ones spend eternity depends on their comparative virtue. In Calvinism it depends entirely on God's grace. In cryonic eschatology virtue has nothing to do with who gets resuscitated. But money does. At present the cryonics specialists must have a down payment of $500. After ten days $2,000 more is required for the initial rites, and following that, $6,000 for the encapsulation in liquid nitrogen for one year. After that it is $500 per year. This rather crass commercialization of the right to immortality recently sparked a science fiction novel, *Bug Jack Barron* by Norman Spinrad, in which a fearless TV commentator takes on the powerful top dog of the freeze business (Luther vs. Tetzel?). Cryonics gives man a new basis for an old, old hope.

The suspension theory is not very new. The Egyptians apparently believed that their pharaohs preserved in pyramidal cryosanctorums would eventually come alive again, not just in a superterrestrial sphere but here where they would need their bowls and dogs. Cryonics is a dramatic example of a problem that theologians have steadfastly avoided. If not nitrogen freezing, what about aging deterrents? If not in the next hundred years, what about the next thousand, or ten thousand? The theological issues fairly swarm over the subject. Do the cryonics people realize, for example, just how *Western* (even Christian) their operation is? There are some religious traditions in which coming back from the dead into *this* world is not at all a desirable goal. The instructions in *The Tibetan Book of the Dead* are specifically written to help the dead man, if possible, to resist and prevent a new birth. Preservation of the body and the rekindling of consciousness are not hoped for at all in religious traditions that view the body as evil and consciousness as illusory. Or consider the fact that for a white male of twenty-five in the U.S.A. today, suicide is the second most probable cause of death (auto accident is first). Presumably only people who choose to do so would be frozen, and suicides would not. But should they be condemned to an eternity of oblivion for one impulsive act? Or should they be frozen and revived when the cure is found, to give them another chance? Not to give them such a second chance would seem to perpetuate the old Roman Catholic teaching (now almost wholly inoperable) that a suicide dies in mortal sin and goes to hell forever.

There are numerous other "religious" questions. If cryonics grows into a more widely practiced art, the rituals and symbolic overtones attached to its equipment, practitioners, and procedures will be fascinating to watch. But the obviously symbolic-religious dimension of cryonics differs only in degree, not in kind, from the same dimensions of other technologies.

When does one begin to pray to the dynamo? Obviously certain technologies are beginning to achieve a ritual significance. They touch our fears and our fantasies at deep levels. They focus our hopes. They sanctify the values that guide our crucial decisions. They provide the ritual means by which a desired state may be attained.

Now I turn from technology as *ritual* (means of grace) to technology as *myth,* the symbolic definition of man's place and purpose in the scheme of things.

If old Henry Adams were to return in the flesh today, one place I would surely take him would be Anaheim, California, for a visit to Disneyland. Nowhere I have ever visited does the merging of memory, myth and machine become so complete. Nowhere do we see such wonderfully clear plasticized surrogates for our myths of origin and destiny.

When you take the famous submarine ride at Disneyland, you actually board an underwater craft that splashes beneath the surface, where you see sharks, octopi, sunken treasure ships and marine flora and fauna of every conceivable description—all rubber and fiberglass but astonishingly real-looking. Then, as the voyage is ending, the taped narrator's voice warns you not to expect to see any mermaids, since they are entirely mythical creatures. Instantly, of course, a covey of lovely sea maidens appears. The passengers chuckle, but nothing really seems amiss. After an hour or so in Disneyland that thin line between reality and artifice, fact and fancy, data and dream, seems to evaporate. Mermaids and giant squid, both plastic, inhabit the same world in what is surely the holy mountain of America's cultural symbols. No wonder Khrushchev wanted to see it. A man of the soil himself, he knew instinctively it was the American equivalent of Red Square, Lenin's tomb and the Moscow Puppet Theater combined. Disneyland is the place where our fondest memories, our mass-media fantasies and our timid hopes for the future are all mythically recreated and re-enacted. It is a consumer's Oberammergau, a permanent tribal dance marathon for middle America.

It is also a triumph. Anyone who minimizes Disneyland out of hand has simply not allowed its underlying vibrations to touch him. What you have to do, I think, is to purchase a Mouseketeer hat with those great protruding ears as you enter. Suspend all critical faculties temporarily and swing with the whole thing. Disneyland is not just for the kiddies. Its amusement park rides and layout can be misleading. It is an inspired repristination of small-town America, a never-ending liturgical celebration of the legend of the American past, and an effort to conjure a manageable future. Over sixty million visitors, so the management claims, have found their way to Mickey Mouse Mecca, and the number of pilgrims grows each year.

Omnia Disneyland *est divisa in partes tres.* There is *Frontier-*

land, where you can watch bloodthirsty Indians burning the cabins of settlers, take a trip on a full-size Mississippi riverboat, stroll through the (re-created) streets of old New Orleans while black minstrels whomp out Dixieland jazz on the street corner, or have a Creole dinner next to a darkened bayou lit only by (electrical) kerosene lanterns and (electrically powered) darting fireflies. The food is real if not particularly gourmet. During your visit to Frontierland, don't let your *knowledge* of American history distract you. We are dealing here not with what *happened* (which fusty antiquarians waste their lives digging up) but with what Americans like to *think* happened. Every tribe needs a myth and Americans are no different.

Now on to *Fantasyland*, the second province, where you will ride the submarine, scale a concrete Matterhorn, get whirled around in teacups, and careen through a scary funhouse, with Snow White's mean old witch cackling and leering at you from every wall. The third province is *Tomorrowland*, and it is by far the saddest. The fact is there is no tomorrow in Tomorrowland. What it dishes up is a tepid extension of today's technology—bigger, shinier but not really different. The charismatic names in Tomorrowland, ominously enough, are not Tom Sawyer or Dopey as they were in Frontierland and Fantasyland. They are Monsanto, GE and Kodak. In the Disney version our future is safely in the hands of the great American corporations. But it is a rather dull future. Monsanto magically reduces you in size by sending you through a miscroscope and allows you to explore the inside of an atom. GE proudly displays the kitchen of tomorrow (which I'm told has to be changed all the time, since today's kitchens are always catching up), and your telephone company displays a 360-degree movie screen on which, however, the movie shows the America of about five years back. You can buy at any souvenir stand in Disneyland a music box which, when opened, plays "Someday My Prince Will Come." But this is as close as Uncle Walt's eden ever comes to eschatology. For Monsanto there is of course no tomorrow. There is only a flashier and more efficient today. Those who hold the reins of power in any society can hardly be expected to envision a future that is very different from the present. They rather like the present. Maybe that's why when Jesus talked about the Kingdom of God he always said that only the poor would know what he meant.

There is no hope in the technological religious vision of Disneyland. For the past there is nostalgia; for the present, sentimentality; and for the future, extrapolation and programming. There is of course a big moon rocket there, but few people seemed interested in it. Unlike the dynamo at the Great Exposition, no one would think of praying to it. There is no charisma in Tomorrowland. Visitors hurry through it and sneak back for a second ride on the Caribbean pirate boat. Disney's bland tomorrow makes anyone prefer the colorful, if legendary, past.

At the center of Disneyland, stretching across its length and linking the three provinces, like the sacred world center in a primitive grove, is Mainstreet, America. It is the heart of Disneyland, an entrancing re-creation, in perfect human scale, of the main street in ten thousand American towns of the 1930s and 1940s—now gone forever. There is the local drugstore and ice cream emporium before Rexall and Howard Johnson. There is the little movie theater, the flower store, the petite shops and bakeries that mass food merchandising has wiped out. That street runs not only through the center of Disneyland but through the racial memory of millions of Americans, still bewildered and disoriented by urban monstrosities and characterless suburban sprawls. Mainstreet invites you to walk down it, to linger, to loaf a bit, to idle. Cars do not drown out the tinkling bell on the door of the jeweler's or gasoline fumes spoil the smell of the freshly baked bread. (Oh I know there *were* cars on Main Street in the 1930s, but Disneyland is interested in the way we would like to remember it.)

There is a gate of course, through which you pass upon leaving Disneyland to find your car in the smog and crawl in bumper-to-bumper traffic, past the giant war industries, back to Sam Yorty's Los Angeles. But don't let the exit mislead you. Disneyland does not stop at the ticket booth. Its aura hangs over all of Southern

California and over our entire Monsanto-Mickey Mouse country. We *are* a people who cannot accept the real story of our past, especially of what we have done to red and black, and who therefore *must* tell ourselves the myth of the Good Sheriff and elect him if possible to govern our state (as Californians have). We cannot manage much real fantasy, so we let Donald Duck and Dumbo do it for us. And as for tomorrow, the technological afterlife erected by the titans of industry seems dull and devoid of attraction. Perhaps the reason is that there are no powerful myths of the future for those who have turned their past and present over to the media.

But fear not. Disney Enterprises knows full well that its *Geist* does not stop at the gate. The company is now planning a full-sized city within the gates of Disney World in Florida, and people will actually reside there. And after that, why not a small state, then a big state? Mickey Mouse might not make a bad monarch after all, considering the competition.

Besides using its techniques to re-create a mythical past and paint an image of the future, technology has also begun to supply the root metaphor by which man understands himself.

The use of machine images to symbolize man has a long history, the classic written statement being Julien La Mettrie's *L'Homme Machine*, first published in 1747. Although his book shocked many of his contemporaries it really should not have, since La Mettrie was merely extending insights that had already been in circulation since the previous century. During Descartes' time (1596–1650) there was a lively interest in comparing men with machines and in making life-sized mechanical replicas of people. Some contemporary observers thought these toy humanoids sacrilegious. Descartes, however, disagreed. He drew the familiar analogy between man who makes automata and God who makes man. The human body, he declared, "is a machine made by the hands of God, which is incomparably better arranged, and adequate to movements more admirable than in any machine of human invention." Descartes added, of course, that the mechanically superior human body was also differentiated by the fact that God had placed within it a rational soul through which man could participate in the spiritual world.

Since Descartes and La Mettrie there has been a continuing tradition—now defended, now attacked—of viewing man *sub specie machinae*. Sometimes man is seen as a machine, sometimes machines are endowed with human qualities. Sometimes the symbolization is negative, at other times positive. The metaphor persists. Its influence can be seen in as widely disparate places as behavioral reinforcement therapies and cybernetic theories of human knowledge and perception.

The symbolization of *society* as a machine is not, however, as easily traceable a tradition. The seventeenth and eighteenth-century deists, influenced by some of the same currents that touched Descartes, liked to refer to the natural universe as a clock God had created, wound up, and left to its own devices. But I can find few poetic or iconic images of society as a machine until the nineteenth century. Poets then began to use technological images, especially of factories and locomotives, to represent the entire new age that seemed to be rushing in. Thoreau felt sure the shriek of the locomotive whistle was the harbinger of a new and undesirable age.

The filmic apogee of the machine-as-society motif is Charles Chaplin's classic *Modern Times*, made in 1936. Here the factory and its machines represent the society Chaplin and many others were beginning to regard with suspicion and distrust. Charlie is a worker who is driven insane by the monotony of endlessly tightening bolts and is finally drawn into the machine as a helpless victim. (Interestingly, he later escapes by skillfully using the machine against his pursuers.)

There is a subtle connection between the depiction of society as a machine and the perennial fear that man may be turned into a machine. As Chaplin himself said, *Modern Times* was an effort to "say something about the way life is being standardized and channelized, and men turned into machines—and the way I felt about it." In Stanley Kubrick's *2001* a computer named Hal takes command of the space ship until a determined astronaut disconnects his circuits. In *The Forbin Project*, released in 1970, the computer wins, making everyone on earth his subjects.

The fear that man could be enslaved by the machine reflects some of the same discomfort we noted in the age of Descartes. No wonder many people still have an uneasy feeling when they watch machines performing humanoid tasks, a fascination tinged with fear. The uneasiness is the obverse of the feeling experienced when we observe muscles or joints and see how they resemble machines. This feeling resembles in some measure the mixture of fascination and horror of the sacred described in Rudolf Otto's *The Idea of the Holy*. Horror films also suggest contemporary man's ambivalence about technology. In the Frankenstein variety of horror film, an invention of either a well-intentioned or a "mad" scientist gets out of hand and threatens to destroy all of life: technology as demon. In the Dracula type, human beings are deprived of their souls by vampires or zombies. In a more recent crossbreeding of these two species, the scientist employs his technology to make docile slaves out of people, usually through injections or electrical control. In either case the loss of "soul" or conscious selfhood is portrayed as worse even than death. (Zombies would *rather* be just plain dead instead of the "living dead.")

The loss of soul through demonic technology is a modern fear. But it has obvious theological roots in this notion that the loss of soul is even worse than death. Still it is important again to notice the ambivalence: terror at the machine's and/or the society's capacity to deprive us of our soul is always mixed with a fascination for that power and the possibility of using it for one's own purposes. "Mechanophobia," the fear of the machine, is a complex compound in which a certain amount of fascination is usually present. The standard line at the end of a hundred horror movies, as the writhing monster dies or the evil lab goes up in flames, is that with a little different luck or a little more virtue the whole thing might have gone the other way.

Technology today is not just something we use. We invest our machines with our deepest hopes and terrors. They buzz and flash through our imagination. They deliver us from danger, threaten to destroy us, steal our souls, trick us into serving them, bewilder and enrage us. In the dream of the Golem or of Hal in *2001* they become men and help us or tyrannize us. In other instances they lure us or coerce us into becoming like them. Whatever else they may be, however, at least in the all-too-real world of fantasy and human symbol, the artifices of technology are certainly *not* just neuter tools waiting to be picked up and used.

What would Henry Adams have thought if he had lived to witness the ritual burial of an automobile, the "die-in" in protest against jet noises at Logan Airport, or the astronaut in *2001* ripping the cells out of the rebellious computer? Adams did not get the whole picture. Perhaps he looked at it too soon. The dynamo today has not just replaced the Virgin of Chartres, it has also replaced the gargoyles, those leering ugly reminders of the Evil One. And that is a lot of symbolic weight for any single symbol to incarnate. Many of the hopes and fears we have in the past directed toward technologies have now become much more intense. We could be entering a period in which the Western attitude toward technology becomes just plain negative instead of ambivalent, in which the demonic face of the machine eclipses the angelic. Maybe in our time the dynamo is becoming more gargoyle and less Virgin.

Adams visited the Great Exposition in 1900. Are we now turning away from the dynamo? By 2000 will the Virgin or some other more recognizably "religious" symbol, in the more conventional sense, have replaced the dynamo?

There is evidence that our culture may be shifting its attitude toward technology and that the result could be momentous. In my own view some corrective is needed, but it would be too bad if what happens is twentieth-century Ludditism. Confronted with a machine in the midst of our garden, we are tempted to seek salvation first in the flowers and then in the gears. But from the perspective of biblical thought, *neither* the garden nor the machine can save man. The Hebrew prophets knew this. There were two major temptations against which they warned the errant children of Abraham. One was the sweet lure exuded by the sacred grottoes of the Canaanites: nature religion. The other was the temptation to fall down and worship the things made with their own hands: idolatry. Yahweh creates man to enjoy and tend the garden, but not to offer sacrifice to it; to make things for his own use, but not to pray to them. The cardinal sin for Hebrew man is to attach religious significance to inappropriate objects. His effort to avoid idolatry produced at once the earthy Hebrew appreciation for food and flesh, but also the constant refusal (albeit with periodic episodes of backsliding) to divinize either. It also produced a healthy capacity to use the things man could make without investing them with excessive hopes. He could build a sturdy ark but not a tower that would touch heaven.

Yahweh fought a constant battle with the nature baalim of Canaan on the one side and man-made idols on the other. The struggle of the creator-redeemer God to purge man of his illusory hopes and ungrounded fears provides the dynamic of Hebrew religion and, to some extent, of its Christian daughter. It has reappeared in various forms throughout Western history: in the medieval conflict between the Cathedral and the Desert, in the American version of the City and the Wilderness, in today's alternative life-style images projected by the astronauts and the rural communards.

The biblical tradition never sanctifies one at the expense of the other. It supports both nature and artifact when they are appreciated as the provisional, limited creations they are. It condemns both insofar as we escalate them into sources of salvation. Theologians (mainly Protestant) have seen some of the same dangers in the Virgin that the Hebrew prophets saw in the baal: the illegitimate sanctification of natural processes. Other theologians (many Catholic) have viewed with distrust the confidence modern man places in his technical prowess. It is thus understandable why Protestants should have endorsed "artificial means" of birth control while Catholics have resented the intrusion of technology into the "natural."

In recent years our heads have been pounded by a wave of writing about technology and society. But in this ocean of print one finds almost nothing about the symbolic significance technologies acquire. The Adamsian sensibility has run thin. Yet because symbols do exercise such massive power, especially in the long run, few areas of investigation are more crucial. If man is to take responsibility for his world, including its symbols, then the question is too important to be left undiscussed or ignored. I do not believe, with Tristan Tzara, that the machine can save man from destiny. Man's only destiny is to use his God-given freedom to shape and achieve his destiny for himself. If he refuses this destiny, then nothing can save him; no Virgin, no dynamo, nothing at all.

CHAPTER TWELVE

The Flintstones in Recife

When the world speaks to us, without our being able to speak to it, we are deprived of speech, and hence condemned to be unfree.
—Gunther Anders

ONE NIGHT a couple years ago I was visiting in the modest apartment of a schoolteacher in the city of Recife in the poverty-cursed northeast of Brazil. We had eaten a fish dinner served in traditional *nordestano* style, quaffed thick black coffee and lit some small cigars. Then it happened: The children flicked on the TV. There pranced onto the screen a cartoon series called *The Flintstones*, made in the U.S.A. a few years before with sound dubbed in Portuguese. It is the story of a modernized Neanderthal family. The script that night had something to do with Fred Flintstone's bowling league. As I watched, my stomach sank. The canned laughter used in the show, the banal situations, the cleverly contrived ads, the lack of contact with life, in Recife or anywhere else, sickened me. It especially upset me that these Brazilian children devoured North American leftovers so hungrily. TV obviously reached them very effectively.

In the United States, mired in the effluvium of a frenzied consumer society, insulated in a thousand ways from our own people's poverty, the Flintstones on TV seem like one tiny insult among others, perhaps a mere venial sin. In Recife, on the other hand, surrounded by sickness, hunger and hopelessness, the humor seemed obscene, a mortal trespass. At my hotel that night

I dreamed about the Flintstones, and in my dream the cartoon TV cavemen reached out of the screen, strangled the children, and ate them.

I left Brazil more convinced than ever that the mass media are distributing a destructive and debasing form of religion. They provide the heroes, myths, sacraments and beatific visions for more and more people every day. The fact that mass-media piety is not recognized as such and therefore not criticized and called to account does not make it any less influential. In fact religion is probably more influential in those cultures where the values it supports are not seen as "religious" but are simply a part of the culture at large. Fish seldom take special note of the water they are swimming in.

This incident in Recife focused for me the need for a theological response to the challenge of mass media. The new media, especially those dealing in pictorial images, are immensely powerful. They have already markedly altered the cultural sensibility of the high-consumption societies and can certainly do so in the poor nations as well. TV reaches us at a level of consciousness below the critically centered intelligence. It inundates us with vivid images. Also the technology of mass media is "one way." It makes us all quiescent consumers of their images and values. It is not true that if we could just use mass TV to transmit something better than the Flintstones, all would be well. It would not. It would still be a monodirectional and therefore a manipulative exercise. The technology of TV has specialized in enlarging the screen, adding color, increasing the broadcast distance. All these developments concentrate more power in the sender but fail completely to enable the receiver to respond. The present technology of the mass media prevents dialogue and emphasizes one-way "communication." There were no technical devices in that simple Recife home to help facilitate communication *among* neighbors. They did not even have a telephone, and such technical possibilities as community TV, feed-back devices, sender-transistors, or easily available and usable TV filming equipment have not been distributed. People are encouraged by the present technology of media to be "listeners" and "watchers," consumers, not creators. Close neighbors can be reached by CBS more easily than they can reach one another. Present mass media not only fail to congeal community, they even increase people's isolation from one another at local levels.

Because of increased migration and the breakdown of traditional values and sources of information, especially in poor countries, the average person must rely on mass media today more than previously. The boom in one-way communication devices comes just as the need for orientation to a new setting is most acute. Uprooted villagers watch TV in the city to find out where and who they are. The result is doubly alienating, since just as the poor nations begin to rely more heavily on mass media, the rich nations are increasing their control of the scope, content and style of the media. Again the "communication" is one way. There is no button a poor Recife family can push to beam a message into the home of a Manhattan script writer or advertising agent.

Perhaps the most unsettling issue raised by the Flintstones in Recife is that such programs produce an inevitable trivialization of human issues. With a few exceptions, divisive issues are avoided, conflict is dissolved into personality differences, the raw edges of life disappear in a sea of gray froth. The media, designed to reach the broadest possible audience, thus discourage consumers from having strong feelings about anything important. It is crucial to keep the political significance of trivialization in mind, since banality seems non-political. The fact is that whenever real issues can be trivialized, the status quo is strengthened.

Finally, there is a close correlation between the images and life styles projected by the media (clothing, family roles, furniture, house design, utensils and utilities) and the advertisements. Even the Flintstones, though a Neanderthal family, had a car, a washer, a refrigerator, a record player and a TV, albeit all cutely hewn from stone. Only adults make the mistake of believing there is a real difference between programs and ads. Children watch both.

Both first create, and then suggest ways to satisfy, human needs. But the process is one of seduction. Genuine human needs are exploited for purposes foreign to the fulfillment of the viewer.

Some of the issues raised by the mass media refer principally to poor countries whose media are owned and operated by rich ones, such as the United States. Other issues obtain primarily in the so-called "advanced" countries that have already attained the pinnacle of consumer culture. But in all societies, rich and poor, the mass media weaken the inner life of individuals and groups and thus increase their vulnerability to outside control.

In a culture inundated by mass media, people are not just informed and entertained by them. They soon begin gauging the significance, and in some sense even the reality, of events on the basis of whether they see them in a magazine or on TV. People who have actually witnessed accidents, for example, have become very troubled if they do not find an account of them in the paper. The disease is progressive. Eventually, even in activities in which the mass media play no direct role, people begin to need more and more confirmation of their inner reality from large outside institutions. The "media culture" then becomes a kind of touchstone for one's own worth and even one's own perception. Abstraction defeats concreteness. People begin to distrust their own ideas and impulses if they are not corroborated by the media. Distrusted long enough, these feelings are forgotten and die. The signals begin to prescribe not only what is good and true, but what is real.

There are those who will say any critique of the media is aimed at the wrong target, that the real villain is not the media at all but the society that has so drained us of inwardness and so decimated our forms of human association that we stand isolated and defenseless against the onslaught of media signals. The mass media, this rebuttal says, merely rush in to fill a vacuum created by much larger enemies of the spirit—capitalism perhaps, or bureaucracy or industrialization.

The skeptics have a point. I do not wish to separate the mass media from the more comprehensive forces that conspire with them to invade and lay waste our psyches. But I suspect the mass media do play a more powerful and independent role than most observers think. In this I differ not only with the media professionals who tell us they are only giving us "what the people want," but also with the radicals who reduce the mass media and their culture to the mere stench exuded by a terminally ill body politic. Both these groups agree, ironically, that the mass media merely *reflect* social reality. The pros are busy trying, through audience polls and viewer ratings, to discover what that elusive reality is, so they can reflect it more accurately and make more money. The rebels are busy trying, through revolution or reform, to change the social reality so that people will want, and presumably get, something different through the media. Both doubt that the media can take initiative or do anything to change the social reality very much.

I disagree with both groups. The media pros are wrong when they say people "get what they want." They get what someone else wants to give them and must be constantly taught by the same media to believe it is what they want. Nor are the rebels right to ignore the mass media until a new society is somehow produced without media help. Against both these groups it must be insisted that the mass media do produce and distribute ideas, values and images—the stuff from which culture is made. And ideas and images do contribute to the altering or preserving of social forms. The media themselves will never bring in the new era, but without them no new era will ever appear.

The mass media and the signals they distribute both reflect and reinforce the underlying social fabric. It is true that our consuming and competing way of life breaks us into isolated atoms and that industrial cities play havoc with the small subgroups where stories are passed on from person to person. It is also true that all these centrifugal forces contribute to our frailty and impotence. But what I am saying here is that the mass media are not just the unfortunate side effect of this crime, they are active accomplices.

So the answer to my question of why we are so vulnerable to their signals is that both the media and the society make us that way. They are co-conspirators who collaborate in rendering us vulnerable. We will cure our deadly susceptibility to media myths only by a counterattack against both the mass media themselves and against the misshapen society they strengthen and speak for.

Our dilemma is a serious one. Cut off by the currents of the age both from my own inner story and from the story of my people, I listen for another story to hear and to tell myself. I listen because I have no real choice. As a Homo sapiens I am an incorrigibly storytelling animal. Literally I cannot live without a story. But I do not have to search long. A substitute is readily supplied. The most powerful technologies ever devised churn out signals to keep me pliable, immature and weak. They hit at my most vulnerable spot. There is still time for us to learn again to tell stories—mine, yours, ours. If we do not, the signals will sweep all before them. Their gentle bleeps and reassuring winks will lull us into a trance from which there is no awakening. If there is any hell where souls are lost forever, that would be it.

Let us turn now from the image of the Flintstones to the image of another family which is also present in the cultural consciousness of millions of people: the holy family—Joseph, Mary and Jesus—in flight toward Egypt. Poor, harassed, displaced and persecuted, they are headed for the awesome uncertainty of a strange land. Surely they represent the deepest fears and hopes of millions of people more than a stereotyped bourgeois consumer family, albeit draped in Neanderthal furs. The holy family must face death, privation and exile. Their lives are anything but trivial. They own no modern conveniences. Yet they live by a hope no tyrant can extinguish. Their story, were they on earth today, would probably either be avoided by the media as too controversial or sweetened into a domestic travelogue.

I do not contrast the Flintstones and the Flight into Egypt to disparage a particular TV serial. I could also have discussed many others, including the Dick Van Dyke show, which is also exported all over Latin America. I am interested rather in showing that both in their content and in their technical structure, the mass media today present an unavoidable challenge to the Christian vision of human life.

The Christian tradition has generated a set of stories, images and values that provides a vantage point by which some judgments can be made about cultural phenomena. As theologians we try to make these judgments as sharply as we can without claiming omniscience. We also recognize that because of the flow of history, the unseen bias in our own perspective, and the constant development of the religious and ethical consciousness, no such judgment can be made once and for all. Still, theology does make critical judgments. It is pastoral and prophetic. When it ceases to do so, it ceases to be theology and becomes an inferior form of sociology of religion.

The Bible contains examples of the communication of messages to all kinds of people, and it sees "God" as the communicator *par excellence*. He is the "Word," indentified in his very essence—*Logos* (Greek) and *Dabar* (Hebrew)—with communication. But it is important to notice how God speaks to man. He does not communicate one way; there is dialogue. God speaks, but man also speaks back. The Creator makes man a responding creature and constantly calls him to respond to the Creator and to his fellow man, hopefully in love, but always in freedom. The thrust of the idea of the Incarnation is that God intentionally makes Himself fully vulnerable to whatever response man makes.

When the Nicene Creed says "true God and true man," what it means is that in the life of Jesus, man not only learns about God, he also learns something important about himself. We could even say that man learns something from the life of Christ about the essential structure of authentic human communication. What he learns is that communication requires the possibility of response. Ultimately, self-communication entails vulnerability. The *mode* of God's self-disclosure to man, in the life of a man who is abused, rejected and murdered, is not accidental to the *content* of that disclosure. God shows Himself to be one who is willing to risk the most dangerous consequences of dialogue in order to make His message known.

In the Hebrew Scriptures the same paradigm of dialogue, vulnerability and the call for response can be seen. Amos, Isaiah and Jeremiah had to struggle with their people, expose themselves to persecution and ridicule, and pay the price of weakness in order to be heard. In this way they were not just God's spokesmen in the content of their message but also in the mode of its delivery. One-way "communication" by decree, fiat or promulgation is viewed by the Bible as the style not of prophets but of tyrants and oppressors. In the New Testament the apostles speak in synagogues and public places. They expose themselves to danger and rejection as well as to authentic acceptance. Jesus himself begins his ministry by reading from the prophet Isaiah in a synagogue and commenting on it in such a way that the response endangers his life. The hearers tried to toss him off a cliff. His final statement to the corrupt religious and political leaders of his day is made through an act of total vulnerability, the cross. The crucifixion eloquently expresses the logic of the biblical view of communication—probably no single event in the history of mankind is so widely known—and it is an event involving vulnerability unto death.

With this biblical model in mind it seems inaccurate to call most of our present mass media "means of communication." In the light of what Christianity teaches about the essential ingredients of communication, they are not means of "communication" at all. They are obstacles to communication and means, mainly, for social control, propaganda and coerced persuasion.

The church itself has rarely modeled its own form of communication on the prophets and Jesus. Preaching, evangelizing and catechizing have often been done in a coercive and monodirectional fashion. Still, by its (frequently ignored) teaching that free consent is absolutely essential to faith, Christianity has preserved a principle of communication that builds in the necessity of response and therefore of possible rejection.

But what is the relationship, if any, between *The Flintstones*, as its message poured into the Recife home, and the communication of a religious message?

We must reject the idea that there is a fundamental difference between religious and secular forms of communication. If Christ's message has any validity at all, it is not as some special esoteric form of "religious" communication. He tells us something about the structure of *all* human hearing and response. Nor can we allow *The Flintstones* and the ads to pass as mere fluff. The programs and commercials, as well as the structure and style of the mass media, preach a cultural religion. It is not the task of the church and of theology merely to interpret or defend Christianity and its institutions. Christianity is obligated by the faith to defend man himself against incursions, belittlements and attacks. The church's task is to be *advocatus hominis*, the advocate of man, especially where man is weak, poor or powerless. Without being arrogant, we must insist that media of so-called "communication" whose structure and content pervert human needs or blunt crucial issues are destructive of man's sanctity. We must also insist that the present technologies of the mass media—because they violate the inherent nature of human communication, isolate man from those close to him, and deepen his powerlessness—are a menace not just to "religion," which has often used just such methods, but to the integrity of man himself.

We cannot, as men and women of faith, merely eschew the use of structurally inhuman media for "religious" purposes, and then believe we have kept ourselves pure. We must oppose the inhumane and unjust dimensions of these media just as we oppose other forms of bondage, oppression and dehumanization. And as people committed to the Kingdom of God and the maturation of the species, we must do more than merely oppose. We must demonstrate the dialogical form of communication with all its risk and promise.

Christianity has been entrusted with a message it believes is crucial for the health and even for the "salvation" of man. The word "salvation" may sound archaic, but what it means is "making-whole," the healing and reconciling, not only of person to person, but of man to God and to the natural cosmos. It means the full liberation of humankind. Christianity makes the message known in four ways. It tells, i.e., teaches, preaches and announces. It *demonstrates* the message by the quality of its corporate life. It is, or should be, "a provisional demonstration of God's intention for all people" (Barth). It is a "sign of the Kingdom." Christianity should also nourish and *support* whatever signs of the New Humanity, whatever strides toward a restored human community, and whatever "first fruits of the Kingdom" it finds. They come not just in the "churchly realm" but in all sectors of the world. The Spirit blows where it lists, and the signs of the Kingdom appear where we least expect them. Finally, Christianity *celebrates* the promise of the message and its partial, periodic fulfillment with song and feasting, with dance and stringed instrument.

Given the importance of the message, one might think that the original "Communicator" would choose any means whatever to make sure it was heard. But it does not happen that way. "The Word was made flesh," the fourth Gospel says, "and dwelt among us." "Dwelling" suggests a long-term permanent commitment to the ambiguities and limitations of the human world. In his ministry Jesus utilized the fabric of images and stories and the institutional networks of communication of his day. But he refused Satan's tempting offer to use coercive power or spellbinding tricks. Most of his teachings are parables and "logia," or sayings. Even his so-called "sermons" are seen by biblical scholars as later assemblages of single utterances arising out of particular human situations. They are not abstract discourses delivered to faceless crowds without reference to particular events. As a celebrator, Jesus deepened moments of joy, anticipation, fear, love and hope through the use of appropriate gestures and words. The style and manner of Jesus' communication closely cohere with the content of his message, that God has come to be with man forever, and because the basic power of the universe is *for* man, no humiliation need be final, no injustice unalterable, no sorrow beyond comfort. Sickness and sin, bondage and despair—all are doomed in the light of the unlimited resources that are made available to man. Man is free to become what he was originally intended to be, a partner in the cultivation and enjoyment of the cosmos.

A theology of the means of communication begins not only in the belief that Jesus demonstrates the essential character of human communication. It also begins with the conviction that man is intended to become a communicator. God, the Logos, creates man in His own image. As Paulo Freire says, "To be a man, a man must say his word." The utter centrality of communication becomes clear when we see that in the biblical view, the purpose of history is the bringing forth of a new community, using the broken, hate-filled anti-communities we now have but purifying and transmuting them into communities of justice and joy. Communication can only occur in community.

This does not mean that the sore issues dividing people today are mere "failures to communicate." The angry hunger of the Third World cannot be salved by a skillful lesson in group dynamics or by another TV satellite. Oppressors and oppressed "communicate" only when the rage of the underdog finally frees him from his exploiter. When real "communication" begins, all parties concerned discover that it is risky and painful. It requires a redistribution of bread and power. The communication of outrage helps build the needed new community by challenging the anti-communities within which people are now trapped. The present bondage of poor nations to rich ones provides a vivid example of this kind of anti-community.

But just as there are anti-communities that pretend to be communities, and must be exposed for the charades they are, so there is a kind of "anti-communication" which pretends to be communication but destroys the only basis on which human communication can possibly occur—dialogue, risks and response. A theology of mass communications media will expose the fraudulence of anti-communication, alert the victims of non-dialogical propaganda, and demonstrate in its own style a risk-taking, response-inducing approach.

Are the present means of "mass communication" then incorrigibly anti-communicative? Does their non-dialogical technical structure inherently prevent reciprocity, feedback, argument, altercation, critical response? Are the "mass media" unalterably destructive of human community?

No. Admittedly the present technical structure and political control of the mass media are largely guilty of the indictment, but I do not believe either the structure or the control is unalterable. I reject the elitist notion that the present forms of media can be utilized for justice merely by throwing out those who now control them and replacing them with more enlightened people. I also reject the notion that the humanizing of the media is merely a technical problem—simply requiring more community antennas, citizen bands, and sender-transistors. Both these ideas fail because the present one-sided technical form of the media results from the political control man has exercised—by rich over poor, North over South, men over women, and white over black. The solution is neither simply political nor simply technical, neither Ludditism nor Leninism (busting the machines or seizing their control). We need to change *both* the way media are controlled *and* the technical composition of the means of "communication" themselves.

In an age of increasing elite power and of the growing authority of the central state, we should stop the further development of broadcast TV and radio, of one signal emanating from a central source to be picked up by numberless receivers. What we need instead are simple easy-to-use means whereby small communities, minority groups, neighborhood unions, and other groups can communicate effectively with one another. We need real "networks," not the vertical conduits that are now inaccurately called "networks." Ordinary people need to develop their competence and confidence in the use of media for their own purposes, to define and celebrate their own lives and concerns, to deepen their awareness, to speak out their anger. We need also means of technical access, so that groups who wish to propose or protest can get their message seen and heard in a dramatic form. We need movie equipment that is cheap and easy to use, so that poor people can tell their story to themselves and others. These technical innovations are all already possible, though underdeveloped for obvious political reasons. If they become as available as TV receivers and transistors they could become a more powerful means than print to help the oppressed of any age claim the promise of liberation.

Churches today often ask what can be done about the media boom, the enormous growth of "the consciousness industry." My foregoing analysis would yield the following tentative proposals:

1) The church should avoid the contradiction of trying to make widespread use of media that are technically non-dialogical and therefore perpetuate passive, quiescent, immature people.

2) The church should demonstrate its own message with radio, TV, festival, dance, film, music and light in ways that elicit rebuttal and response. This acceptance of vulnerability is an essential part of the message itself.

3) The church should bless and support those groups that are trying to alter the monopolistic policy control of the media and distribute it more widely. In general, the closer the source of control is to those who eventually hear the message, the better it will be.

4) In its schools and parishes the church should encourage people to develop a critical, suspicious attitude toward mass media. The images and values of the media can be sifted and resisted most easily if recipients have an ample chance to discuss them among themselves and, most importantly, produce counter-images. People still trust primary nets of information more than media.

5) The church can demonstrate in its own life a style of

communication that is participatory, response-inducing and vulnerable. This suggests discarding some present forms of totally teacher-controlled teaching or totally preacher-controlled preaching. People who learn in school or parish to respond, criticize, and formulate their own ideas are not as subject to the seduction of media as those who have learned to be docile and quiescent.

6) The church can encourage the further technical development of more community-building forms of media, devices more accessible to ordinary people. This has a special importance for church-owned radio and TV stations.

7) The church can oppose the further enlargement of one-way media systems, especially in countries where the die is not yet fully cast. For Latin America, for example, to duplicate the monodirectional structure of North American (and most other) TV systems, would be a disaster. Instead, why not more video-tape, closed-circuits, community antennas? This idea will probably be opposed not only by outside imperialist groups who want mind-capturing devices to control the masses but also by some change-oriented national elites who still want to speak *to* the people without listening. The real political question is not only how the control of media can be wrenched from "outsiders," it is how it can be put in the hands of the people themselves. This means going far beyond the nationalization of media. It means striving for their decentralization, politically *and* technically.

8) In the present political and technical structure, before the needed changes are made, the church can use the time it gets on the media to provide opportunities for groups that are otherwise voiceless or powerless. This is clearly only an interim tactic, but it is also obviously the church's right and its role as *advocatus hominis*.

A theology of the media begins with a vision of what human communication entails. But we need not accept this vision merely on blind faith. It is confirmed in our own experience. We learn time and again what it costs to say a word that is really heard. But such a theology must move on to examine and evaluate what now passes for human "communication" in our world. What facilitates it? What prevents it? What falsifies it? The full realization of total human communication will probably never come. Still, even in this "fallen" age, we can occasionally experience it, and once we do we can never settle for pseudo-communication again.

CHAPTER THIRTEEN

The Future of Theology: A Poetic Postscript

GEORGE SANTAYANA once remarked that to try to be religious "in general" is like trying to speak language in general. It cannot be done. We speak one language or another and we are religious in this way or that way, not in general. Santayana was right. The holy makes itself felt in human life in this vase, that hymn, this myth, that rite. It appears "in, with and under" specific earthly acts and artifacts. The infinite is known through the finite, the transcendent in the immanent. So to disparage the *particular* rites and practices by which real people have encountered the divine, as intellectuals often do in their quest for some distilled essence of religion beyond its flesh and blood incarnations, seems to me not only condescending but also ultimately illusory.

In this book I have explored some of the grisly, earthy ways in which what I call "people's religion" helps individuals and human groups to survive psychic invasion, to retain a hold on the past and to stoke the flames of hope when they flicker. I have tried throughout to avoid equating the voices of the spirit with the particular forms in which those voices have spoken, a mistake made by dogmatists of all faiths. But I have also tried to avoid belittling the importance of the concrete shapes the spirit has taken, an error made by the spiritists and Gnostics of all ages. After all this is said, however, we are still left with the vexing question of the relationships among this bewildering plethora of rites and creeds, devils and divinities. We are left with the age-old questions of pluralism, relativity and truth.

Here too, however, I find Santayana's analogy from language a suggestive one. It helps us not only to appreciate the concreteness and particularity of religious faith, it also helps clarify the relationships *among* and *between* the different visions. For example, speaking English does not preclude my learning to talk in French and perhaps learning to understand a little of several other tongues. Indeed, learning another language frequently helps us to learn the limitations of our own and to appreciate its positive qualities more. This is also true of faith. In addition, as one hears and learns more languages, one discovers that the human reality they encode and express is shared by all people. But one also finds out that the variety of human languages is not just an inconvenient misfortune; it reminds us that there are actually multiple forms of consciousness, and that no single thought-word system could possibly encompass the infinite ways reality can be grasped and symbolized. All this holds as well for the variety of forms the spirit assumes. Finally, just as Esperanto, the ill-fated attempt to concoct a synthetic language from the elements of living ones, was a miserable flop, so attempts to paste together a synthesized world faith are also doomed to failure. Thus the foregoing pages are in part a defense of the extravagant variety of forms religious expression takes against those who would like to tailor the spirit to precut patterns—a defense, if you will, of schism, heresy and heterodoxy. It is also a defense of the reality of religion against those who dismiss it as delusion, superstition or opiate.

In my saner moments I doubt very much that such defenses are actually needed. The human spirit will undoubtedly continue to spawn myths and weave symbolic meanings, without much regard either to intellectual attacks or to zealous defenses, as long as the species exists. Though in the short run the spirit is catastrophically subject to trickery, coercion and exploitation, in the long run it can neither be exterminated nor domesticated. It is, as St. Paul says, "Persecuted but not forsaken, cast down, but not destroyed." But if my role as *advocatus spiritis* has helped even a little bit, I am glad.

The future of theology, however, does not seem as secure as the future of the spirit. The religious evolution of humankind began millennia before theology appeared and will presumably continue long after theology disappears. True, as long as human beings continue to be both religious creatures and thinking creatures they will inevitably think about their religion. But the question is what *form* human thought, about religion or anything else, might take. I doubt that such thought will be "theological" in the present sense of the word. Theology, after all, is the expression of a particular form of thought—reflective, analytical, objective—that has arisen only in recent centuries and will probably not last forever. Sciences, mental forms and modes of thinking come and go, but the creativity of the spirit continues. We can be thankful that the future of the spirit and of the race does not depend on the eternal survival of theology. What then, in the light of all that has gone before, should the future of theology be?

The theology of the future should be a kind of play. In an earlier chapter of this book I showed how the "theology of play" and the "theology of revolution" complement rather than undercut each other. But there I was discussing the theology *of* play, not theology *itself* as a playful activity, as an activity endowed with a certain kind of "ludic consciousness." Here I would like to take that next step, to suggest the possibility that what theologians should be doing in the future can most easily be understood as itself a form of play. I mean play in three senses of the word: play as "making fun of," play as "making believe" and play as "useless" or non-productive activity. The case for such a harlequinesque theology runs something like this:

1) As "making fun of," theology is a satirizing activity which debunks destructive myths. It criticizes the cramping symbols that keep people busy turning the wheels of grandiloquent institutions and bowing down before bloated cultural and political tetrarchs. The theologian's job is to be a persistent muckraker of spurious mystiques. He is the "demythologizer," the exposer of fraudulent meanings and pasted-on values. He is the theologian as jester or holy fool, the one who pricks pretenses and shouts out for everyone to hear that the king has no clothes. I call this "making fun of" because I believe lampoon is one of the most effective forms of cultural demythologizing. Denying the power-

ful their mystique destroys the fear they must nurture in the souls of the powerless. Dismantling and deflating auras, halos and nimbuses is part of any theology devoted to human liberation.

History abounds with precedents for this debunking role of the religious critic. There are many stories of Zen masters who burn statues of the Buddha to shock their followers out of their blind awe. The Hebrew prophets spoofed the claims of the kings, and the early Christians punctured the sacred legends that sacralized the Roman emperor. The Russian holy fools parodied bishops and czars in public. Luther told bawdy stories about the pope. All "critical" theology is an attempt to advance the freeing of the human species by undercutting the magical authority of sacred texts and the spurious legitimacy of proud rulers. This does not mean that religious traditions or secular states are divested of *all* claims to loyalty, but it does mean they cannot base their claim on ignorant deference, obfuscation or deception.

We should never doubt that the jester's job is a "serious" one. This "making light of" is itself a heavy responsibility. Under his painted grin the clown often bears a sad face, and the treatment meted out to the most inspired clowns of our own day should teach us why. Charlie Chaplin was hounded out of America during one of our periodic "anti-subversive" panics and returned only as an old man to be honored. Buster Keaton died in penury. Lennie Bruce was driven mad by a calculated legal inquisition into his "obscenity." Fraudulent power rests on intimidation by razzle-dazzle, and it never likes its props revealed in public. "Making fun of" may not be fun for the one who does it, but it is an integral part of the theologian's calling. And insofar as every thoughtful man or woman of faith is also to some extent "a theologian" (I do not believe theology should remain forever the province of an elite), this risky fun making is the calling of all.

2) Theology is play not just as making fun of but also as "making believe," as fantasizing, pretending or imagining. Theologians should be transmuting old symbols, exploring alternative metaphors, juxtaposing unlikely concepts, playing with new and improbable images of man and woman, God and world, earth and

sky. The great theologians of the past have not merely examined and systematized existing religious patterns. They have ventured new ones. They have invented new pictures, woven new connections, spun new ideas. Admittedly constructive, imaginative theology has been neglected for a long time. This is partly due to the century-long reign of critical theology. Consequently theologians today would sometimes prefer to use another word for the fanciful side of their activity—maybe "theo-poetics." Some purists argue that the "ology" part of the word "theology" makes it a science in which imagination and fantasy would naturally be out of place.

But I disagree. The "ology" part of "theology" (as in "biology" and "geology") comes from the Greek *logos* ("word," "meaning," "significance"). To banish the imaginative side of life to the il-logical in-significant or meaning-less is to accept a crippling restriction on what counts as meaning or on what is "logical." I believe, on the contrary, that play, pretending and imagining are alive with meaning and significance. Only a prosaic definition of what is "logical" could deny that play is "logical." Our whole age is bogged down by just such restrictive nomenclature. Happily the condition may be temporary. Some of the best thinkers in modern science are beginning to notice again how essential the imaginative component is in any science.

The most winsome recent example of this playful-aesthetic element in science is James Watson's *The Double Helix* (which I hear he first wanted to entitle *Lucky Jim*), about the discovery of the DNA "key" to the genetic code. Watson tells, in an appealingly lighthearted way, how luck, jealousy, make-believe and a kind of aesthetic intuition entered into his success. My colleagues at M.I.T. who assign *The Double Helix* to freshmen tell me that nothing works so fast to blast away their pious high school image of The Scientific Method. They are then ready for the whim, luck, intuition (*and* hard work) that are essential to any scientific endeavor.

It is both sad and ironic that just as some biologists and physicists are beginning to welcome the place of play in their disciplines, theologians, who have labored so arduously for decades to have theology accepted as a "science," now cling to a rigid no-nonsense view of theological method. It is sad because it so badly constricts the scope and style of theology. It is ironic because theology in the past has often made its most decisive contributions in the writings of people who were not afraid to admix metaphysics, autobiography and fantasy. A history of theology purged of its prayers, confessions, visions, imaginary dialogues, improbable puns and wild speculations would be a dull and misleading one. When I plowed through some of the many volumes of Karl Barth's *Church Dogmatics* as a graduate student, what I liked best were his frequent quips, asides, digressions and rambling comments on politics and music—usually set by the editors in small type. I have told my own students that the best way to read Barth may be to skip the text, or skim it, and read only the small print. What I mean is that theology is not at its scientific best when it is shorn of subjective caprice or quirky impulses. Pretending is an essentially personal activity. So are believing and dying, as Luther once said. And so, in a sense, is theologizing.

When children "make believe" they often pretend they are someone else. This suggests another significant job that theology as "making believe" has to do: exploring and relating to one another the various alternative forms of human consciousness.

More and more frequently nowadays theologians are urged to get to work and build a twentieth-century *Summa Theologica*, a new medieval synthesis which this time would have to integrate not only Christ and Aristotle, as St. Thomas' *Summa* did, but all the major non-Western traditions plus kundalini yoga, Sufism, bio-energetics, Tarot cards, the nature mysticism of the Dakota Indians and, if possible, the *I Ching*. This hope for an updated version of the thirteenth-century synthesis is most frequently voiced by imaginative moderns like William Irwin Thompson who feel the pain of the present spiritual fragmentation and long for a new civilizational faith in which each altar will have its place. My view, however, is that it is not only impossible now to construct a new comprehensive religious metaphysic but that even the attempt to do so represents an early medieval answer to a late postmodern question. Admittedly system construction can also be a form of play, as anyone who has toyed with an erector set or built a sand castle knows. But the devising of a new synthesis is still mainly a job of intellectual planing and joining, and at this pivotal stage in the evolution of religious consciousness what is most needed is not a neatly carpentered system. What we need rather is to learn how to experience one another's spiritual traditions from the inside. What we suffer from most is not a poverty of intellectual competence in theology but an erosion of experience and a failure of imagination. Few people who consider themselves "non-religious" today reject faith because it seems unreasonable. They reject it, or rather ignore it, because it does not seem to touch or intersect their own experience. The blame for this lies not so much with religion as it does with the numbing and anesthetizing of the psyche which is the price our civilization has paid for industrial affluence and the technical mastery of the world. People who are taught from their earliest years to stifle and distrust all feelings that are not "useful" or "productive" soon grow incapable of experiencing most of what the religious traditions of history are all about. A population that has been trained to compete and accumulate will inevitably become blind and insensitive to vast ranges of experience still available to people who have not been so hardened. One cannot, as Jesus said, serve both God and Mammon.

The theological problem is twofold. Some people feel alienated from their own religious tradition and intrigued only by exotic import models, but incapable of experiencing them at any depth. Other people feel equally estranged from any religious experience at all: God is a cipher, mystics and saints are harmless psychotics, and religious celebration is a dangerous surrender to impulse and irrationality. For either group even the most brilliant and persuasive new theological synthesis would elicit only another jaded yawn.

"Make-believe" involves setting aside for a brief period the role, self-image, identity and world view within which one operates most of the time and trying out another way of being. Children do this quite easily. People who for one reason or another have escaped the standard industrial form of consciousness and can still experience transport, ecstasy and trance do it too. But most adults in highly organized bureaucratic societies find it virtually impossible to do. They go through life with an antenna tuned to one or two wavelengths when there are hundreds or maybe even thousands available. What is the future theologian's responsibility to such lost sheep as these?

It is not, in the first instance, I believe, to elaborate a new comprehensive system. Even a system which somehow integrated the thousand wavelengths would remain opaque to people whose receivers are turned off. No, the first job theologians have is to learn from the shamans and the gurus how to help people encounter and experience the vast solar systems of reality they are now missing. And this means that the "compleat theologian" must first learn, as every guru must, how to travel to these worlds of meaning himself. Only then can he learn how to guide others. Like a vaudeville trouper or a repertory player, he must master the technique of moving in and out of different religious traditions without losing his own psyche in the process. Such a course will be perilous, but without this personal exploration of the terrain, any *Summa* he might eventually assemble would turn out to be an airy mental vehicle, as fragile as a floating soap bubble, just as lovely perhaps but also just as evanescent. There can be no short cut. Tomorrow's theology must move from experience to exposition, from testimony to text, from *Confessions* to *Summa*. It cannot move the other way and still be the theology we need at this historical moment.

This still does not solve, of course, the conundrum of the one and the many or the danger of nihilism, which is always posed by radical pluralism. William James confronted that issue by serenely assuring us that since we live in a pluralistic universe we need not bust our heads over how it all goes together. I suspect that James may have been right, but whether he was or not, I suspect also that the way we will cope with the radical diversity of meaning-worlds in the coming epoch will *not* be to assign each a place in some large whole. Rather, we will cope with it by evolving a form of human consciousness which can move from one world to another without panicking or falling to pieces. Thus the next *Summa* might consist not of a thousand chapters but of a thousand alternative states of being, held together not by a glued binding but by the fact that all thousand are equally real.

Imagine what kind of world it would be if instead of merely tolerating or studying them, one could actually *be*, temporarily at least, a Sioux brave seeing an ordeal vision, a neolithic hunter prostrate before the sacred fire, a Krishna lovingly ravishing a woodsful of goat girls, a sixteenth-century Carmelite nun caught up in ecstatic prayer, a prophet touched by flame to go release a captive people. One need not be a follower of Carl Jung and believe that all these figures are already present in our archetypal unconscious waiting to be awakened, though that might very well be true. Even if it is not, we still have enough records, cave scrawlings, memoirs, amulets and oral reports to help us find our way into these people's lives, if we would let ourselves. And we still have, in however precarious condition, people's religions, the infinitely valuable unabsorbed traces of forms of consciousness that are older, richer and more complex than ours.

Admittedly the trek from our present infinitesimal range of consciousness and our ingrained terror of unknown psychic states to the pluriform future I have just described will be an arduous one. And the only place I know to begin is with our nearly forgotten childhood capacity to make believe we are someone else. But that, after all, should not come as a total surprise. Someone did say once, "Except ye become as little children, ye can in no wise enter the Kingdom of Heaven."

3) Theology can become play in a third sense, namely as non-instrumental, non-productive, "useless" activity. As an enterprise which, like play, serves no goal beyond itself, theology rightly defies the modern prejudice which decrees that only useful things have a right to exist.

I first became aware of the invaluable uselessness of theology when a few years ago I attended a five-day conference sponsored by the World Council of Churches on the ethical problems posed for the modern world by scientific technology. We heard papers and reports; discussed and debated; listened to technical experts, political advocates and theological interpreters. There were many eloquent pleas for the churches to become "relevant," to say a significant word to the technical society, to learn to speak in the idiom of the industrial-technological world. Everyone seemed earnest, serious and determined.

All through the conference there sat just in front of me a venerable bishop of the ancient Ukrainian Orthodox Church, vested in flowing robe and long beard, trying manfully to listen to the thousands of words pouring into his headphones from the simultaneous interpreter in the glass booth at the side of the hall. He never said a word throughout the whole five days. At the end of the conference, when all our heads were buzzing with ideas, arguments, charts, trends and graphs, someone apparently thought it would be a nice idea to ask him to pronounce the benediction. When he had listened to the translation of the request and was sure he knew what was expected, he rose to his full height, smoothed his robe, beard and long flowing locks and strode to the front of the hall, his bishop's miter in hand. He stood facing the assembly, an icon of the Mother of God swinging from a golden chain around his neck, and blessed us all with a sweepingly expansive sign of the cross. Then, holding his hand high, he began to pray in a language I had never heard. Apparently few others had ever heard it either, because the simultaneous translating receivers went dead. People at first switched frantically from channel to channel, then stopped. The interpreters in the glass booths looked at one another in panic, shook their heads and then sat silently. The bishop's prayer swelled and receded like ocean waves. After several minutes it stopped. I later found out the language in which the bishop had prayed was Old Slavonic, the archaic liturgical language of his church. Not only did the Russian interpreters not know it but I was told that even in the Ukraine very few people know it. No wonder the earphones had gone silent in defeated exasperation. With another wide sign of the cross, the bishop then walked—"recessed" is the proper word—back to his document-cluttered desk. There were embarrassed coughs and throat clearings. The well-known "irrelevancy" of the Eastern Orthodox Church and the equally notorious irrelevancy of prayer had once again been irrefutably documented in our midst.

Or had they? I felt, on the contrary, that we had just witnessed the most significant episode of the conference. I went immediately to the bishop and thanked him for his prayer. He seemed surprised but grateful. He even gave me a special individual blessing then and there, making a sign of the cross that was a shade smaller than the one he had bestowed on the multitude. For some reason I felt closer to the bishop at that moment than I did to any of the other participants. Only later on did I come to know why.

Unwittingly, I am sure, the Ukrainian Orthodox bishop had demonstrated that one of religion's most important features is its intractable irrelevance, its eccentricity, its downright inconvenience. Religion is an antique settee on the freeway, an almost indecipherable old song disturbing the bleep of the computers. Try as anyone will to doll it up, it is never fully "up to date," and to my mind it should not be, which is why I've never liked the word *aggiornamento* ("bringing up to date") to describe what the church allegedly needs.

The greatest danger posed by the technological world we were discussing at that conference is precisely that it infects our language and our images. It gets into our heads and our words. It levels down our cultural quirks and our religious peculiarities. It produces an increasingly uniform world with less and less place for oddness, transcendence or deviancy. It dismisses as "irrelevant" those impulses and idioms that cannot be tailored to its Procrustean couch of efficiency. It defines what is "useful" and then makes usefulness the ultimate test of value and validity.

I often think of that bearded old patriarch with his timeless icon of the Theotokos dangling on his midriff. He had said a wholly irrelevant, and therefore gloriously "relevant" word. Though he was probably unaware of it, he had reminded us that there are areas of the human life which are simply not reducible to technological or even political relevancy. He had spoken to us in the idiom of the spirit, and those who were attuned to it knew what he was saying even though the words never came through the transistor headsets. He had said his piece in a language of costume, gait, gesture and sign that keeps alive a dimension of human spirit now fatally threatened by the very technical reality to which some people wanted him to be "relevant."

Theology is play in the sense that it is not just useful, relevant or productive in the way those words are understood in societies organized around efficiency and getting results. It represents a stubborn holdout among the "sciences," and when it accepts the industrial-technical closure of the world of human meaning, or tries to blend into the one-dimensional flatland, it betrays itself. As a holdout theology has, paradoxically, something important to say to technopolis. It has an eschatological word, a kind of summons to mankind to decide about its future. The paradox is that something which seems so *out* of date, so strangely held over from such a remote past, *may* be in the only possible position to postulate a radically alternative future. The technical mentality deprives us of a sense of the past. But when a person or a society is robbed of its past, it has that much less chance to bring any critical perspective to bear on the present.

Of course it does not *necessarily* work that way. A church (or anything else) that lives wholly in the past may be so insulated from the present that its memory does not create any friction.

Still, one purpose of memory is to remind us that the present moment is not all there is, and to provide a source of alternative images of the future. Without memory there would be no discontent, no awareness of oppression, no hope for a changed future. The marvel of play is that it reminds us that productive work is not the ultimate end of man. Man was made not just to shape the world but to delight in it, not just to glorify God but "to enjoy Him forever." Play, among other things, is something we do for its own sake, with no extrinsic goal in mind. It is something we do just for the hell of it, and so is theology. It is not only, as St. Thomas said, the intellectual love of God, it is also a kind of intellectual delighting in Him, and in His world, forever. My hope is that, in this sense, theology will always be a little useless.

If theology itself is a form of play, then one must be careful not to end a theological book on an overly portentous note. Hence I conclude with this doggerel, the only "poem" I have ever published or probably ever will. I include it here, as a kind of benediction, with the hope that both in its style and in its content it will indicate what the "future of theology" should be about.

ON CHRIST THE CLOWN

Stop that man!
The painted juggler with the idiotic grin,
And all his motley gaggle
Of harlequins, fat ladies and sword swallowers.
They're all fakes, I think.
At least they're unwelcome intruders into our well-calibrated,
Surprise-free universe.
We had read that he was dead.
Can't believe anything you read these days, but we did,
Despite the lilies and anthems and all.
Oh, we knew our noses were itching for something,
With all the beads and mantras and incense.
But he was so gray and unavailable.
Embalmed by church and state. To be viewed on high unfestive
occasions.
Is the minstrel really back? That inept troubadour whose
unpolitic legerdemain
Finally got him lynched
By the imperial security forces?
Back? Not a chance. Though there are these funny rumors,
But they come from the usual unreliable sources: spooked-out
undependable
People, notorious liars. Ladies of shady repute. Sleight-of-hand artists.
They let on he lives, like love and laughter and man's eternal
gullibility.
But who can believe people like them?
Children do, and fools. Maybe a few meter maids.
But who else?
Who else?

Notes on Sources

CHAPTER ONE

Dubos, René, *A God Within*. New York: Scribner's, 1972. An answer to ecological critics of Christianity.

Erikson, Erik H., "The Development of Ritualization" in Donald Cutler, ed., *The Religious Situation 1968*. Boston: Beacon Press. A brilliant note on the psychological basis for human ritual.

Gray, Francine du P., *Divine Disobedience*. New York: Knopf, 1970. On Mendes Arceo, the Berrigans, Ivan Illich and Emmaus House.

———, *Divine Disobedience: Profiles in Catholic Radicalism*. New York: Random House, 1971.

Henderson, Joseph L., *Thresholds of Initiation*. Middletown, Conn.: Wesleyan University Press, 1967. An insightful psychiatric view of puberty rites from a Jungian perspective.

Illich, Ivan, *Deschooling Society*. New York: Harper, 1971.

McHarg, Ian, *Design with Nature*. New York: Doubleday Natural History Press, 1971. The author believes biblical faith is responsible for our negative view of nature.

CHAPTER TWO

Baker, James T., *Thomas Merton, Social Critic*. Lexington: University of Kentucky Press, 1971.

Buber, Martin, *Paths in Utopia*. Boston: Beacon Press Paperback, 1958.

Ellul, Jacques, *The Meaning of the City*. Grand Rapids, Mich.: Wm. Eerdmans Publishing Co., 1970.

———, *The Political Illusion*. New York: Knopf, 1967.

———, *The Technological Society*. New York: Knopf, 1964.

Greeley, Andrew, *Unsecular Man*. New York: Schocken, 1972. A somewhat shrill but often persuasive attack on the "secular" theologians, including myself.

Hardin, Garrett, *Nature and Man's Fate*. New York: Mentor Books, 1959.

Leiss, William, *The Domination of Nature*. New York: George Braziller, 1972. Chapter 2 covers "Mythical, Religious and Philosophical Roots."

Mumford, Lewis, *The City in History*. New York: Harcourt, 1961.

Newman, John, *Apologia Pro Vita Sua*. London: Longman's, 1891.

Sennett, Richard, *The Uses of Disorder*. New York: Knopf, 1970.

Soleri, Paolo, *Arcology: The City in the Image of Man*. Cambridge, Mass.: M.I.T. Press, 1961. Soleri's oversize utopian fantasy of the future city.

Strong, Josiah, *The Twentieth Century City*. New York: The Baker & Taylor Co., 1898. A choice example of turn-of-the-century evangelical anti-urbanism.

White, Lynn, Jr., "The Historical Roots of Our Ecologic Crisis," *Science* 155: 1967, pp. 1203–1207.

The most quoted article on the religious basis of hostility to the earth.

White, Morton and Lucia, *The Intellectual Versus the City*. Cambridge, Mass.: Harvard University Press, 1962.

CHAPTER THREE

Cloud of Unknowing, introductory comment and translation by Ira Progoff. New York: Julian Press, 1957.

Elwood, Robert S., Jr., *Religious and Spiritual Groups in Modern America*. Englewood Cliffs, N.J.: Prentice-Hall, 1973. An able survey with a comprehensive bibliography.

Gandhi, Mohandas K., *Mahatma Gandhi, His Own Story*, ed. by C. F. Andrews. New York: Macmillan, 1930. Material selected from Gandhi's autobiography.

Keddie, Nikki R., ed., *Scholars, Saints and Sufis: Muslim Religious Institutions in the Middle East since 1500*. Has articles on Sufis by B. G. Martin and Vincent Crapanzano.

Rubenstein, Richard, *My Brother Paul*. New York: Harper, 1972. A brilliant combination of autobiographical and historical interpretation.

Tillich, Paul, *The Courage to Be*. New Haven, Conn.: Yale University Press, 1952. My late teacher's most unforgettable book.

Watts, Alan, *In My Own Way*. New York: Random House, 1972. The autobiography of an eccentric but intriguing figure in recent religious history.

CHAPTER FOUR

Marx and Engels on Religion, introduction by Reinhold Niebuhr. New York: Schocken Books, 1964.

McLuhan, T. C., *Touch the Earth*. New York: Pocket Books, 1972. Pictures and texts illustrating the faith of native Americans.

CHAPTER FIVE

Bakan, David, *Sigmund Freud and the Jewish Mystical Tradition*. Princeton, N.J.: Van Nostrand, 1958.

Bonhoeffer, Dietrich, *Letters and Papers from Prison*, the enlarged edition. London: SCM Press, 1971.

Maslow, Abraham, *Religions, Values and Peak-Experiences*. Columbus: Ohio State University Press, 1964.

May, Rollo, *Power and Intelligence*. New York: Norton, 1972.

———, *Love and Will*. New York: Norton, 1969.

CHAPTER SIX

Between Honesty and Hope. Documents from and about the church in Latin America, issued at Lima by the Peruvian Bishops' Commission for Social Action. Maryknoll, N.Y.: Maryknoll Documentary Series, 1970.

Castaneda, Carlos, *The Teachings of Don Juan: a Yaqui Way of Knowledge*. New York: Ballantine Books, 1969. See also his *Journey to Ixtlan*. New York: Simon & Schuster, 1972.

Gutierrez, Gustavo, *A Theology of Liberation*. Maryknoll, N.Y.: Orbis Books, 1973.

Martin, David, *The Religious and the Secular*. London: Routledge & Kegan Paul, 1969.

CHAPTER SEVEN

Birnbaum, Norman, *The Crisis of Industrial Society*. Oxford University Press, 1969. Includes an excellent analysis of the Paris May of 1968.

Cohn, Norman, *The Pursuit of the Millennium*. New York: Harper Torchbooks, 1961. Revolutionary messianism in medieval and Reformation Europe and its bearing on modern totalitarian movements.

Cone, James H., *The Spirituals and the Blues: An Interpretation*. New York: The Seabury Press, 1972. A theological interpretation of a "people's religion."

Friere, Paulo, *Cultural Action for Freedom*. Cambridge, Mass.: Harvard Educational Review and Center for the Study of Development and Social Change, 1970.

———, *The Pedagogy of the Oppressed*. New York: Herder & Herder, 1970.

Greenberg, Louis, *Sisters of Liberty*. Cambridge, Mass.: Harvard University Press, 1970.

MacEoin, Gary, *Revolution Next Door*. New York: Herder & Herder, 1972. Includes good sections on the Latin American church.

Mutchler, David, *The Church as a Political Factor in Latin America*. New York: Praeger, 1971. Very critical of the institutional Catholic Church in Latin America.

Sanders, Thomas, "Catholicism and Development: The Catholic Left in Brazil," in Kalman H. Silvert, ed., *Churches and States: The Religious Institution and Modernization*. New York: American Universities Field Staff, Inc., 1967.

Stewart, Zeph, ed., *Essays on Religion and the Ancient World by Arthur Derby Nock*. Cambridge, Mass.: Harvard University Press, 1971.

Teilhard de Chardin, Pierre, *The Phenomenon of Man*. New York: Harper, 1959.

Vijayavardhara, D. C., *Revolt in the Temple*. Colombo: Sinha Publications, 1953.

CHAPTER EIGHT

Miller, Perry, *The Life of the Mind in America*. New York: Harcourt, 1965. For an account of the impact of revivalism on American culture.

Miller, Stuart, *Hot Springs: The True Adventures of the First New York Jewish Literary Intellectual in the Human Potential Movement*. New York: Viking, 1971.

Welch, Claude, *Protestant Thought in the Nineteenth Century*, Vol. I: 1799–1870. New Haven, Conn.: Yale University Press, 1972. For a short but lucid account of the origins of pietism.

CHAPTER NINE

Durkheim, Emile, *The Elementary Forms of the Religious Life*. London: George Allen & Unwin, 1915.

Gottwald, Norman, *The Church Unbound*. Philadelphia: Lippincott, 1967.

Greeley, Andrew, *Why Can't They Be Like Us? America's White Ethnic Groups*. New York: Dutton, 1971.

Metz, Johannes Baptiste, "The Church and the World," in T. Patrick Burke, ed., *The Word in History*. New York: Sheed & Ward, 1966.

Novak, Michael, *The Rise of the Unmeltable Ethnics*. New York: Macmillan, 1972.

CHAPTER TEN

Adams, James Luther, *Paul Tillich's Philosophy of Culture, Science and Religion*. New York: Harper, 1965.

Freud, Sigmund, translated by Joan Riviere, *The Ego and the Id*. London: 1927.

Langer, Susanne, *Problems of Art*. New York: Scribner's, 1957.

McLuhan, Marshall, *Understanding Media*. New York: McGraw Hill, 1964.

Mumford, Lewis, *Technics and Civilization*. New York: Harcourt, 1934.

Read, Herbert, *Icon and Idea*. New York: Schocken Books, 1965.

Robinson, W. R., "The Movies, Too, Will Make You Free," cit. in *The Cosmos Reader*, ed. by E. Z. Friedenberg, et al. New York: Harcourt, 1971.

Tillich, Paul, *Theology of Culture*. London: Oxford University Press, 1959.

CHAPTER ELEVEN

Becker, Ernest, *Angel in Armor*. New York: Braziller, 1969.

Campbell, Joseph, *Primitive Mythology*. New York: Viking, 1959.

Durkheim, Emile, *Elementary Forms of the Religious Life*. New York: Free Press (Macmillan), 1954.

Eliade, Mircea, *Patterns in Comparative Religion*. New York: Sheed & Ward, 1958. See Chapter IV, "The Moon and Its Mystique."

Huff, Theodore, *Charlie Chaplin*. New York: Henry Schumann, Inc., 1951.

Immortality, A monthly. 9 Holmes Court, Sayville, N.Y. 11782.

Killinger, John, *World in Collapse: The Vision of Absurd Drama*. New York: Dell, 1971.

Malinowski, Bronislaw, *Magic, Science and Religion*. Boston: Beacon Press, 1948.

Otto, Rudolf, *The Idea of the Holy*. London: Oxford University Press, 1923.

Slater, Philip, *The Pursuit of Loneliness*. Boston: Beacon Press, 1970.

Spinrad, Norman, *Bug Jack Barron*. New York: Walker, 1969.

Vartanian, Aram, *La Mettrie's "L'Homme Machine": A Study in the Origins of an Idea*. Princeton: Princeton University Press, 1960.

CHAPTER TWELVE

Buber, Martin, *Between Man and Man*. New York: Macmillan, 1965.

———, *The Prophetic Faith*. New York: Harper, 1966.

Burke, Kenneth, *Language as Symbolic Action*. Los Angeles: University of California Press, 1966.

Havelock, Eric, *Preface to Plato*. Cambridge, Mass.: Belknap Press, 1963.

Ong, Walter J., *The Presence of the Word*. New Haven: Yale University Press, 1967.

Stahmer, Harold, *"Speak That I May See Thee": The Religious Significance of Language*. New York: Macmillan, 1968.

Index

Aaron, Raymond, 189
Academics, 106, 274
Acquiescence, 46 ff., 63, 75
Activity, 46 ff.
  autonomous, 11, 17
  urban life and, 63
Adam, fall of, 64, 66, 75
Adams, Henry, 262, 280–81, 288
Adams, James Luther, 264
Adler, Felix, hymn by, 53
Adolescence, puberty rites and,
  40–41
Advertising, images and, 266, 267
Africa, 141, 170, 216
  monogamy and, 235–36
African Methodist Episcopalians,
  29
Afro-Brazilians, 215–16, 250
Aggiornamento, 327
Agni Purana, 53
Ahab, Captain, 271
Altizer, Tom, 174
Ambiguity of the sacred, 282–83
A.M.E. church, 29
Amos, 309
Anaheim, California, 292
Anders, Gunther, 302
Angel in Armor, 285
Anglo-Saxons, 241
Anthropology, 145, 146
Apprentices in learning, 146, 147
Aquinas, Thomas, 265, 322, 329
Arcologies, 82–83
Arminius, Jacobus, 73
Armstrong, Neil, 275
Arrogance, city crises and, 76
Artists, commercial, 266

Assumption of Mary, 175, 177,
  192
Augustine, St., 72, 73, 77, 92, 98
Autobiography, 9, 97
  corporate, 115, 117
  interiority and, 107
  theology and, 109–11
Autonomous activities, 11, 17
Aztecs, 119

Baal, 300
Baba, Meher, 222
Bakan, David, 139
Baptism, 37–39
Baptist(s), 35 ff., 124, 253
  black, 30
  ministers, 43–45, 50
  ritualism and, 43
Barrio in Sante Fe, 115–16
Barth, Karl, 322
Baths, nude, 205 ff.
Becker, Ernest, 285
Beckett, Samuel, 285
Berlin, 123–25, 127, 142
Berrigan, Daniel, 42, 218–19, 222,
  223
Bethlehem, 197–98
Big Sur, California, 197 ff.
Birth, radical theology and, 174
Black Christianity, 29–30, 117, 119
  identity and, 240
  women and, 248–49
Black Elk Speaks, 110
Bodily metaphor, 216–17
Bondage, extrication rituals for,
  284 ff.

Bonhoeffer, Dietrich, 123, 125 ff., 226
Book-and-print culture, 276–78
Boston Tea Party, 156
Brave New World, 108
Brazil, 131, 141, 173
    television in, 302
    Umbanda movement in, 215–216, 250
Brecht, Bertolt, 125, 271
Broadacre City, 67, 80
Brooke, Edward, 240
Bruce, Lennie, 320
Bruno, Giordano, 281
Buddhism, 138, 170, 201, 210
Buñuel, Luis, 285
Byzantine Easter, 156 ff.

"Calling" of pastors, 44–45
Calvin, John, 178
Calvinism, 70, 72, 74, 75
Camara, Dom Helder, 131
Cambridge Institute, 84
Camera, 270–71
Campbell, Joseph, 286
Canaan, 300
Castenada, Carlos, 144, 145–46, 150
Cathari, 92
Catholicism, Roman. *See* Roman Catholic Church.
Chaplin, Charles, 297, 320
Chartres, 280
Cheyenne puberty rite, 40
Chicanos, 116–17
Chinese body manipulation, 199
Chinese Cultural Revolution, 187
Christ, 307
    cities and, 71–72
    as clown, 330
    communication and, 311
    family life of, 230

Christ (*cont.*)
    as Second Adam, 66, 75
    touching by, 216–18
Christianity
    activism and, 63
    black, 29–30, 119
    cities and, 69
    communication and, 308 ff.
    ecology and, 61–62
    essence of, 153
    family in, 227 ff.
    Gnostics and, 101–2
    iconoclasm in, 268
    Indian and, 121
    liberation as purpose of, 153
    male dominance and, 232
    Marxist dialogue, 123 ff.
    message of, 311
    non-religious interpretation of, 125 ff., 142
    rebellion and, 63
    socialism and, 127
    striations of, 121
    touching in, 216–18
Church, 13
    experimental liturgy in, 161–62
    family as substitute for, 227 ff.
    new. *See* New church
    radical, 172
    rural-urban communities planned by, 87
    small-town, 27 ff.
    universal, 251–53
    wealth of, 244–45
Cities, 53 ff., 69
    acquiescence in, 63
    arrogance and, 76
    building of, religious-group involvement in, 85–87
    civility of, 88
    contemplation and, 68
    elitist thought on, 76
    ethnicity in, 237–38

Cities (*cont.*)
  future of, 79 ff.
  as holy experiments, 78
  Jesus and, 71–72
  nature and, 60–62, 82, 85–86
  opposition to, 66 ff.
  planning of, 79 ff.
  pluralism of, 59, 80
  rebellion and, 63, 72
  self-image in, 63–64
  sharing life in, 77
  spiritual vision and, 78–79
  as symbols, 68, 72, 77
Civility, 88
Civil polity in new church, 247,
    252, 253, 254
Civitas Dei, 78
Clark, Joe, 54
Class, 27 ff.
  ancient texts and, 190
Cleanliness, compulsive, 284
Clockwork Orange, A., 66
Clothes, meaning of, 212–13
Cloud of Unknowing, The, 92
Cluster family, 235
Cohn, Norman, 178
Collective interiority, 117, 226 ff.,
    248 ff.
  ethnicity and, 236 ff.
  family and, 227 ff.
  group consciousness and, 221–
    222, 223, 248
Colombia, 191
Columbia, Maryland, 84
Commonweal, 244
Commune, Paris, 189
Communication, 308 ff.
  by books, 276–78
  with God, 308–9, 311
  mass media and, 276–78, 303–4,
    309–10, 313
  Scriptures and, 308–9
  signals and, 11–12

Communication (*cont.*)
  symbolic, 134
  vulnerability and, 308–9
Communion, 217
Communists, 123 ff., 129, 130–32
  radical theology and, 190, 191
Community, 246 ff.
  communication and, 312
  dream-sharing in, 136
  ethnic, 237, 240
  interiority and, 95–96
  liberated, 249
  non-exclusivity of, 251
  particularity in, 249–50
  rural-urban, 85, 86
  technology and, 288–89
Condomblé, 216, 250
Conscientization, 173, 176
Consciousness, 82, 183, 185, 187
  group, 248, 249, 254
  Third World, 170, 172–73
  universal, 151, 152, 154–55
  visual images and, 265
Constantine, 57
Contemplation
  cities and, 68
  guided, 138
  rebirth of interest in, 94–96
  technology and, 270
Control
  cultural, 170, 171
  vertical, specialization and, 106
Convents, medieval, 179
Convergence in traditions, 155,
    167
Conversion, Third World, 171,
    172–73
Coordination, specialization and,
    104, 105, 106
Corporate
  autobiography, 115, 117
  consciousness, 82
  evil, 73, 74, 75

Corporate (*cont.*)
   extinction, 119
   grace, 75
   neurosis, religion as, 129
Cosmopolitan man, 59–60
Counterculture, 174
Courage to Be, The, 98
Cox, Harvey
   baptism of, 37–39
   boyhood of, 23 ff.
   city experiences of, 53–55, 89
   at Esalen, 197 ff.
   ethnic background of, 241–42
   hometown of, 23 ff., 51–52
   in Latin America, 171–72, 215–216, 302–3
   in Marxist-Christian Dialogue, 123 ff.
   as teacher, 97 ff., 109 ff.
Cox, John Foreman, 28, 35
Cox, Maud, 29, 30, 35
Cox, Nancy, 123, 125, 212
Cox, Phil, 31
Creation, 74, 75
Creativity, human, 48–49
Critical theology, 319–20
Cryonics, 298 ff.
Cuernavaca, Mexico, 175
Culture, 262 ff., 273 ff.
   book-and-print, 276–78
   borrowing, 151
   change in, 267, 278
   control through, 170, 171
   definition of, 263
   diversity in, 239, 240
   healthy, 17–18
   mass media, 14–15, 277, 305–6
   popular, 266, 274
   revolution in, 267, 275, 277
   visual, 269 ff.
   Western, 46–48, 86, 170
Czechoslovakia, 187

Dabenton, Jeanne, 178
Daly, Mary, 181
Dancing, 157, 216
Dark Night of Resistance, The, 223
Death, 289 ff.
   radical theology and, 174
   suspension theory of, 291–92
"Death of God," 169, 174, 177
DeGaulle, Charles, 188
Deity. *See also* God.
   feminine qualities of, 180–82
Delegation, 104, 105
Deliverance, technology and, 284 ff.
Demian, 137
Demon, technology as, 298
Demonstrations, 221
Denominations, 247, 251, 252
Descartes, René, 296–97
Deschooling Society, 47
de Stefano, Mary Ellen, 31
Director society, 170
Disciplines, 106
Disneyland, 292 ff.
Divorce, Scriptures and, 229
Domination in institutions, 231–232
Double Helix, The, 321
Dracula, 298
Draft-card burning, 41, 42
Dreams, 13, 133 ff.
   technology and, 286
Drugs, 40–41
Dubcek, Alexander, 187
Durkheim, Emile, 226, 282–83
Dynamo, 280–82, 299

Easter, 152–54, 156 ff.
Eastern Orthodox Church, 326, 327

Eastern Orthodox Church (*cont.*)
  icons, 269, 291
  Mass, 162–63
East Germany, 123, 124, 127
Ecclesiasticism, 154
Eclecticism, 243
Ecology, 46–47, 61–62, 82, 85–86
Eden, 64
Education, higher, 204
Edwards, Jonathan, 220
Eichmann, Adolf, 104–5
Electronic technology, 262, 273.
  See also Mass media; Technology.
Elementary Forms of the Religious Life, The, 282
Eliade, Mircea, 43, 280
Elitism, 76, 154, 277, 313
Elliot, Charlotte, 23
Elliott, Ebenezer, 113
Ellul, Jacques, 69 ff.
Emancipation. *See also* Liberation.
  radical theology and, 195
Emerson, Ralph Waldo, 97
Emotional health, 132–33
Encounter-sensitivity movement, 197 ff., 219 ff.
Ephesus, Council of, 73
Epimethean Man, 47, 62–63
Episcopal church, 29
Erikson, Erik, 132–33, 248
Esalen Institute, 197 ff.
Essence of Christianity, 153
Ethnicity, 236 ff.
Evaluation of religion, 142, 150
Evil, 72, 73, 74, 75
  kinship of, with good, 282
Exodus, 152–54, 229
Exousia, 72, 75
Experience in religion, 203
Experimental liturgics, 155 ff.

Extinction
  corporate, 119
  of human species, 85, 87
Extrication rituals, 284 ff.
Extrinsic theology, 48

Fall of man, 64, 66, 75
Family, 227 ff.
  cluster, 235
  holy, 307
  monogamy and, 229, 235–36
  nuclear, 227 ff.
  residual, 228
Fanon, Franz, 67
Fantasy
  Disneyland, 292 ff.
  guided, 138
  religion and, 13, 118
  symbols and, 133
  in theology, 320 ff.
Fatima, 181
Feast of Fools, 117–18, 140
Federalism, world, 255
Feelings, personal, 148–49
Feminine elements of deity, 180–182
Finney, Charles Grandison, 220
First Baptist Church of Malvern, 35 ff.
Flintstones, 302–3, 310
Folk religion, 10, 167
  Mariachi Mass, 176–77, 192
Foot washing, 217–18
Forbin Project, The, 298
Frankenstein, 298
Freedom. *See* Liberation.
French May (1968), 188–89
Freud, Sigmund, 73, 265
  on religion, 129–30, 133, 134, 139–40

Freire, Paulo, 172, 173, 312
Frozen dead, 289 ff.
Future of an Illusion, 130

Gandhi, 98, 151
Ganesha, 242
Gdansk, Poland, 55
Georgi, Dieter, 190
Germany, 123 ff., 127
Gerson, Charlier de, 178
Gestalt therapy, 135–36, 138
Gestures, 41–42, 221
Ghettos, 55, 237
Ghost Dance, 120
Gilson, Étienne, 78
Ginsberg, Allen, 200, 201
Gleichschaltung, 236
Global village, 278
Glorification, 50
Glossolalia, 141
Gnosticism, 101–2, 107, 109
God
    communication with, 308–9, 311
    "is dead," 169, 174, 177
Golconda Movement, 191
Good, moral, 73
    kinship with evil, 282
Gospel, non-religious interpretation of, 125 ff., 142
Gossner center, 123, 124
Grace, 74, 75
    means of, 14, 45. *See also* Ritual(s).
    sin and, 70
Gramsci, Antonio, 131
Great Awakenings, 220, 224
Greeks, 46–48
Greenberg, Louis, 189
Group(s)
    consciousness, 117, 248, 249, 254
    encounter. *See* Encounter-sen-

Group(s) *(cont.)*
    sitivity movement.
    ethnic, 236 ff.
    identity, 167, 238
    loyalty conflicts and, 248–49, 251, 255
    massage, 208–9
    silence and, 223
    therapy, 136–37
Growth centers, 203, 204
"Guernica," 265
Guevara, Che, 67, 116
Gurus, 222, 324

Happy Days, 284–85
Hardin, Garrett, 87
Harvard University, 97, 109
Haussmann, Baron, 79
Hegemony, 232, 267
Heretics, 190
Hermeneutics, participant, 146 ff.
Hesse, Hermann, 137
Hidalgo, Father, 193
Hinduism, 210, 283, 290
Hires ruin, 24, 25
Hispanic Catholicism, 171 ff.
History
    book-print culture and, 278
    radical theology and, 190, 193
    sharing of, in ritual, 249–50
Hitchcock, Alfred, 266
Holy family, 307
Hominisation of reality, 173
Homo faber, 48–49
Homo nuovo, 173
Homo urbanitas, 56
Human potential movement, 197 ff.
Hus, Jan, 178
Huxley, Aldous, 108, 109
Hymns, 34–35, 36

Icon and Idea, 261, 264
Icons, 262, 266 ff., 291
Ideal possibilities, 14
Ideas, images and, 261, 265 ff.
Identity, 167, 238–39, 240
Idolatry, 300
Illich, Ivan, 47, 48
Illusion, religion as, 129–30
Images, 261–62, 265 ff.
  cultural revolution from books
    to, 277
  machine, 296–98
  mass media, 303, 304, 306
  suspicions of, 267–68
Immigrants, 237–38
Immobility, technology and, 284–
  285
Immortality, assumption vs., 177
Immortality, 289
Imperium, 88
Indians
  American, 57, 120–21
  Yaqui, 145–46
Indochinese war, 105
Industrialization, 85, 274–75
Information
  overload crisis, 101, 102 ff.
  significance of, 305
  specialization in, 102 ff.
Informed heart, 100
Initiation rites, 43
Institutions
  domination within, 231–32
  new church and, 252
  player-revolutionary and, 186
Intellectual Versus the City, 67
Interiority, 93 ff.
  collective, 117, 226 ff. *See also*
    Collective interiority.
  participatory hermeneutics and,
    148–49
  repression and, 111
  in teaching, 109 ff.

Interiority (*cont.*)
  testimony and, 96
  theologians' lack of, 98, 100, 107
Interpretation, 125 ff., 142, 148–49
Invasion of the Body Snatchers,
  The, 108, 109
"Investigating" vs. "learning
  from," 145
Involvement, 287–88
Irrelevance of religion, 327
Irvine, California, 84
Isaiah, 309
Islam, 180–81, 198
Isolationism, 255

Jackson, George, 111
James, William, 91, 325
Jeremiah, 309
Jerusalem, 71
Jesus. *See* Christ.
Jet travel, 285–86
John of the Cross, 93
Joseph, 307
Juan, Don, 146
Judaism
  family and, 228–29
  women and, 181
Judge, good, 100
Jung, Carl Gustav, 117, 132, 251,
  325
"Just As I Am," 36
Just City, 78, 89

Kafka, Franz, 266
Keaton, Buster, 320
Khrushchev, Nikita, 293
Kierkegaard, Søren, 98
King, Martin Luther, 130, 151
Kingdom, Creation and, 74
Knowledge, 101
  specialization in, 102 ff.

Kriebel, Mr., 37, 38
Kubrick, Stanley, 66, 298

La Mettrie, Julien, 296
Langer, Susanne, 134, 266
Language, 317–18
Latin American Catholicism,
    171 ff.
Learning, 146 ff.
    objectivity and, 149
    personalization of, 100–102, 104
    response and, 149 ff.
    stages of, 147
"Learning from" vs. "investigat-
    ing," 145
Left, myths and, 186–87
Lenin, 131
Liberals, technology and, 73
Liberation, 129, 152 ff.
    community and, 249
    group consciousness and, 248–
    249
    male, 236
    of mass media, 278
    play and, 186–87
    universal, 231
    women's 180. *See also* Women,
        liberation of.
Life history. *See* Autobiography;
    Testimony.
Light, word vs., 268
Literature, 268, 276–78
Liturgics, experimental, 155 ff.
Liturgy. *See* Ritual(s).
Losers, 190, 196
Love and Will, 133
Loyalties, group, 248–49, 251, 255
Loyola, St. Ignatius, 138
LSD, 201
Lucrum Salax, 244–45
Ludic consciousness, 185, 187

Machine(s), 296–98
    meaning of, 269, 271
    model, 107
Macumba, 216
Magazines, 14, 305
Make-believe, 14, 320 ff.
"Making fun of," theology as,
    319–20
Malcolm X, 111, 130
Malinowski, Bronislaw, 283, 290
Malraux, André, 188
Malvern, 23 ff., 43–45, 241
Manhattan Project, 105
Manic-depressive, 63, 65
Manifestations of religion, 194
Mao Tse-tung, 187
Mariachi Mass, 176–77, 192
Mariology, 177 ff., 190–91, 280
    change in, 192–93
    prayer and, 183–84
Market mentality, 86
Marriage, 229, 235–36
    mixed, 240–41
Marx, Karl, 62, 73, 169
    on religion, 129, 130, 190, 192
Marxism, 74, 129, 130–32
Marxist-Christian dialogue, 123 ff.
Mary. *See also* Mariology.
    Assumption of, 175, 177, 192
    of Valenciennes, 178
Masculine religions, 180–82
Masks, 271
Mass
    Eastern, 162–63
    experimental liturgic, 157
    Mariachi, 176–77, 192
Massage, 208–9, 214–15
Mass media, 12, 14–15, 272 ff.
    access to, 314, 315
    communication and, 303–4, 309–
    310, 313
    contempt for, 273–75
    culture, 305–6

Mass media (*cont.*)
destructiveness of, 303
elite and, 313
enthusiasm for, 275–76
"high" culture and, 273–75
liberation of, 278
participation and, 277
power of, 303
promise of, 276–78
reality and, 305–6
sensationalism of, 108–9
signals, 14, 306–7
theology of, 312 ff.
trivialization of issues in, 304, 305
Mastery, compulsion to, 46 ff., 66, 103
May, Rollo, 132, 133
McHarg, Ian, 47, 49
McIntyre, Carl, 246
McLuhan, Marshall, 266, 286
McLuhan, T. C., 120
Mead, Margaret, 235
Meaning, personal, learning and, 148–49
Meaning of the City, The, 69
Mecca, 198
Mechanophobia, 298
Media, mass. *See* Mass media.
Medieval convents, 179
Meditation, 199, 222
rebirth of interest in, 94–96
Melville, Herman, 271
Memory, 14, 265, 328
Men
dominance by, 180–82, 232–34
liberation of, 236
rituals and, 251
Mendes Arceo, Don Sergio, 175, 176, 192, 193
Merton, Thomas, 68, 69, 110
Messages, meanings of, 146 ff.
Metanoia, 172, 173

Methodist church, 34–35
Metropolitan man, 63–64. *See also* Cities.
Ministers, Baptist, 43–45, 50
Mob rule, 67–68
Moby Dick, 271
Modernism, liberation and, 153
Modern Times, 297
Mondlane, Eduardo, 130
Monks, 138
Monogamy, 229, 235–36
Moon, frozen dead on, 290–91
Moral good, 73
Moslems, 180–81, 198
Movements, problems of, 219 ff.
Movies, 272, 276–77
horror, 108, 298
literature vs. 268, 276
machines in, 297–98
Mumford, Lewis, 77, 270
Murphy, Mike, 199
Music, 34–35, 36, 156, 157, 158
Mystics, 93 ff., 222, 223
Myth(s), 14
death, 290
fall of man, 64, 66
national, 254
psychoanalysis and, 133
radical theology and, 183, 185–187, 191–92
ritual and, 41, 42
as symbols, 284
technology as, 292 ff.
Myths, Dreams and Mysteries, 280

Naked revival, 197 ff.
National basis for new church, 247–48, 251–52, 254–55
Nature, 60–62, 300
technology vs., 269–70
Nature and Man's Fate, 87

Nazis, 125, 267
Neurosis, symbols and, 134
New church, 226 ff.
  bases for, 247 ff.
  ethnicity and, 237 ff.
  family as, 227 ff.
  group consciousness and, 248
  politics and, 246 ff., 253, 256
New City, 78 ff., 89
New Jerusalem, 70, 74, 78
Newman, John Henry, 98
Newspapers, 305
New York City, 68
Nicene Creed, 308
Nicodemus, 134
Niebuhr, H. Richard, 100
Niebuhr, Reinhold, 98
Nietzsche, 62, 174
1984, 108
Nock, Arthur Darby, 194
Nodal events, 81–82
Non-productive theology, 325 ff.
Non-religious interpretations of
  Christianity, 125 ff., 142
Nuclear family, 227 ff.
Nude baths, 205 ff.

Objectivity, learning and, 149
Observation, participant, 146, 148
Omnipotence syndrome, 80, 106
"On Christ the Clown," 330
Oppression, 129, 130–31
  group consciousness and, 248,
    249, 254
  liberation vs., 119
  meditation and, 95
  of preliterates, 180
Optical memory, 265
Oral communication, 276
Organized religion, threat of, 12,
  15
Orgy, religious, 140

Original sin, 64, 75, 106
Orthodoxy, 163, 269, 291, 326, 327
Orwell, George, 108, 109
Otto, Rudolf, 298
Our Lady of Guadalupe, 116, 180,
  193, 232

Paoli, Pennsylvania, 23, 29
Paris May (1968), 188–89
Parochial schools, 30
Participant hermeneutics, 146 ff.
Participation, 195, 277
Particularistic pole, 152 ff.
Passion, experimental, 157 ff.
Passover, Easter and, 156
Paul, St., 75, 236, 289, 318
Paul VI, 244, 245
Pauline-Augustine Reformation,
  72–73
Peace movement, 41, 42
Pelagius, 73
Penn, William, 88
Pentecostals, Black, 117
People's religion, 115 ff., 169 ff.
  definition of, 10
  group identity in, 167
  learning from, 144 ff.
  Mariology and, 177 ff., 190–92
  new forms for, 226 ff.
  repression and, 140
  revolution and, 193
  sharing history in, 250
Perls, Fritz, 133, 135–36, 138
Personal life, 93 ff.
Peyote cults, 120
Philadelphia, 53 ff.
Photography, 270–71
Physical contact, 214 ff.
Pietism, 204, 211
  group encounter, 220, 222, 224
  mass media, 303

Pike, James, 198, 200, 201–2
Pius XII, 184
Place, experience of, 57–58
Planning, city, 79 ff.
Play, 184 ff., 319
  theology as, 319 ff.
Pluralism, 59, 80
  ethnic, 240, 242
  radical, 324–25
Political Illusion, The, 77
Political Testament, 131
Politics
  ethnic, 239–40
  of gestures, 41–42
  group movements and, 221, 223
  images and, 267
  new church and, 246 ff., 253,
    256
  play and, 185 ff.
  radical theology and, 170, 174,
    191, 192–93
  of revivalism, 224
  specialization and, 106
  trivialization and, 304
Poor people
  mass media and, 305, 312
  religion of, 118, 169 ff., 191. *See
    also* People's religion.
  touching among, 216
  wealth of churches and, 244–45
Popular culture, 266
Popular religion. *See* People's re-
    ligion.
Power, quest for, 232, 256
Powerlessness, technology and,
    284–85
Prayer, 140, 183–84
Preachers, 43–45
Prehistory, 147, 149
Preliterate religion, 60, 180
Presbyterian church, 28
Pride, city crises and, 76
Primitive Mythology, 286

Primitive religion, 180
  dead in, 290
  sex roles in, 251
Privacy, 287–88
Problems of Art, 266
Progoff, Ira, 133, 137–38
Prometheus, 47, 62–63, 75
Protest, religion as, 193
Protestants, 67–68, 268
Provincialism, 150, 154, 170, 171
Pseudospecies, 248
Psyche, ritual and, 141
Psychodrama, 189
Psychotherapy, 132 ff., 138, 139,
    140
  acting out dreams, 135–37
  visual images and, 265
Puberty rites, 40–41, 42
Pulpit committees, 45, 50
Purification rituals, 284
Puritanism, 204
Pursuit of Loneliness, 287
Pursuit of the Millennium, 178

Quakers, 28, 96, 241
Quetzalcoatl, 116, 119
Quietism, peril of, 221

Race, 239, 247
Radical theology, 169 ff.
  in America, 194
  Communism and, 190, 191
  disputes within, 184
  emancipation and, 195
  history and, 190, 193
  losers and, 190, 196
  Mass and, 176–77, 192
  myths and, 183, 185–87, 191–92
  participation in, 195

Radical theology (*cont.*)
 play and, 184 ff.
 pluralism and, 324–25
 politics and, 170, 174, 191, 192–193
 women and, 177 ff., 190–92
Radio, 272
"Rain and the Rhinoceros," 68
Ricoeur, Paul, 284
Read, Herbert, 261, 264, 265
Reality, 173, 195
 masks and, 271
 mass media and, 305–6
 play and, 185
Rebellion. *See* Revolution.
Recife, Brazil, 302
Regression, prayer and, 140
Relevance, 221, 326–28
Religion, 13. *See also* Christianity;
 Church; Fantasy; Mariology;
 New church; People's religion; Radical theology; Rit-
 ual(s); Theology.
 components of, 14
 emancipation and, 129
 evaluation of, 142, 150
 folk, 10, 167
 future of, 129, 130
 good-evil poles in, 282–83
 as illusion, 129–30
 irrelevance of, 327
 meaning of the term, 13–15
 nature and, 60–62
 negativity of, 128–29
 non-religious interpretation of,
  125 ff., 142
 as oppressor, 119, 129, 130–31
 organized, threat of, 12, 15
 as protest, 193
 psychotherapy and, 132 ff.
 response to, 149 ff.
 role of, 17–18
 seduction and, 16

Religion, (*cont.*)
 space-time and, 57–58
 stories in, 9 ff.
 urban, 56 ff.
Repression, 111, 132–33, 139–40
Resettlements, 57
Resignation, 46 ff., 63, 75
Resistance, 223
Response, learning and, 149 ff.
Reston, Virginia, 84
Resurrection, 177
Revivals, 219 ff., 224, 226 ff.
Revolt in the Temple, 170
Revolution, 63, 72, 74, 319
 cultural, 267, 275, 277
 play and, 186–88, 189
 power and, 256
 resignation vs., 46
Ritual(s), 39 ff.
 baptismal, 37–39
 dancing in, 216
 ethnic history and, 249–50
 experimental, 156 ff.
 extrication, 284 ff.
 group therapy, 137
 initiation, 43
 juxtaposition in, 161, 162
 length of, 160–61
 manipulative threat in, 165, 166
 participation in, 166, 167
 physical contact in, 214 ff.
 psyche and, 141
 puberty, 40–41, 42
 purification, 284
 repression of, 140
 setting of, 161, 214
 sex roles in, 251
 as symbol, 283–84
 technologies as, 284 ff.
Robert Hart, 51
Robinson, W. R., 268
Rocha, Glauber, 193

Roman Catholic Church, 30 ff.,
    50, 253
    in Latin America, 171 ff.
    Mass, 157, 176–77
    wealth of, 244–45
Roszak, Theodore, 101, 131
Roxbury, Massachusetts, 55
"Ruach," 64
Ruether, Rosemary, 181
Rural-urban communities, 85, 86
Russia, 141

St. Patrick's Church, 30, 32–33
Salvation, 91–92, 219, 311
Santayana, George, 177, 317
Sante Fe, New Mexico, 115–16
Sartre, Jean-Paul, 266, 285
Satirizing, theology as, 319–20
Schimel, Robert, 290
Scientific method, 321–22
Scottsdale, Arizona, 82
Scriptures
    communication and, 308–9
    family and, 228–30
Second Adam, 66, 75
Secular City, The, 128, 272
Secular man, 59–60
Seduction of the spirit, 16, 118
Seignioralty, male, 232–34
Selection device, 102, 104
Self
    conversion and, 172–73
    play and, 185
Self-consciousness, 59–60, 81–82
    ethnic, 239, 240
    national, 247–48, 254
Self-image, 63–64
Sennett, Richard, 79–81, 237
Sensitivity movement, 197 ff.
Sermons, 311
Setting, 147, 148, 161

Seven Storey Mountain, The, 110
Sexual basis of new church, 247
Shamanism, 286–87, 324
Shekinah, 181
Sherson, Jacob, 25
Shiites, 181
Sight, sound vs., 269
Signals, 10 ff.
    mass media, 306–7
    meditation and, 94
    specialization and, 106, 107
Silence, 222–23
Sin, 64, 70, 72, 73, 75, 106
    encounter movement and, 219
Sisters of Liberty, 189
Slater, Philip, 287
Snyder, Gary, 200, 201
Social experiment, liturgics and,
    156 ff.
Socialism, 127, 170, 187
Social problems, revivalism and,
    221, 224
Social reality, 305–6
Society of the Poor, 178
Socrates, 285
Soleri, Paolo, 79, 81–83
Solomon, 228
Soul, 94, 121
Sound, sight vs., 269
South America, 171 ff.
Sovereign states, new church and,
    247–48, 251–52, 254–55
Space-time, religion and, 57–58
Spagnola, Nicholas, 31
Speaking in tongue, 141
Specialist mentality, 104
Specialization, 102 ff.
Species, extinction of, 85, 87
Speech, sound of, 269
Spinrad, Norman, 291
Spirit
    ethnic expression of, 243
    seduction of, 16, 118

Spirit of Liberty, 178–79
Spiritual vision, 78–79
Spontaneous activities, 11, 17
Stories, 9 ff.
    interiority of, 93 ff.
    mass media and, 307
    means of communicating, 12
    place and, 57
    signals vs., 10 ff.
Strong, Josiah, 67–68, 69
Structures, man's use of, 75
Students, 109 ff.
Study of religion, 145, 150. *See also* Theology.
Subjectivity, 94, 222, 223
Suburbia, 80
Sufis, 95
Suicide, 292
Summa Theologica, 265, 266, 322, 324
Suspension theory, 291–92
Symbol(s), 265 ff.
    ambiguity of, 283
    city as, 68, 72, 77
    clothes as, 213, 214
    communication and, 134
    machine, 296–98
    masculine and feminine, 180–82
    myth as, 284
    psychotherapy and, 133, 135–36
    ritual as, 41–42, 283–84
    sacredness of, 282–83
    seduction of spirit and, 118–19
    setting and, 161
    technology and, 280 ff.
    visual, 265 ff.
Symbolism of Evil, 284
Syncretism, 243
Synthesis, 322–23
System(s), 73, 75
    coordination, 105, 106
    new, 323, 324

Tai Chi, 199
Tantric tradition, 210
Teaching, 109 ff.
Teachings of Don Juan, 144, 145
Technics and Civilization, 270
Technique, la, 72
Technological Society, 72
Technology, 48, 72, 262
    bondage and, 284 ff.
    community and, 288–89
    death and, 289 ff.
    as demon, 298
    images and, 269, 270, 296–98
    liberals and, 73
    as myth, 292 ff.
    nature vs., 269–70
    neutrality of, 73
    personal life and, 94
    as ritual, 284 ff.
    symbolism of, 280 ff.
    television, 303
    theology and, 326, 327
    woman's role and, 233
Teilhard de Chardin, Pierre, 48, 81, 173, 209
Television, 273, 302 ff.
    elite power of, 313–14
    enthusiasm for, 275
    images, 303, 304, 306
    promise of, 276–77
    threat of, 12, 14–15
Ten Commandments, 229
Terrestrialization, 155
Testimony, 9, 91–93, 96, 97. *See also* Autobiography.
    silence and, 223
Texts, 146 ff., 278
Theology
    autobiography and, 109–11
    of communication, 312 ff.
    critical role of, 319–20
    of culture, 262 ff.
    descriptive aspect of, 151

Theology (*cont.*)
  of encounter movement, 219 ff.
  fantasy in, 320 ff.
  future of, 142, 318 ff.
  iconology and, 262
  interiority in, 98–100, 107
  liberation and, 153–54
  "making fun of," 319–20
  manifestations of religion and,
    194
  non-productive, 325 ff.
  play and, 184 ff., 319 ff.
  provincialism of, 150, 154, 170,
    171
  radical, 169 ff. *See also* Radical
    theology.
  as response, 150, 151–52
  technology and, 326, 327
Therapy, 132 ff.
Thinking, visual, 265
Third World, 170–71
  communication and, 312
  conscientization, 173, 176
Thompson, William Irwin, 322
Thoreau, Henry David, 297
Tillich, Paul, 98, 133, 262 ff.
Togliatti, Palmiro, 131
Tonantin, 180
Tontin, 116
Torres, Camillo, 116, 191
Touch the Earth, 120
Touching, 214 ff.
Tradition, 150, 152 ff.
Travel by jet, 285–86
Tribal village, 23 ff.
Trobriand Islanders, 283
Truth, Christianity and, 101
Twentieth of July Movement,
  125
2001, 298, 299
Tzara, Tristan, 301

Ukraine, 326
Ulbricht, Walter, 127
Umbanda, 215–16, 250
Unconscious, 117, 136, 265
Universalism, 152, 154–55, 251–
  253, 255
Urban man, 63–64. *See also* Cities.
"Useless" theology, 325 ff.
Uses of Disorder, The, 79
Utopianism, ceremonies and, 250

Vahanian, Gabriel, 174
Value systems, 15, 86
Verbal, visual preceding, 265
Vijayavardhara, D.C., 170
Village, 23 ff., 278
Violence in cities, 80
Virgin. *See* Mariology.
Vishnu Purana, 197
Visions, massage and, 209
Visual images, 261–62, 265 ff.
Vulnerability, 308–9

Waiting for Godot, 285
War, specialization in, 105
WASPs, 241
Watson, James, 321
Watts, Alan, 222
Wesley, John, 98
Western culture, 46–48, 86, 170
Where the Wasteland Ends, 101
White, Morton and Lucia, 67
Whole, learning from, 147, 148
Women
  black, 248–49
  differences from men, 236
  Islam and, 180–81
  Judaism and, 181
  liberation of, 180, 231, 232–34
  men's domination of, 232–34
  poor people's religion and,
    177 ff.

Women (*cont.*)
  rituals and, 251
  Ten Commandments and, 229
Word, images vs., 268, 269–70
World Council of Churches, 123,
  244, 325
World federalism, 255
Wounded Knee, 120
Wright, Frank Lloyd, 67, 80

Yahweh, nature and, 300
Yaqui Indians, 145–46
Yoga, Maharishi Mahesh, 222

Z, 158, 160
Zapata, Emiliano, 116, 193
Zen, 201